Thirty-Seven Ideas For Tactical Managers*
*Improve Your Project and Process Management Skills!

By:

Ron Parker

ISBN: 978-0615652061
LCCN: 2012949465

Operation Improvement Inc.
Flat Rock, North Carolina

Table of Contents

Dedication

To Mom and Dad, who prepared me well for life.

Acknowledgements

James. C. Abbott of Abbott Associates gave me the opportunity to teach and consult with business audiences. I have yet to find productive work that I enjoy more.

Working with James over several years and many projects accounts for a *cross-pollination* of skills as I gained experience and maturity.

I worked with James when he pioneered computer training and consulting for accountants, engineers and executives. When public education caught up and began offering computer training for all, we moved ahead.

Drawing on our engineering, mathematics and science backgrounds, we offered services in Manufacturing and Statistical Quality Control.

When the Deming inspired *quality improvement* impetus morphed into an industry appetite for brand name *quality certification* programs, we re-focused our teaching and coaching on development of new techniques for project and process managers.

As US manufacturing increasingly moved offshore, we turned our attention to the *back office* and to the *service side* of business, including: customer service, accounting operations, case handling, *technology* help desks and call centers.

Had I not met James, I would most likely have confined my consulting to technology projects. I would have missed the diversity of experience and the broad overarching view of operations: from engineering to production, from customer service to the back office.

Finally, this book would not have been possible without the help and encouragement of my wife, **Trudy**. She has been a patient reader of early drafts and has helped me to turn the rough drafts into a more polished result that can be released in book form.

Introduction

Tactical management is the planning, organization, direction and supervision of available means to a chosen end.

Project Management and Process Management are more than certifications or job titles. They are tactical management *Skill Sets*. Like a left hand and a right hand, they are complementary and most effective when their relationship is understood and exploited.

The end result of a project is a deliverable, usually tools, intentional methods, or a facility that will be integral to new processes. Projects have a beginning middle and end. When the deliverable has been achieved, the project is over.

The end result of a process is *readiness,* an ability or capability of consistent product creation – provided that it is fed appropriate raw materials. Those raw materials could be orders, specifications and physical materials in a manufacturing environment or customer requests in a service environment.

Unlike projects, processes do not end. If unmanaged, they can fall into dis-repair. They can fail to sustain their readiness to deliver the chosen output. They can drift off target or produce undesirable results when fed improper raw materials. They can be dismantled, mothballed and shut down.

The responsibility of the tactical manager to the process is to sustain an optimum state of readiness. The responsibility of the tactical manager to the project is an on time deliverable that meets or exceeds performance specifications at or below budget.

Unfortunately, many larger companies have come to associate project and process management principally with accounting, diagramming and chart-making techniques and computerized record keeping. There are several factors driving this trend:

New words for old concepts. Software for tracking projects is more powerful and more complex each year. The learning curve is steep and each new generation incorporates more esoteric analytical tools. This results in *jargon-creep,* a proliferation of new words and terms that creates an artificial barrier and improper compartmentalization of work.

Unintended Consequences. Human Resource departments respond to this complexity by relying more and more on certification programs. Unfortunately, there is, in my experience, abundant evidence that knowledge of technical terms and techniques does not imply proficiency as a tactical manager.

So, what is an HR department supposed to do if the company's best project managers cannot run the latest software that produces all those reports that top management thinks they need?

They create a job title, hire based on certifications and computer competencies and assign these "project and process managers" to teams and undertakings where they may bring *only* those project accounting skills.

This breeds an "I do not need to understand it to manage it." attitude. With little or no knowledge about organization and manufacturing lines, operational mergers, or customer relations – they find themselves at odds with those on the team who do have management and subject matter experience or aptitude.

Responsible but not truly in control, these project managers have difficulty defining tasks, identifying comparables, estimating durations and partitioning work along rational lines of segmentation.

Perhaps a better job description for these corporate resources would be project/process coaches, or project/process administrators.

Some of the more fashionable techniques taught by certification organizations are simply wrong. It is vital that an experienced tactical manager preside over the project or process, and carefully judge the appropriateness of the "latest and greatest" analytical tool.

The purpose of this book is to establish a *solid-ground* framework for process and project management. Through small and easy steps, you will increase your knowledge of tactical management and your confidence in evaluating the latest and future techniques of analysis and reporting.

1: Ends And Means

Here are four situations:

- A Clerk is assigned a project. The objective: re-organize the file room.

- An Engineer is assigned a project. The objective: increase the rate of production of a manufacturing line from 800 to 1200 units per day.

- An Executive is assigned a project: The objective: merge the business operations of an acquisition into the principal company.

- A Program Director is assigned a portfolio of projects; the goal is the research, development and deployment of a new and revolutionary spacecraft.

All of these example have two things in common. 1) There is a gap between the implied current state of affairs and what is desired. 2) A responsible person is charged with managing change. This duty has a beginning, middle and end.

An illustration of this idea might look like this:

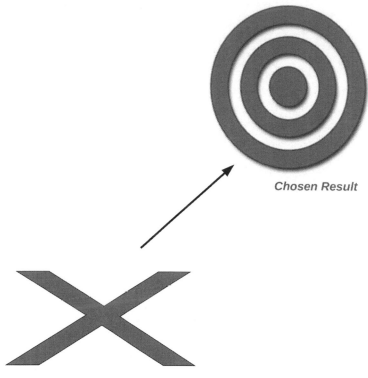

Chosen Result

Current State

ENDS AND MEANS

In reality, the actions and consequences of work are one. If one digs a ditch, the eventual result begins to take shape with the first shovel of dirt.

"**Dig** a ditch." and "Dig a **ditch**." are simply two mental perspectives on the same thing. From one perspective we are focusing on the work, the actions, the *verbs*. From the other perspective we mentally focus on the result, the deliverable, *the noun*.*

The most complex management techniques and tools build on this most basic skill; the ability to organize our thoughts around *ends and means*.

This need to shift perspectives shows up in every aspect of managing work. When one delegates, for example, are you delegating the *digging*, or the *ditch*? (Hold your answer until we discuss Delegation and Teams.)

An illustration of the mental separation of ends and means might look like the one on the next page. It emphasizes the idea that time must first be taken to understand the objective.

Then we turn our focus over to the tasks that we believe will bring us to the objective. The end result dictates what tasks are necessary and sufficient for completion.

Here is a simplified example:

Objective: 10 Feet Long, 1 Foot wide and 1 Foot Deep Ditch.

Tasks:

- Rent Tools

- Measure and Stake Ditch Location

- Dig

Notice that *rent, measure, stake, dig* are all verbs. *Ditch* is a noun. This may seem trivial, but this simple distinction will help you to understand the most common errors tactical

13

managers make. It goes to the root of the question, *"What, as a manager, can you really control?"*

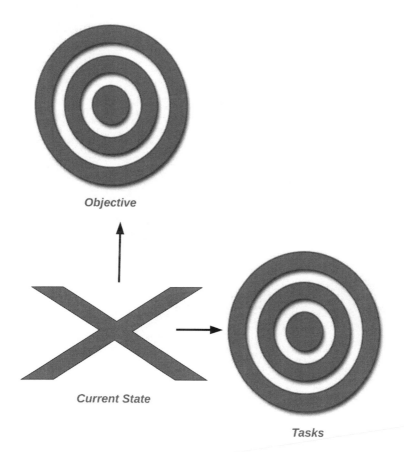

Objective

Current State

Tasks

SO WHAT'S WRONG WITH DIVING IN?

Some would prefer to keep things simple. Starting from the current state, they dive in, swimming for the destination. For the simple and self-evident, there is no real problem with this, but we often work with others, and coordinating our work with others is an essential aspect of tactical management..

While it is clear that 100% of your time spent in planning and none in execution will not achieve results, experience has taught us that a little forethought before diving in is worthwhile. When there is a possibility of great waste and error, time spent thinking and planning work can easily pay for itself.

Anyone you expect to contribute to your project will become frustrated and will ultimately be ineffective if you do not take the time to separate out and define work from these two perspectives.

If you have been disappointed with how associates have performed on your projects in the past, perhaps the root of the problem lies here, and not in psychology, attitudes and motivation.

ENDS, MEANS AND PROCESS MANAGEMENT

The mental distinction of ends and means is similar in process management. The terminology is a little different. Instead of objectives and tasks, a process approach mentally separates the *process* from the *product.* Once again, the tactical manager is thinking about verbs and nouns.

We have often diagrammed the process and product relationship like this:

15

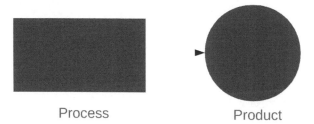

Process　　　　　　　Product

Our classic example of process is baking biscuits. (Ovens are rectangular and biscuits are round.) This separation helps to clarify cause and effect relationships. *Baking* (a verb = the process) takes place for a certain time and a certain temperature, and *Biscuits* (a noun - the product) may be perfect or burned.

MUST I DRAW PICTURES?

Well, no. However, with experience, I think you will find diagramming techniques a helpful brainstorming, documentation, and training tool.

We will build on these simple diagram techniques throughout this book. You certainly should feel free to pick and choose those which are most helpful, given the circumstance.

2: Metrics And Measures

For many people, metrics seem like report cards. Who will get a bonus or promotion? Who will not? Who is in compliance with policy, contract or regulation? Who is not?

The Peanuts characters never heard a word the teacher said, "Wha Wha Whaaa. Wa Wa-Wa". To Charlie Brown and his schoolmates, adult talk was sound from another world, and not intelligible or relevant to *their* world.

Some managers feel this way when they see or hear the word *metrics*. The PowerPoint slides, the tables of numbers and reports may seem important and meaningful when presented, but they often do not seem actionable.

This mis-perception is a lost opportunity

GREAT METRICS REPORTS:

- Pay for themselves by improving decisions at all levels of the organization.

- Can flow automatically from existing business systems.

- Offer fresh data each day, or even each hour or minute as necessary.

- Are accessible to managers and supervisors real-time – as decisions are being made.

- Help everyone understand the current state of the business real-time – as decisions are being made.

- Clearly highlight moments of change across time.

- Clearly highlight individual cases that are objectively atypical.

- Clearly highlight opportunities for improvement, and not just more of the status quo.

- Are the essential companion to clearly defined correct processes.

- Metrics make consistent processes possible.

Good Metric reports often surprise us by revealing many things that are not obvious with simple observation, but they should never flat out contradict what one sees firsthand.

Seeing is believing, but not everything we see is automatically retained, integrated and related to other observations in other places and at other times.

METRIC REPORTING

Most people refer to company metrics when they really mean metrics *reports*. A good report contains a presentation of statistical results in an easy to understand format. The best reports will present the *ideas* conveyed in the statistics. An audience not skilled in statistical techniques should be able to grasp the *ideas* that the statistical analysis supports.

The statistical analysis depends on numbers. Numbers depend on measurements that quantify *a metric*, an important quality or characteristic of a product, process, objective or task. Measurement depends on good measurement *method* and on *observation*.

Every element of a good metric report must be traceable back to some thing or some action that can be directly or indirectly observed. *Floating abstractions* are results that cannot stand up to a rigorous audit and should be considered *arbitrary.*

This is the most fundamental reason why we do **not** endorse a common attitude of some analysts: *"I do not need to understand where the numbers come from in order to analyze them."*

It is possible to perform very advanced statistical *calculations* on numbers but a statistical calculation is just one link in a chain. This is a subtlety of *applied* mathematics that those with advanced degrees in theoretical mathematics and little subject matter experience will sometimes miss.

Good Metrics reporting is the end product of a careful sequence that brings facts up from the front lines of work. It cannot be emphasized enough. Metrics reporting finds and highlights *actionable ideas.* It is not principally about PowerPoint, Minitab or SPSS expertise.

I have a preferred format of presentation that retains this perspective. The title of a slide poses a question. The subtitle answers it, and the graph or exhibit answers the question, "How do we know?"

Measures such as inches, degrees Fahrenheit, and minutes help us to quantify metrics.

 Our process diagramming techniques can help us to organize, inventory and share what we know about the process. Adding metrics and measures to our biscuit and oven diagram would look like this:

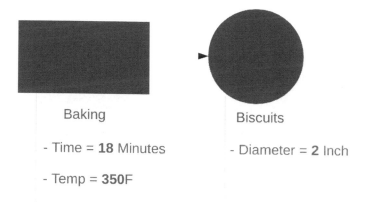

Baking

- Time = **18** Minutes

- Temp = **350F**

Biscuits

- Diameter = **2** Inch

PROJECT METRICS

For our ditch digging project, we can qualify and quantify the objectives and tasks. This will help us to better manage.

Objective: 10 Feet Long, **1 Foot** wide and **1 Foot** Deep Ditch.

Tasks:

- Rent Tools – ESTIMATED COST:**$75.00**

- Measure and Stake Ditch Location
  – ESTIMATED TIME:2p x 1 Hrs.

- Dig
  ESTIMATED TIME:1p x 4 Hrs.

Metrics for project objectives are typically organized into four dimensions: performance, time, cost and risk. When a project is conceived, project sponsors will often consider various trade-offs of performance, time, cost and risk before settling on a final version.

A deep, wide and long ditch is a ditch qualified by adjectives, and "feet" is an obvious way to measure these metrics. These are typical *performance* metrics.

We want to complete tasks quickly and cheaply. Cost and time are typical task metrics and can be measured in dollars and hours. The heart of this little project, *digging*, sounds like something we might manage as a process! Wouldn't a metric like *digging speed* in feet/hour be useful?

We will dig deeper into metrics in a later chapter. Now, let's not forget that working effectively with other people is central to tactical management. It is important to bring some of those issues into play next.

DEFINITION BY DECREE

By the power vested in me as the author of this chapter, I shall decree a team to be two to five people, with six being a border-line case, and a one man team a special case.

Certainly, when one person can easily do a job, there exists a training opportunity for an apprentice; there is no point in saddling them with a partner if no partner is needed.

I shall try to be consistent in usage through each chapter in this book, and delegating a task to a team will mean "two to five people".

The team is typically too small a unit of organization to require a separate role, "Supervisor". A team may have a team leader, or captain, but a team leader's work is largely the same or similar to other members of the team. They may have a few administrative duties and might need to speak for the team at larger assemblies. I think of these leaders as senior members of a team. Often team leaders are the more experienced core personnel around which a team is formed.

I offered guidelines on how to select team members in different circumstances in a previous book, and I will repeat them here. Teams need to be formed in such a way that they exploit one of several established principles of productivity.

1. **Division of Labor.** It has been known for generations that cooperating specialists can be more productive than generalists, *if* there is sufficient work to keep the specialty occupied. If there is not sufficient work, then the specialty work is absorbed into the closest skill match.

You can take advantage of this principle by staffing a team with _different_ backgrounds and skills. A team with a diversity of skills can maximize productivity if there is sufficient work to justify each specialty.

2. **Many hands make light work.** There are many jobs that are unpleasant, tedious and boring. Nevertheless, they must be done. A single good trooper who is assigned to _swamp draining_ duties may intellectually appreciate that every job is important, but a long dreary task can sap the morale and productivity of the best.

    This kind of assignment generally calls for _similar backgrounds and skills_. A friendly peer is the best kind of team member to have by one's side when there is an undesirable assignment to be slogged through.

3. **Perspectives Generate Ideas.** Once again, here is a reason to staff a team with individuals selected for their _different backgrounds and skills_. There are times when we are _idea poor_ and are looking for a fresh approach to a market, to a new product or for a problem solution.

    Teams of like mind tend to hash over the same old talking points and repeatedly converge on the same solution. Worse, as a result, they may deem their conclusion the best alternative because they do not have the benefit of a radically different perspective.

4. **Safety in Numbers.** A team can be more productive than individuals if teams are formed as a _risk reduction strategy_. Think of this as adding a _Co-Pilot_

conceptualize their responsibilities around a kitchen *work-center* consisting of three biscuit-making *work-stations.*

In our example, the conceptual view of the process helps in delegation of work, explanation of responsibilities, and the coordination of each worker's activities to each other and to the final product.

I have applied this technique in large work forces and I can only describe worker reaction to this method as joy. In some cases, they had worked for years at a single task and a single workstation with *no concept* of how their work contributed to a larger whole and to company profits.

PROCESSES AND TEAMS

What is the size of our biscuit kitchen? Moderate? Perhaps a team of two to five can manage the entire work center. Team members with different aptitudes and skills would be required.

There would be some manual dexterity required of the team member responsible for forming and placing raw biscuits.

The team member responsible for the oven might need a more analytical nature if the reading of gauges and oven adjustments are called for.

Is our kitchen huge? Perhaps it would be appropriate to place a small team with similar skills at the oven. A different team might be responsible for mixing, etc.

If we have done our homework and partitioned the work appropriately, then authority will be commensurate to responsibility.

Many discussions of teams fall into the side issue of morale, motivation and other attitude issues. I am of the opinion that managers can only do so much to marginally improve the attitude of a fairly paid worker who chooses to be a part of a company.

On the other hand, managers can do tremendous *damage* to morale. There is a tremendous benefit to "cease and desist", to stop being an impediment. Many workers simply wish their managers would get out of their way and let them do their job.

The list of management sins is a long one. But, if you can describe the work in terms your teams can understand and provide appropriate tools to to the job, then you will go a long way towards keeping the attitude of your co-workers positive and productive.

DELEGATION AND PROJECT MANAGEMENT

At this early point in the book, there are two major issues that need to be introduced. Each will be examined in greater detail in subsequent chapters.

First, there is the question of appropriate level of detail in describing work. There is some flexibility into breaking down the work into three tasks or ten. One can define the objective as a single deliverable, or a series of smaller incremental sub-objectives.

Errors are made with too much or too little detail. The criteria for success is clarity. Dr. Charles Hobbs tells us, "If people do not have a clear picture, they do not act."

A businessman might say *"We need a bigger oven."* Not constrained by available means, they consider a range of alternatives even if they cannot immediately afford the purchase.

> *"Shall I take a business partner? Should I borrow the money? Can I pay the money back? Do I want the oven enough to pay the interest on the money? Do I want to share decision-making with a partner? Maybe I could lease an oven! "*

The same kind of weighing and balancing of alternatives will happen if a couple chooses to commission a project to build a custom home.

> *"A larger house may be harder to sell. A smaller house may mean we have to move sooner if our family grows."*

Once a decision has been reached, the strategic decision-maker provides not only the available means for the tactician, *but the* **motivation!**

IN A THOUSAND YEARS, WHO WILL CARE?

Tacticians can easily be disheartened with a casual *"So What?"* The web site is 10% faster. *So What?* The filing system has been purged of dead wood files and folders. *So What?*

"In one thousand years, what will it matter?" Tactical managers cannot answer such a philosophical question without deferring to the strategic thinker who says, "It only has to matter *to me!*"

Strategic thinking weighs values and risks, clarifies goals and establishes tactical objectives. Meaningless work is work that has lost its connection to a broader vision. It no longer can be connected to strategy.

While strategy imbues tactics with meaning, it is tactics that bring desires to life. Tactics bring realization to the hopes and dreams of strategy.

EXACTLY HOW DOES ALL OF THIS WORK?

I prefer the term *"Goal"* to refer to an end or outcome at the strategic level. Consistent use of a different word with a similar meaning is a good way to remind ourselves that strategic thinking about goals is different from tactical thinking about objectives.

Goal implies a broader scope, a longer range and more abstract thinking. Instead of thinking about a house with 2000 square feet and three bedrooms, one may think about a home big enough for family, overnight guests and the occasional small party.

Achievement of a goal might require completion of a single specific objective or an entire portfolio. A lofty goal such as *"The cure for cancer"* or *"Astronauts on Mars"* would imply dozens of particular objectives. Some of these objectives would research and identify promising approaches and seal off dead ends. Other objectives would develop and deploy key technologies and processes.

PRINCIPLES OF ACTION

One cannot mentally leap from a strategic end (*a goal*) to objectives in a single bound. Even at this abstract level, ends and means thinking is required. Knowledge of cause and effect must be called into focus before objectives can be defined and commissioned.

To move from goals to objectives you need to draw on a wide body of knowledge. If possible, you draw on all that is known about the relevant subjects.

If the goal is medical, you talk to doctors, nurses, patients, medical manufacturers and more. If the goal is Mars, you consult aeronautical engineers, materials experts, and so on.

All of this knowledge is condensed and organized into *principles of action, **or a strategy**.* Here is a speculative example that will help you get the flavor of this kind of thinking and planning.

For an expedition to Mars, your plan of action may begin with this:

> *"We will need some way to provide food for months in space instead of days. We will need a new energy source capable of flight across the solar system. We may need way-stations if the trip cannot be achieved in a single voyage."*

Notice that this kind of planning is packed full of s*ome* one and *some* how thinking. It is similar to the relationship of algebra to arithmetic. Principles of action create a mental scaffold from which specific research, development and implementation objectives can be defined.

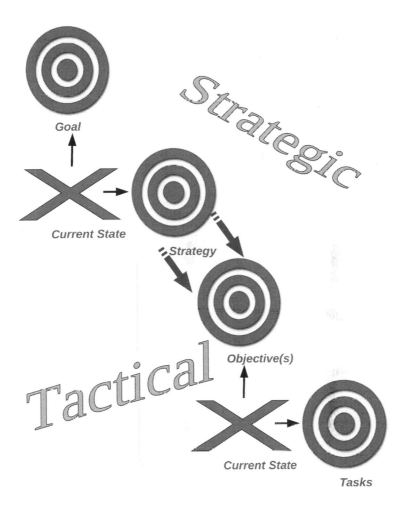

ARE YOU STRATEGIC OR TACTICAL?

Are you strategic or tactical? At any one time, most of us will find ourselves predominately in one or the other role. There are some situations, particularly in small business and in engineering disciplines, where we wear both hats.

We will make better decisions and choices if we can keep the distinction. Ask yourself, am I faced with a decision or a choice? Am I dealing with a concrete objective and available means, or am I weighing values and risks? Do I need to think now in terms of specific people, times and tasks, or should I be thinking *in principle* about how to achieve a goal?

THRASHING

Things change. As you will see in future chapters, planning is essential precisely *because* things will likely not go according to plan.

As things change, tactics change. Good tactical managers have one fundamental mechanism for coping with and managing the unexpected. They *re-deploy* resources.

A strategy, however, requires a longer term commitment. If you bail out of your strategy at every adversity and setback, you will undermine the morale and destroy the tactician's ability to work. Strategy has to be, at least for a period of time, **solid ground.** Plan your work and work your plan is good advice.

Like a pilot on instruments, you must have a certain level of confidence or faith in your strategic judgements. Trust and verify, but trust you must. Strategic thrashing makes any achievement almost impossible.

STRATEGY AND TACTICS NEED EACH OTHER

Like a Navy and Marine rivalry, tacticians and strategists need each other, but sometimes must be reminded of it.

Without a context of values and risk and without principles of action, tacticians could be off chipping away at a continental canal with picks and shovels while wondering *"What's the point?"*

If there is no one in particular to move the first and last shovelful of dirt, then the most beautiful strategic plan for an inland waterway will never materialize.

Both strategists and tacticians can take pride in their contribution to work, but both must realize that objectives without values and planning without execution is sterile and futile.

Although this book is principally about tactical management, the distinction between strategy and tactics will be an important concept in several future chapters.

Standards of Time and Risk are more complex to define. For now, we will set aside risk, and then reintroduce it when one is managing a portfolio of projects.

It is best to think of time as a *bullseye*. A too-early completion can detract from the project value and a too-late completion can have penalties as well. The relationship of Time to Value is a subject that deserves at least a chapter of its own.

6: Specifications and Targets

Every product or service today is subjected to measurement. Call centers, for example, want to know if *prompt service* is provided. "Prompt Service" is an example of a metric, or what James Abbott calls a *study area*.

The first measure that comes to mind is not necessarily the best. What is used in one industry, business or department is not necessarily the right measure for all. Particular measures can become negotiation points, contractual requirements and even regulatory obligations.

If the things that you measure do not accurately track the metric, you will have gaps between your performance as scored on paper, and performance as scored by the customer. Being contractually bound to measure and exceed the wrong measures only makes a bad situation worse.

PROMPT SERVICE

For a call center, prompt service begins with measures of Call setup time, answer time and wait time.

Setup time could be measured in seconds. It is the time between the last digit dialed and the first ring heard by the customer. Even though telephone service is a common utility, you should be aware that this time represents a cost to the customer. You may assume or may have been told that it is a factor beyond your control, but there are still reasons to be aware of that delay and there are reasons to measure it.

Answer time is generally measured in *rings*, or seconds. The number of *rings* until answer is a measure that will most likely make your measures commensurate with the customer. *"I let the phone ring seven times!"*, a customer might say.

Modern telephone customers are delighted with immediate answers, but typically expect and tolerate a short queue time, provided that it is actually short. There is no single answer, though, as to what *short* is, in seconds or minutes.

A complex transaction such as the booking of a three week safari will take considerable time. Callers who anticipate these complexities may wait a bit longer than someone calling an information line to check on flight delays.

Customers who are making high value purchases might expect the vendor to spend a little more on call center alacrity than the customer who queues up for the discount deal of the day.

Of course, every customer deserves prompt service, but before I actually mention a specific number – I want to make sure that we understand that prompt service is *contextual*.

SPECIFICATIONS, TARGETS, TOLERANCES.

Specifications have two components: Targets and Tolerances.

- Targets tell tactical management what to aim for. They are the standard of success.

- Tolerances are the standard of failure.

Some companies only use tolerances in metrics. This is a mistake. Like an academic PASS/FAIL grade, measuring against tolerances does convey actionable information. One never knows how close to target, or how close to failure a passing grade represents.

A COMMON MISTAKE

There is a systemic flaw in the way tactical teams are trained and directed. I conclude this because, in my experience, 99% of the personnel I have trained must *unlearn* what they think they know about targets and tolerances.

Here is the mistake:

If told that the target for wait time is 0 seconds, and the tolerance is 20 seconds, most will strive to *not* let a call go unanswered for more than 20 seconds.

If told that a part should have a diameter of 2 inches and a tolerance of 0.1, most will strive to *not* make a part with a diameter of less than 1.99 or more than 2.01.

Their mind's eye is not on the target! Their head is filled with what they *don't* want, and not with what they *do* want.

The importance of the correct approach lies in a deeper issue; what you can and can*not* control and *how* one exerts control as a tactician.

This issue will become clearer in the next chapter when we introduce the performance chart.

7: Measuring Performance

The *Performance Chart* is the one measurement reporting tool every tactician should be familiar with. It is not the end and ultimate; it is simply a sound beginning.

To illustrate this technique, we will imagine a company that serves a small community with cable TV service. *"Prompt Service"* is important to their customers. The company advertises prompt service and sets customer expectations. They even obligate themselves to this performance in their brochures and contracts.

THE METRIC AND THE MEASURE

Acme Cable, Inc. advertises, *"Order service today and receive prompt installation!"*

You think, *"Great! There is a big game being broadcast tonight. I'll call later this afternoon."* Then you read the fine print: *"Service in seven days or installation is free."*

Now, a target of immediate service fulfillment has been established. "Prompt" may take three days, but two days, one day or same day service will always be *more prompt*, closer to the target, and measurably better performance. Think of this not as PASS/FAIL, but a score of B, B+, A or A+.

A tolerance has also been communicated. The customer who reads the service offer will know that although *"prompt installation"* has been promised, service could take up to seven days.

The target of immediate service and the tolerance of seven days together make up the specifications and set certain expectations in the mind of the customer.

There is also something else hidden in this offer. It is called a Service Level Agreement, or SLA. You know that a target is the standard of success and a tolerance is the standard of failure.

Business agreements between vendors and customers typically recognize that failure sometimes happens, and an occasional failure *may* be tolerated. An agreement may include an SLA – a standard below which the vendor is judged nonperforming and forfeits all or part of any fees.

In our Acme Cable service offering, our tolerance is also our SLA. Installation is *free* if it is not provided within seven days.

TRADITIONAL REPORTING

The traditional approach to measuring and reporting performance is preoccupied with the tolerance, the SLA, and a PASS/FAIL approach. Someone will usually take a time period (*"Last Quarter"*) and simply count the number in each category – perhaps adding a percentage column.

Since the number of service requests may vary from quarter to quarter, percent is used as an attempt to standardize the report from period to period. The traditional report may be a table or bar chart and it often looks like this:

and metrics reporting – proper grouping is the key to clarity, decisiveness and success.

NO TWO SNOWFLAKES ARE ALIKE

"No two snowflakes are alike, unless you compare them to a canned ham." Compared in pairs, it is said that no two snowflakes are alike. It takes the qualities and characteristics of a third contrasting item to underscore similarity. The third item can be physically present, or drawn from experience and memory.

I sometimes present this material in class at break or lunch. As props, I may set a slice of pie and a piece of cake in front of the group. I ask the group to set aside any associations from their own mind and just look at the objects presented.

If I add a paperweight as a foil, the idea *"food"* emerges in everyone's mind – since you cannot eat paperweights. Then, I substitute the meal's main course, and the more specific idea of *"dessert"* emerges.

The same kind of exercise can be done with soda bottles. A Coke and a Pepsi soda are obviously different until a contrasting element is introduced – a clear soda for example. Colas, and clear, carbonated and flat, large and small, Brand X and Brand Y – all of these conceptual groupings arise from the observable contrasting characteristics and qualities of the items under discussion.

As tactical managers warm to this way of thinking, they begin to see finer distinctions. They see this production batch versus that batch, products made on this equipment line versus the other, biscuits baked at a higher temperature or lower.

Morning, late night and daytime workloads and staffing requirements, and so on.

This ability to see and group, the ability to *point* to an idea, is a skill that improves with practice and with work experience.

PART NUMBER DISEASE

As a consultant to tactical managers, it has often been more important to tackle how associates have conceptualized the business before any other priority. I can tell if this need is critical if the organization has symptoms of *part number disease*.

If everyone complains that work is unmanageable because manufacturing has *"a million part numbers"*, or because no two calls to the customer call center are alike, then there has been a failure to properly conceptualize work.

It is amusing that the exact opposite self-assessment indicates the same diagnosis. If everyone observes that all calls to the call center are really the same, or if all production simply boils down to production of "parts" and "part numbers" - then part number disease is indicated.

"Parts are parts and they are all basically the same", and "No two are alike." indicate that no one has really thought about objective similarities and differences to gain a wholesale advantage on management decision-making.

I believe that part number disease has become rampant due to early automation techniques. Spreadsheet *row numbers* and database SKU number data structures preceded modern object-oriented data representations.

Later generation systems developers may have better tools, but there is still a *red zone* – a gap between systems developers and customers where each expects the other to conceptually structure the data in a way that captures and retains business knowledge.

FACTORING

I have never seen automation clean up the mess of part number disease, although many attempts have been made. Systems Developers have proposed and implemented search and filtering tools, product *"configurators"*, and more – but none equip the tactical manager and his team with the kind of product confidence that pre-automation generations knew.

Using James Abbott's "t-shirt" example, a customer service rep may search a database of thousands of SKU numbers attempting to match a particular item to customer needs.

If the product offerings have been properly grouped, the agent will know that they are dealing with ten sizes, two and only two collar styles, six colors, two kinds of sleeves, regular and long waist, two fabric blends, and an optional breast pocket.

Nearly two thousand *entirely different* t-shirts can be mentally grouped by: SIZE, COLOR, COLLAR, SLEEVE, WAIST, FABRIC AND POCKET. One thousand nine hundred and twenty SKU numbers can be reduced to just seven *factors*. You may also notice that these factors can also be thought of as key *product metrics*!

Identifying the seven factors behind two thousand variations is what we call *factoring* the product. We borrowed the name from mathematics. Two, Three, Five, Seven and Eleven are *factors* of two thousand three hundred and ten, because the large number can be reduced and represented as a product of these small quantities.

Factoring simplifies work and gives every member of a tactical team the power to think more clearly about the work and the intended outcome.

The benefits from factoring, and periodically re-factoring work are so great that I suspect you would find my own personal anecdotes unbelievable. I have personally seen it slash wait times and dramatically improve customer satisfaction at call centers in a matter of *days*. I have seen it virtually eliminate scrap and reduce setup time from hours to minutes in manufacturing.

Do not underestimate the degree to which correct ideas about work empower the mind of the individual and the effectiveness of a team *as a cohesive unit*.

9: Grouping And Process Management

Remember this diagramming technique for processes?

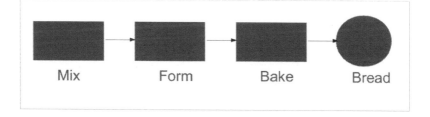

| Mix | Form | Bake | Bread |

When finished, these diagrams sometimes seem overly simplistic – stating what is only obvious. However, when confronted with a blank piece of paper, most realize that creating dependency diagrams is harder than it looks.

With manufacturing work, people often take a hint from the work that plant engineering has already done. Workstations have been created and procedures are established. A first draft seems like an easy matter of documenting what is known. The challenge is to dig deeper and describe not what is, but what *should* be.

In service work, methods are *too* pliable. They are not constrained by the speeds and cycles of conveyors or machinery. Tactical managers are often reluctant to establish a consistent method, a *process*, by which every call is handled.

"No two calls are alike.", they say. The hope and prayer is that team initiative and individual good intentions   will

suffice and that no one will have to sort out the mess conceptually.

With prodding, a service team will reluctantly produce an initial process dependency that looks something like this:

1. Answer the Phone.

2. Talk To The Customer

3. Hang up

The product of this process will at first be vague and undefined in the service team's mind.

To get past this beginners mistake, I sometimes compare this outlining task to that of preparing a good after-dinner talk.

Many speakers begin with, "I have five main points". Certainly there will be no more than five and no less than two in a clear and concise presentation. The speaker is trying to create a mental scaffold under which every specific point can be properly filed. The speaker is trying to *group* what may be dozens of ideas in a useful and retainable manner.

Answering the call center phone is definitely important, but surely it is not the one that captures the important first idea of customer contact.

PROPER PROCESS SEGMENTATION
A second iteration might look like this

1. Greet The Customer.

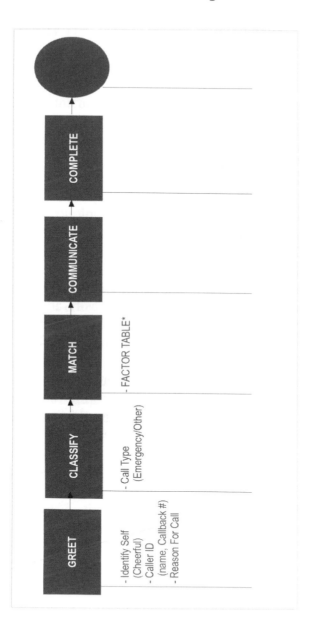

INCOMING AND OUTGOING PRODUCTS

Tactical management of a call center process is not about completion of any single particular call, it is about *readiness*. Although we may collect data on individual calls such as wait times, processing times etc., the management perspective on such data is that it tells us about the *capability* of our process to deliver results correctly and consistently.

Capability is the *woodchuck* question. *"How many call requests can a call center handle, if a call center could handle calls."*

Processes are the money-making engines of business. Like a mechanic tuning an engine, the capability, duty cycle, input requirements (fuel), and operational parameters of the process are our proper concern.

The call center manager might describe our process as *"Request Triage"*. The incoming product is a customer request, and the outgoing product is a *classified and routed request*. Given the available facility and staffing, this little engine has a measurable throughput. It can handle a quantifiable number of requests per hour or per day.

After a couple of brainstorming attempts to describe a process, I recommend that you **start** a final draft by specifying the end product, then add the incoming product. Finally, refine the process in a way that the entire scheme is described in three to five key ideas.

TRANSIENT PRODUCTS

Each process step in a dependency diagram *could* be drawn on a separate page. A resulting product could be shown for each process step, and that product could be shown as the key ingredient, or incoming product to a subsequent step.

Instead, these transient products are typically not shown, unless a deeper level of detail is really required to understand the work. Process steps are connected one to the next and these *transient* products are implied in the diagram.

The calculation of gross revenues produces a product: a dollar sum. That dollar sum is the *input* to the calculation of a per cent management fee.

> *If a transient product is flawed, all subsequent process steps are voided!*

That is to say, a dependency diagram reminds us that a correct percentage calculation *depends* on a correct sum of the monthly revenue. If upstream processes are incorrect, all downstream processes are *null and void*.

It is an understandable mistake to think that dependency diagrams show time sequence, but the deeper interpretation is that a bookkeeper must *know* the monthly revenue sum *before* a correct management fee can be calculated. It is in this sense that dependencies illustrate *knowledge* dependencies.

When I validate a process, I ask myself, *"What do we know and when do we know it?"* and, *"What is the transient product at this step in the process?"*

PERT CHARTS

Knowledge dependencies may be clearer if we take a look at PERT CHART techniques in project task scheduling.

In a systematic scheduling of tasks, task relationships are typically described as *predecessor* and *successor* tasks. Tasks are related in one of four ways: Finish-Start (FS), Start-Start (SS), Start-Finish (SF) and Finish-Finish (FF). In addition, a gap or overlap is specified as *lead* or *lag* time.

Novice schedulers just "know" that Task A (Build Forms.) should happen on Monday and Tuesday, and Task B (Pour Concrete) should follow on Wednesday and Thursday.

If they use a software package, they fiddle with task dependencies and leads and lags until the two tasks appear on the calendar where they intended. This is *not* how these powerful tools were meant to be used.

The concrete contractors, let us say, are our most difficult to schedule workers. They have *promised* to bring concrete to our work site on Wednesday. *That* is the predecessor task. It is a bit of certainty that the rest of the schedule builds on.

Based on the knowledge that the concrete will be delivered on Wednesday, we establish a relationship to the *successor* task. We calculate that the building of forms to hold wet concrete must be *finished* before concrete is delivered on Wednesday. That is a *Start-Finish relationship.*

Since construction of footings is expected to be a two day process, we determine a starting date for *that* task by the powerful mathematical technique known as *subtraction.* We work backwards on the calendar to find the Monday starting date of Task A.

The GANTT chart shows the time sequence, A precedes B, but the PERT chart preserves the *knowledge dependency relationship.*

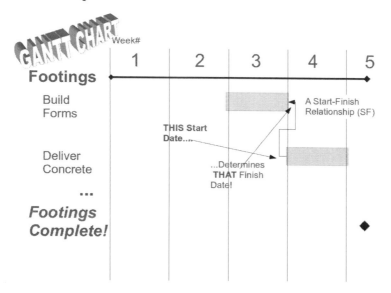

On the PERT chart view, Task B (Concrete) comes first, and Task A (Forms) follows. This is because we *know* with some certainty when concrete will be delivered, and we are planning the other tasks accordingly.

We plan because there <u>will</u> be change. Things <u>will</u> <u>not</u> always go according to plan. If the concrete contractors reschedule, the PERT chart and the Start-Finish dependencies in our scheduling plan remind us *which* tasks must be rescheduled.

A PERT Chart is a Dependency
Diagram That Documents the Order
In Which Scheduling Decisions Are
Made, Facilitating Rapid Review And
Re-Scheduling.

2 Days   2 Days

The dependency diagram retains a record of causality in our decision-making. *"Why did we schedule form construction when we did? Because the concrete contractors go on the schedule first, and other tasks are scheduled and re-scheduled accordingly."*

CRITICAL PATH

Dependencies are used sparingly in project scheduling to represent *real* constraints. In our example, the difficulty of scheduling concrete had an impact on at least one other task.

A prepared bed for concrete complete with forms is something that may be perishable. Perhaps we do not want that work completed and left exposed to the elements for too long before concrete is delivered. There is a definite reason to incorporate this dependency in scheduling.

Other tasks are scheduled later by analyzing available resources. The limitation of workers and equipment keeps us from tackling every task simultaneously, and a project manager will work that out in a second phase of scheduling.

For now, these tasks that are independent are left on the schedule to start ASAP (*as soon as possible*). Resource limitations will cause some of these to be delayed.

At this early stage of scheduling, something called a **critical path** emerges. It is possible to identify a sequence of tasks that determine the *minimum total duration of a project*.

If there are *no* dependencies in a project and everything is scheduled *ASAP*, the critical path is simply the time it takes to complete the longest task.

When *product* and *knowledge* dependencies are identified and incorporated into the schedule, a realistic time line of the project begins to take shape.

Novice misuse of scheduling software and dependency-based scheduling often results in *everything* being linked into a too-long critical path. This creates unrealistically long estimates of the total project duration and leads the manager to think their only means of improvement is *more resources.*

Proper and sparing use of dependencies and *ASAP* scheduling gives the tactical manager options. They can choose where and when to deploy and *re-deploy* resources. They can lengthen non-critical tasks, and shorten tasks on the critical path.

When things change, when things *do not go* according to plan, the most powerful tool in the tactical manager's kit is the power to *re*-deploy resources. A good plan establishes contingencies in advance.

THE FACTOR TABLE

Dependency Diagrams are not flow charts. They represent a planning of work that proceeds from certainty to certainty, from correct product to correct product.

How then, can such a simple method for diagramming processes be made *flexible* enough to accommodate *variability and unknowns?*

Many are tempted to turn dependency diagrams into *flow charts.* They want to introduce *decision box symbols and branching and looping lines and arrows.* This is not only unnecessary, it is a mistake that will have a negative impact on the ability of a tactical team to work confidently, correctly and consistently.

In our call center example, we were to greet and identify the caller, and then *match* the call request. Callers can call about a multitude of things. Even if we *factor* the types of calls into a smaller and manageable number, how then does the manager maintain a sense of orderly correctness with a simple dependency diagram?

If we decree that there are a dozen different *types* of calls, do we make a dozen dependency diagrams to plan and describe our process – the way in which it handles each variant?

The answer is no, and the solution is something called *Factor Tables.* A discussion of factor tables deserves its own chapter later in this book. Once mastered, you will never be tempted to turn dependency diagrams into flow charts.

12: Root and Other Causes

Any intentional method that is designed, implemented and operated *correctly and consistently* will have some risk of failure.

No matter how many times we perform a *Causal Analysis*, the same risk of failure remains inherent in the process unless something about the process changes. New variables must be incorporated into our process design and managed if positive change is to occur.

The responsibility of the tactical manager is to deploy *available means* as effectively as possible in order to run the process correctly & consistently. With new knowledge, the definition of Correct will change.

Root Cause Analysis is a strategic approach intended to aggressively identify unknowns and care must be taken not to let it drive bad tactical behavior.

DEFINING "CAUSE-EFFECT"

In its most fundamental sense, *Cause- Effect* is the distinction we make thousands of times each day; every time we distinguish the "Actor" (noun) from the "*Action*" (verb) in the world around us. Nails *pierce* (tires, balloons). Dogs *bark* (at cats). Loose mechanical parts can *rattle.*

This may sometimes be referred to as the *immediate cause.* That *barking* sound is caused by dogs. The flat tire is *caused* by a nail. Why? Just Because. Because that is what dogs and nails *do*. They *act in accordance with their nature.* Causality does not demand anything more or less.

As my first dependency diagrams took form almost twenty five years ago, I toyed with the idea of a third diagramming symbol. There was, of course, no need for a decision-block. Dependency diagrams are *not* flow charts.

I briefly thought that something like nails and balloons should be brought together in an *interaction* box prior to a balloon *deflating* process. Since deflation *is* a nail piercing a balloon, this error seemed to demand that a nail do more than just *be a nail.* This misleading approach was quickly discarded.

CAUSE AS THE ACTOR – IMMEDIATE CAUSE

When there is unexpected behavior, we want to identify some new facet of the nature of things, and the proper starting point is: "What in particular is acting in some new, unexpected or unusual way?

The dog did *not* bark at the cat. *Why?* The nail did *not* pierce the tire. *Why?* What is *that* cause?

To a doctor, it is not helpful at all to know that "someone" has a new and unexpected ache or pain. It is more helpful to know that it is Jane Smith, that the pain is in Jane's foot. Further, that it is the *left* foot, and that it is a dull ache inside in the vicinity of a particular bone of the arch.

Regardless of how much or how little is known about anatomy, this kind of detail is where a causal analysis must start. Think about *Who-What-When-Where-How.*

The doctor who thinks this way is hoping to find cause in the form of a *new actor*, a spur of bone or a rock in a shoe.

By this method, we hope to discover a new agent, or a previously unknown fact about the nature of a familiar one. "*Dogs do not bark <u>when they are sleeping</u>. Nails <u>made of rubber</u>* will not pierce a tire. A bone spur can cause pain in one's foot."

CAUSE AS A LINK IN A CHAIN

A deeper analysis asks: "*What precipitated the new behavior? What set it off?*" Once again, this is a process of naming particulars.

A Nail punctured my tire.
Why?

The roofer's truck spilled nails crossing the intersection.
Why?

The roofer drove over a tree limb he could not see.
Why?

The recent storm broke tree limbs, and many fell onto the road.

Like a row of falling dominoes, this is potentially an endless series. It is a chain, a sequence of things acting in accordance with their nature that forks and terminates in both the infinity of the Universe just being *what it is*, and in *root causes.*

At some point, we reach the limits of our current abilities to command nature, and we have to let this investigation of a *causal chain of events* go.

CAUSE AS A KIND OF THING

The doctor who diagnoses a common ailment in the context of a wealth of medical knowledge has the luxury of classifying "one sample" as a "kind of thing". The doctor could say about the foot pain, *"It is a stress fracture"*, and classify the cause as a "kind of thing". This is the *grouping* issue discussed in a previous chapter.

A tire or balloon can be deflated by a nail, or by a *kind* of thing – a *hard, sharp and pointy* thing. Such is the nature of tires. If this idea is a useful, we may give it a name – deflater would be a choice word to refer to those things which can flatten a tire.

Thinking in principle can open up process improvement possibilities. *"What <u>else</u> could be used as a <u>deflater</u> that would be faster, safer, cheaper than what we use today?"*

CAUSE AS "REASON".

People can be actors in the causal chain; and when they are, we often talk about the cause of their action. Many times, this cause is something abstract or symbolic: a *reason*.

We talk about computers in this manner as well. Sometimes the "effect" we are trying to explain is the result of misinterpretation.

"I drove forward because the light looked green".

"The computer program stopped because it interpreted data as a return code".

"I scheduled construction of concrete forms based on assumptions about the availability of the concrete crew."

When things go wrong, this kind of *cause,* is sometimes called *an error of knowledge.*

ROOT CAUSE - CAUSE AS "CHOICE"

As Actors in the causal sequence, humans have a unique prerogative; they can *choose.* This is a starting point for a sequence of events, a *first cause.* In root cause analysis, this is the end result. After "Cause as Reason" has been studied, only *cause as choice* is left.

There is such a thing as understanding choices in terms of "what is in character" for a certain individual; but we all know no one is absolutely bound by this. *Choice is the kind of behavior one expects from beings that think.*

When we *don't* think, our actions can be reduced to the same kind of dependent causality as everything else. We become just another link in the chain. When we *do* think, we generate outcomes that were *not* inevitable. We can choose to reach into a process and *stop* a domino from falling.

There are always choices we make in the design and implementation of a process that could have been made differently. In Information Technology, there are choices such as: build versus buy, centralized versus distributed, redundancy versus contingency, and so on.

Within the scope of our authority to make decisions, Root Cause Analysis should identify the one or more points at which Strategic choices could have been different, and it should offer alternatives for the future.

When a strategic decision maker asks for _root_ causes, they are effectively saying:

> _Give me options. What are the_ <u>_man-made_</u> _aspects of our operation that could be different, if we so choose?_

There are a number of technical approaches to problem solving and brainstorming: failure mode analysis, the venerable fish-bone analysis, and more. You will find all of these tools more effective when placed on a firm foundation, a proper understanding of _cause._

13: Variability

Shoes in the shoe store were just not selling. After a careful survey of available shoe sizes (6, 8, 10 and size 12) and customer feet (7, 9 and size 11) we happily conclude that the average shoe fits the average foot. *What did we miss? Variability.*

MANAGING VARIABILITY

The shoe store has some control over the variability in shoe sizes when orders are placed, but tactical management of variability is much more subtle. There are things that you can control, and things that you can't. In project and process management, the inability to tell the difference makes things worse and can even end in failure.

There is an old and silly joke about the man who tells the doctor, *"It hurts when I poke my finger in my eye."* The doctor of course, says, *"Well, stop doing that!"* **Learn how to properly manage variability.**

It is often but not always easy to manage known causes of variation. In one copper coil winding and insertion operation studies revealed a one per cent chance of coil failure when current was applied.

How we learned the cause is another story, but the explanation was simple. Copper coil windings varied in how tightly packed the coils were. Some were wound a little looser and some a little tighter. On average, the tightly packed copper bundle was a perfect fit into the intended machine slot.

The looser coils were problematic. About one percent had to be forced into position with the only tool available to the assembler – a screwdriver!

The problem could have been solved far upstream by a product redesign or by re-engineering the coil insertion process, but the simplest answer could have been tactical management of variability.

NO SILVER BULLET

"Surely", many managers think, *"there is a product, maybe hardware, maybe software...something that will solve my variability problems for me."*

While tools can be helpful, there is only one alternative to learning about the nature of variability, how to measure it, and how to manage it. The alternative is to suffer through it.

Many try to punt this issue into the Information Technology department. In call centers, staffing never seems to match call variability, so fortunes are spent on scheduling software and overly complex telephone load leveling systems.

The common result is that calls are dispatched and routed in an inscrutable and unmanageable manner. Service quality suffers because calls are not routed to the right people. (*"But we bought skill-based routing!"*) Caller wait times still have unacceptable peaks and valleys.

Parts assemblers with average sized cylinders to be inserted in average size openings fiddle with stacks of slightly under-sized and slightly over-sized *"within specifications"* parts and wonder why items that meet tolerances won't fit together. Without a proper understanding of variation, managers direct purchasing to tighten the tolerances and buy more expensive components – raising the cost basis of the product they want to sell.

BE CAREFUL WHAT YOU ASK FOR...

You may get it! One cannot apply brute force, one cannot decree that workers stop producing results that have variability. It does not work, and only makes things worse. (James Abbott calls this mistake *Forced Capability - a violation of the principle of Division of Labor in decision-making.*)

One tactical manager tried to eliminate variability by decree. He told his three shift managers, *"Do whatever it takes."* One shift manager performed measurably worse after the order. We called him the **Good Trooper** because of his story.

> *"Of course I'll do what the boss said. I was in the army. I learned that when the boss says jump you ask how high."*

The other supervisors performed more or less as they did *before* the manager's new rule. They said,

> *"He doesn't understand what we can and can't control down here, and he won't listen. I guess whether or not I keep my job depends on chance.*
>
> *There is a chance my variability numbers will be bad, but there is also a chance they will be good. I'll take the credit if they are good, and risk the consequence if they are bad. I know I'll only make things worse if I don't leave what is currently working alone."*

response – they will be beyond the scope of a tactical decision.

The important thing is to maintain a mental readiness, an awareness of the difference between the things you can control and those things that you cannot.

In our previous chapter on causal analysis, we portrayed cause-effect as a potentially infinite chain of events with a decision fork in the alternatives where a human being has made a choice.

One decision fork in the analysis pursues the nature of things are far as we can until we rest our case with this conclusion, *"And that's just the way things are."*

The other decision fork terminates in human choices and actions. Of course, our past choices and actions as historical facts become a given that no power in the Universe can change. They are as indisputable as the fact that nails are pointy and will deflate a tire.

But, we can shift our perspective on human events and submit them to the judgment of hindsight. Why did we decide? Why did we choose? What would the outcome have been had we acted differently? Will we have the knowledge, *when and where we need it,* the next time a similar decision is made?

These are the questions we must ask if we are to incorporate and use new knowledge. These are the questions that highlight what, in the future, we may be able to manage and control.

14: Measurement *Processes*

Temperature cannot be measured in inches, feet or pounds, but it can be measured. Color cannot be measured in kilowatts, but it can be measured a variety of ways including units of temperature and length!

Anything which can be directly or indirectly observed, can be measured. It is simply a matter of choosing an appropriate standard.

Measurement should be thought of as a process, in the same sense that we have discussed in every preceding chapter. It is an intentional method that begins with an input product, a particular metric to be measured.

The process can and should be diagrammed and documented with appropriate metrics. We will talk more about appropriate metrics for measurement processes in the chapter on Measurement Capability and Quality.

The process produces a product, a measurement. One could think of measurement quality (precision, etc.) as *metrics* of the measurement result.

WRITTEN RECORDS

The measurement process is not complete until the result is recorded by pen and paper, by data recorder, or by some reliable means that does not depend on our memory of the result.

MEASUREMENT ERROR VERSUS BLUNDER

Measurement by a correct and consistent process will show variation. I remember a new machine operator who rushed into the quality manager's office to report that they had measured *twice* with the same gauge and had gotten different results! Surely, he thought, this proves that the gauge is broken.

In fact, such encounters with measurement error are common and manageable, particularly as we make precision measurements below the threshold of perception.

On the other hand, there is such a thing as measurement *blunder*. The product of blunder is an *arbitrary result*. Arbitrary results are discarded from reporting and further analysis.

An arbitrary result is not simply an out-lier, an undesirable or an unusual result. It is the product of serious, documented and flawed method. It is the equivalent of a hand on the scale when weights are taken.

SYSTEMIC ERROR

You may be tempted to rehabilitate a special kind of blunder known as *systemic error*. Perhaps you left a 10 pound weight on the scales and conclude that all of your data can be salvaged by subtracting ten pounds.

If we are weighing fifty or one hundred pound sacks of grain, this might be plausible, but there is something called *nonlinear* effects that make even this simple adjustment dangerous, especially when dealing with extreme precision.

ATTRIBUTE MEASUREMENTS

The simplest form of measurement is attribute measurement. Although many examples of this form of measurement are reported as *Pass/Fail*, it is a mistake to think is this solely in terms of defects.

We set up our measurement and records to count the *exception* rather than the rule. A student report card with a check mark for each day of attendance and an **X** for each absence is an example of attribute measurement.

A chicken farmer who grades eggs as regular size or *large* would likely make an **X** for the less likely.

A palette of standards helps simple *Pass/Fail* measurement evolve into discrete measurement across a range of values.

Farmers might grade eggs into small, regular, large and jumbo. Teachers could keep records that discriminate between simply being present and *attending* to the class lessons.

THE IMPORTANCE OF STANDARDS

For measurement to be objective and repeatable – for a number to truly qualify as measurement - there must be a standard that is accessible to all who measure and compare their results. For primitive measurement one need not use an internationally recognized standard, but there must be *some* standard.

With students, we must know whether a partial day counts. With chicken eggs, a large egg is large *compared to what?*

There must also be a standard for dealing with borderline cases. If, for example, an egg appears to be *identical* to the standard, shall we consistently call it regular or large?

Geologists and rock collectors hoping to stumble across a gem one day are probably familiar with Mohs scale of mineral hardness. A pocketful of items like a bit of copper (3), quartz (7), and diamond (10) establish materials hardness on a discrete scale of one to ten. It is a standard gimmick in old action movies; real diamonds scratch glass, but fakes do not.

CONTINUOUS MEASUREMENT

Most of us are more familiar with well researched and universal measurement methods and units of measure. Length, Weight, and Time and their corresponding units are what most of us think of as measurement.

In fact, these measurements are so common, people are often puzzled by my insistence on unconventional examples. I have found that unless people take time to think about these more creative approaches to measurement, they will tend to give up on important metrics as *"unmeasurable"*.

They may be unmeasurable in the conventional sense. There may not be an established and universal measurement method and standard similar to the inch or meter, the pound or the gram. Still, many things can and should be measured, if we as tactical managers intend to manage and reduce variability.

METRICS AND MEASURES REVISITED

This is an appropriate place to emphasize again the distinction between metrics and measures.

A cookie company had their packaging redesigned. The new container was distinctive and stood out from the competitors on the grocery shelf.

"How much space is in the box?", management asked. *Space*, of course, is the metric.

Three different approaches were used. One lab tech filled the box with sand and reported that the box would hold 600 grams of fine sand. The sand was then placed in a graduated cylinder and a second answer was reported in cubic centimeters. A third tech experimented with the company's main product and was able to report that no more than 10 cookies would fit in the box without breaking.

There were three different measures of the one metric. The units of measure ranged from grams, to cubic centimeters, to unbroken cookies.

A measure is a number based on a standard unit. It is arrived at by a correct and consistent method. It *quantifies* a metric. In the packaging business in particular, and generally in any given situation, one form of measurement is more useful than the rest. Whether we think of space in a box in grams, cubic centimeters or a discrete measure like *cookies*, is almost always determined by the decision the data helps us to make.

ACCOUNTING VERSUS MEASUREMENT

If you have experience in accounting, you know the significance of a penny difference in a total. If we divide an odd dollar figure between two accounts we have some discretion over where to credit the fraction of a cent. There is *no* such discretion in a penny difference.

Like a pilot flying on instruments, we must rely on an absolute compliance with method and on mathematical analysis to obtain accurate results and to quantify precision.

We will work through these complications of measurement one step at a time in subsequent chapters, starting with a discussion of variability.

15: Measuring Variability

MEASURE TWICE, CUT ONCE

Carpenters have a saying, *"Measure Twice. Cut once."* Given the likelihood of error, if measurement is cheap *enough* and mistakes are expensive *enough*, then this can be a reliable tactic for reducing costs and maximizing value.

But, what if repeated measurement gives *different* results? It has been said that a man with two watches never knows what time it is. Is this how we think about repeated measurement? Is this an example of the more we know, the less we understand? Should we measure once, and then quit while we are ahead?

ASSIGNABLE CAUSES AND RANDOM CAUSES

When rough measurement varies, the cause or causes are large enough to see, hear or touch. There could be a noticeable burr of metal on a machined part. There could be a substantial bend or kink in a ruler or tape measure.

Of course there are an uncountable number of causes of variation that are *too* small to see. For example, the slightest breeze or a speck of dust has the potential to affect a weighing scale, but in rough measurement, too small to see is too small to matter.

An uncountable finite number of tiny, independently acting unknown things with a collective impact are called *random* causes. Because they are so many and so small (below the threshold of perception), we experience the effect of these things in aggregate. Just we cannot experience the individual

103

While they prepared bigger and bigger capital expenditure requests to tackle what they thought was the common weakness in the ten packaging machine, we dug deeper into the data.

The average of nine zeros and a ten is *one per cent! The* engineers had committed a grouping error. Marching off together in search of a fix based on what the ten machines had in common, they had failed to focus on the idea that one machine was *different.*

MEASUREMENT RANGES

Sometimes grouping errors are hidden within the data. Suppose we reconfigure our experiment to study only 20 ounce bottles.

If we measure and find a cluster of measurements in a range in the neighborhood of 19.5 and another cluster of measurements in a range around 20.25, then we would be wise to describe these as two groups, even if there is no immediate assignable cause.

Uncountable, infinitesimal, unknown and independently acting causes will *blur* measurements into a range. They do not produce distinct clusters of values like 19.5 and 20.25 inch bottles. Only a few, relatively large causes have this kind of impact. Unknown by itself does not mean random.

VARIABILITY

Variability (a metric) refers the amount of spread in a range of measurements. If our 25 bottles all measured the same, then the variability would be zero *by any measure.*

If the measurements ranged from 20.21 to 20.29, then variability would be a small positive number. Twenty-five measurements in a range from 20.011 to 20.49 would be an even wider range *by any measure*.

There are several ways that variability is measured. The simplest calculation takes the largest number in the range and subtracts the smallest.

A more useful and sensitive measure is called *standard deviation*. Standard deviation is *zero* if there is no variability, and the standard deviation calculation produces larger and larger values as variability increases.

SIMPLE EXAMPLES

To illustrate the arithmetic we have been discussing, let's take a simple example and pretend that we are describing the capacity in ounces of five soda bottles.

Here are the measurements:
20.21, 20.23, 20.25, 20.27, 20.29

Here is the Average:
(20.21+20.23+20.25+20.27+20.29)/5 = 20.25

(Note that no one value occurs more than another. There is no *Mode*. The middle value (*Median*) also happens to be 20.25.)

Here is the Range:
(20.29-20.21) = 0.08

Here is The Standard Deviation:
SquareRoot((20.21-20.25)^2+(20.21-20.25)^2+(20.21-20.25)^2+(20.21-20.25)^2+(20.21-20.25)^2)/4)

Whoa! Standard deviation calculations are not so simple, even with just five measurements! For this reason, we often use the Range calculation as a rough measure of Variability when we need a quick *pen and pencil* answer. We use standard deviation for a more sensitive measure of variability when time and computing resources permit.

Every spreadsheet program calculates averages and standard deviations with simple built-in formulas. The formula is typically STDEVS or STDEV(Spreadsheet Range). If there is more than one STDEV calculation, test it on these five numbers. The correct answer is 0.31623.

A WORD ABOUT THAT *OTHER* STANDARD DEVIATION CALCULATION.

That *other* Standard Deviation calculation found in calculators and spreadsheet programs is called the *population* statistic.

It is intended to summarize the variation in a complete finite group. This can be thought of as a hindsight or *postmortem* statistic. *"The 42 widgets we shipped to ACME corporation had a Population Standard Deviation of 6.3"*

The difference between the two calculations diminishes as larger and larger data sets are examined.

16: Correct and Consistent

The responsibility of the tactical manager to the process is to sustain an optimum state of readiness in the face of variability and change. We plan precisely because things *don't* always go according to plan.

An operational plan gives us a baseline of operations. Change is managed as exceptions. When possible deviations from the plan can be anticipated, prepared contingencies are possible.

THE VIRTUOUS CIRCLE

Many people **underestimate** the potential of effective tactical management to improve quality and lower costs. Instead they reach only for expensive capital intensive solutions, or do without.

The tactical management of variability and change as outlined in the last chapter are intended to create a *virtuous circle*, where success and improvement breeds more of the same.

The foundation for this engine of continuous improvement is the principle of correct and consistent operation.

TARGETS

We gardened when I was a child. The ideal was straight maintainable rows of corn, beans and other vegetables. Until I learned a couple of tricks, my rows were anything but straight.

I might start with the intention of a straight row, but a rock or clod of dirt would subtlety send me off course. Looking back on a freshly planted row, I could see why I had failed. Hindsight, they say, is 20/20.

"Pick a target", I was told. A tree or stake in the ground would represent a point to which I could extend my row and keep it straight. This is the essence of *correct operation* – *process targets*.

The science of tactical management recognizes that *process* targets are things we can directly control.

In the call center, our staffing target may be a 65% utilization. In the kitchen, our baking ovens may be a target temperature of 375 degrees.

In the call center, we cannot *directly* control rings to answer, caller hold times and busy/no-answer. In the kitchen, we cannot *directly* control whether or not some of the biscuits are burned. In fact, products that fail to meet targets, *once they occur*, are beyond anyone's ability to control.

An exploitation of cause/effect relationships and *process target* control is the *only* way we have of affecting product outcome. This is what is meant by Francis Bacon when he said, *"Nature to be commanded, must be obeyed."*

CONSISTENCY & FRESH DATA

My childhood garden rows were improved with a target, a stake in the ground to which I could direct my planted rows, but they were perfect when I added a piece of string and a second stake.

Every time I dug into the ground I got *fresh data*. I could see where *this* seed would be planted in relation to the string which marked a straight line.

Tactical operations achieve the same result by observing and *writing down* actual process values *as work occurs.* Everyone prefers an automated system, but this record-keeping is essential. *Use a pencil and paper if you must.*

If you manage the bakery, set your oven on target temperatures, and periodically *measure and record* the actual temperature in the oven. If you manage a call center, staff to a utilization target and then *measure* utilization throughout the workday.

Beginners often measure only the product. (We call these *"burnt biscuit"* reports.) It's at least a start. Just as one might infer something about an unseen animal from footprints, s*ome* information can be gleaned about a process by looking at the *imprint* it leaves in production.

CONSISTENCY CHARTS

Consistency is analyzed graphically in the form of a *time series* chart. *Time Series* means that the data is plotted in the order of events. Time is the 'X' axis of the graph.

111

Thirty-Seven Ideas For Tactical Managers*

This is yesterday's data summarized as control limits:

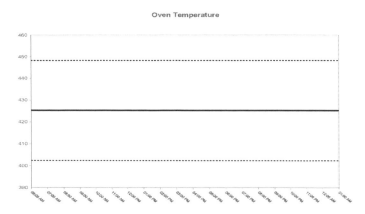

This is today's data illustrating consistency:

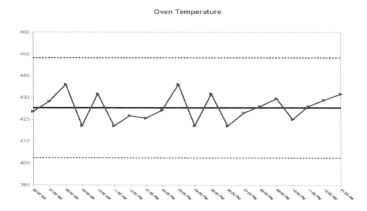

And finally, this is data that *shows change*:

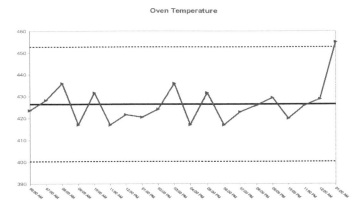

Oven Temperature

Consistency charts document a baseline of process consistency, and then highlight exactly when and where change occurs.

Knowing when and where to look for a previously unknown and unmanaged aspect of a process is the key to the virtuous circle.

NEW KNOWLEDGE

New knowledge does not come automatically. However, if tactical management creates and uses a tool that highlights when and where to look, new knowledge can be found.

You will remember that we described random causes in a previous chapter. Random causes are not infinite in number; they are finite but uncountable.

When Mathematicians think *in principle* about the collective behavior of random causes, they will push the number of

115

causes to infinity in their calculations – but that does not change the fact that in reality there is an uncountably large finite number.

A measure that shows variation and consistency like the graphs above is said to show *random* variation. The measurement is just being blurred by the combined effect of many tiny things.

Mathematicians also push the effect of any *individual* random to *zero* in their calculations. If any cause exists, and it contributes something to variation in our process, then its individual effect is certainly *not* zero. The individual effect is, however, typically masked – hidden within the collective effect of many tiny causes.

When a consistency chart shows change, the largest and potentially manageable of these random causes stands out a bit from the crowd. A change in the time series is an imperative to *look now* for some previously unmanaged aspect of the process that might be controlled to make a better product.

MANAGED CHANGE

What accounted for that surge in call volume at the call center? Was it a new product announcement? An INTERNET outage? A product recall? A change in call routing?

What caused that subtle shift in the temperature readings of the baking oven? Was it the *quantity* we attempted to bake at one time? Was an over door left open? Is it a gas-fired oven? Has the BTU content of the gas supply mix changed?

These are the kinds of questions you should be asking when consistency monitoring shows that something about the process has changed.

To truly improve, you must identify the cause of the change, assess its impact, add it to your dependency diagrams – and manage it. This new knowledge becomes a part of an improved baseline – a better understanding of what is *correct*.

You can see now why I strongly recommend the use of tools such as dependency diagrams. As an inventory of knowledge, they should grow in detail, by adding metrics, measures and target values each time something is learned.

Show me a dependency diagram of your process today and that of last year, and I can tell if you have improved your business.

17: Project Tracking

Many projects have a *Phase I, Phase II, Phase III* structure. The plan details a long series of tasks for the first phase, and then continues into subsequent phases as though all knowledge of tasks and dependencies are known at the project's commencement.

Some call this a *waterfall* schedule because of the way the task plan looks on a GANTT chart. The task bar durations look like a series of steps – a terracing pattern down which water could cascade.

As these projects are tracked, unknowns *do occur.* The result is that unplanned tasks must be added, contingency resources must be deployed, and so on. The manager's goal is to see the project through as close to the original plan as possible.

The key control points in a waterfall approach are the sub-objectives. A sub-objective dictates a duration and the necessary and sufficient tasks.

ITERATIVE APPROACHES

An iterative approach is different. Instead of managing the project from sub-objective to sub-objective, the driver is a constant interval of time.

Instead of asking, *"How much time do we need to complete the next sub-objective?"*, we ask *"How many tasks can we complete in a constant interval of time, e.g. in the next week?"*

Iterative projects are still guided by the final objective, a deliverable constrained by performance, time and cost. The development of a task plan is more fluid and tends to grow in detail concurrently with execution.

In R&D and software development projects, this approach is sometimes called *growing* a program. All information necessary to plan and execute the project are *not* collected and available at the beginning.

Each iteration solves one or more technical issues, and generates fresh facts that help the manager and tactical team to adjust and detail the tasks in the next iterations.

Development work is sometimes shopped on the basis of the hourly rate of technical staff. In my experience, bill rate does not correlate with productivity.

Short interval iterative project tracking permits productivity of knowledge workers to be continually assessed. One is less likely to spend eighty per cent of the time and money budgeted, only to find that eighty per cent of the work remains to be done.

NINETY-FIVE PER CENT COMPLETE
In either approach to task tracking, nothing is more deadly than the ninety-five per cent complete syndrome.

A one hundred foot trench that has five feet of excavation remaining is ninety-five per cent complete. Only tasks that have such definitive and measurable partial completions should be scored in this fashion.

Many tasks that are paused and then resumed are not "partially *complete*". They are simply not done at all.

Much of the cost of time in many tasks is simply the overhead involved in opening up the work. A painter, for example, must prep the areas to be painted. Brushes must be clean. Paint must be color matched and recently mixed. Surfaces must be clean.

A painter who interrupts their work when *"95% complete"* incurs considerable overhead to stop and then begin again at a later time.

If a task like painting spans days, it is better to organize the tasks into smaller tasks that *can* easily be tracked as completed or not. *Paint the house interior* becomes multiple tasks: *Paint Bedroom 1, Bedroom 2, Living Room*, etc.

TRACKING AND THE CUSTOMER

Customers love vending machines. They insert a coin, push a button, and receive a product. What happens in the soda machine is an unimportant curiosity.

Process matters to the *customer* only to the extent that it defines the product. When a two by four is cut, customers care about the process used to cut it only in how it affects the final result. Is the finished cut rough or smooth? Did the cutting process discolor or soil the wood with oil or burn marks?

Project tracking with the customer is an important aspect of project management, but you must remember to keep the focus on deliverables: the objective, sub-objectives and their metrics.

If a leg in the project took longer than planned, you should document it by adding and highlighting the unplanned but necessary tasks that were added to the project time line. This is especially important if these tasks are triggered as a result of changes requested by the customer.

Tasks are *your* responsibility. Values and risk are always in the mind of the customer, the sponsor of your project. They are weighing and re-weighing the initial decision to commission the project.

Remember: If a project does not meet its deliverables, or if external circumstances change, it is the customer's prerogative to *quit while they are behind*, and only pursue a project as far as contractually required.

TRACKING FREQUENCY

There should be a relationship between the frequency of task tracking with a project team and the frequency of deliverables tracking with customers and their financial partners.

If customer-side tracking occurs monthly or quarterly, task tracking on a weekly or bi-weekly basis gives several control points for the tactical manager to assess and redeploy resources as needed.

The capacity to deploy and re-deploy resources is the single most powerful mechanism the tactical manager has to cope with change and the unexpected. You want to create multiple opportunities to exercise that capacity in the intervals between customer reviews.

CRISIS AND TURN-AROUND

Crisis and turnaround projects do not have the luxury of time. When rapid results are required, iterative project management can require a decision cycle measured in hours instead of days.

A five minute task review every hour is sometimes warranted by extreme circumstances. Such tight control can produce amazing results in a short period of time, but it is extremely stressful to the entire project team.

This amounts to a *duty cycle* in excess of what can be sustained by an average human being. If the concept of duty cycle is new to you, you can read more about this important concept in a later chapter.

TAKING THE LOSS

If you have one hundred miles to drive, and an hour to make your appointment – *you are already late*! Most people do not *"take the loss" when this realization sets in.*

In the United States, safe and legal speed limits are typically no more than 75 miles per hour. Our late driver has two choices:

He can take the loss, and use the one hour of time to the best contingent advantage; he can make a phone call, set up a video-conference, nominate a delegate to the meeting on his behalf, or take some other mitigating action to minimize the loss.

Alternatively, he can be tempted to speed.

Variations of this dilemma occur every day. Paint needs adequate drying time before another coat is applied. Food requires adequate cooking time if it is not to be served raw.

How tactical managers cope with this dilemma is a test of wisdom and character.

Do we take the loss as soon as we know we are late and use the time wisely to minimize the consequences? Or, do we speed? Do we leave off a specified second coat of paint? Do we serve hamburger raw?

One could hardly make a good case for serving raw meat or for slacking on a paint job, and one has to reach for a fantastic circumstance to justify a one hundred mile per hour road race.

The tactical manager is bound by the directive of correct and consistent execution and there is no choice from this perspective. But, when we place ourselves in the role of a strategic decision-maker things occasionally look different.

I don't want to legitimize flouting what one knows to be correct, but remember that strategic decision makers weigh values and risk. They sometimes must make difficult choices, and they must be prepared to live with the consequences.

TIME IS THE OPPORTUNITY FOR ACTION.

In movies of the action thriller type – the hero says *"we are out of time"*, thirty seconds before the explosive detonates. Why? Because defusing the bomb takes longer. *The opportunity for action has been lost.*

You will find it extremely useful to put aside arcane and niche definitions of time in favor of this straightforward and

You can expect that individuals will bring expectations of privileges and entitlements based on position, rank, class, education, and need as well as merit. The challenge is to create an environment where extraneous differences can be respectfully set aside, leaving only issues pertaining to the common goal: *to work productively together*.

A HARMONIOUS WORKPLACE

Despite the fact that people come to the workplace with different expectations, it is still possible to create an environment in which you can earn the coveted title of *tough, but fair*.

When someone steps up to play a new sport, they expect to have to learn new rules. In soccer, the use of hands is penalized. In basketball, *traveling* with the ball is not allowed.

In a new work environment, people are receptive to receiving and abiding by a work-specific set of ground rules for behavior.

You have to remember, though, that *Money Talks*. "*I did not pay them to be rude to customers!*", said one manager. "*But you did!*", I reminded him. "*Yesterday was payday! Didn't they get paid?*"

If a referee never calls fouls, players feel free to commit them. If there are no consequences for negative behavior, associates will assume that *correct and consistent process* is only a suggestion.

DALE CARNEGIE

How to Win Friends and Influence People was a salesman's bible for many thousands in the last century. His most memorable advice was to *"Never, Never Criticize."*

This advice is closely tied to the theme of this chapter. Many times, people experience criticism as an injustice. Coaching can be different. Coaching deals explicitly and exclusively with what an individual acknowledges they can control.

A barrage of criticism generally provokes resentment and not change. *"What can I do about spilled milk? Water under the bridge? Someone else was at least partly at fault."*

You cannot help someone else clarify their thinking as to what they can and cannot control unless you are crystal clear on this distinction yourself.

Don't forget that we are talking *is* and not *ought*. What someone *ought* to be able to control *somehow* is not the clear and detailed thinking of a good tactical manager. The next chapter on the principle of Division Of Labor in Decision-Making will delve deeper into this subject.

ERRORS OF KNOWLEDGE

Our earlier chapter on variability introduced the idea that experience should result in increased knowledge. One important *take-away* from this book should be several techniques for retaining and organizing that knowledge.

From the dependency diagrams, to factor tables and visual documentation techniques, to proper methods of organizing metrics to highlight the *ideas* hidden in data – I encourage

129

you to take advantage of these as are appropriate for your situation.

It is usually inadequate to simply *tell* an associate some fact, policy or other guidance as to how to perform their job. They are as likely to remember seventeen workplace rules as they are likely to accurately retain seventeen digit part numbers.

The best pilots still use preflight *checklists* no matter what their level of experience. Good tactical managers should not simply rely on associates *remembering* everything that is important about their job.

SEX, POLITICS, AND RELIGION

Sex, politics and religion are the original big three *verboten* topics during business hours. The list is a little longer today.

Although there is a great pleasure in seeking out and sharing time and conversation with people who share our philosophical perspectives on life, it is *still* asking for trouble to open up these issues at work, unless these matters *are* our work. The subject of sex will inevitably come up in some form at the condom factory. It need not be discussed at the furniture plant.

Setting aside these issues in the workplace is a contract to *agree to disagree*. It is a respectful attitude that acknowledges the different opinions we hold regarding the earned and deserved, but sets them aside for our common virtue – the desire to be productive.

GETTING "PLAYED"

If you take fair treatment of customers and associates seriously, you must be on your guard against those who play on your sense of Justice.

Did you make a mistake? Did you mistreat someone or are you being played? Unearned and deserved guilt feels exactly the same.

Your commitment to know your own mind, to fully understand what you can control and what you cannot, what *others* can control and cannot, and your willingness to correct your thinking when you are wrong is your only defense against getting manipulated by cynical opportunists whose ideas about justice are, shall we say, *flexible*.

FINAL THOUGHTS

Resist the urge to cultivate a parent-child relationship with people who report to you. This can cultivate a culture of entitlement along the lines of Judith Bardwick's *Comfort Zone*.

There *is* an element in supervision that we call *air cover*. Good managers watch for and intercept pressures and events from above and from outside the team that can undermine associates ability to focus on their tasks. Although this feels like parenting, it is simply part of the job of a good tactical manager.

Resist the urge to characterize your management style as democracy or dictatorship. Concepts of politics do not belong in business. It is reasonable to poll associates and vote on serious matters in which they have a personal stake, but it is a mistake to call the question on every trivial matter, particularly if the result is a foregone conclusion.

Keep the distinction between perks and privileges, compensation and generosity. If you provide a free lunch to squeeze a few extra minutes of time from staff during a crisis, don't spin it as generosity or a privilege. At best you will fool no one. At worst, you will modify employee expectations. When free pizza lunches go away, someone will feel cheated.

I'll never forget the restroom signs to employees in a large manufacturing plant: *"We have generously provided these facilities here for your convenience."* Really?

Legalities and building codes aside, just how *convenient* would it be for the business if there were *no* facilities? A sign that said *"We provide these restrooms close to your workstation so you can get back to work ASAP."* would be more honest, but does the obvious really need to be said?

19:Division of Labor In Decision Making

James Abbott has devoted considerable work to the development of what he calls the Division of Labor in Decision Making.

James spent considerable time studying the concepts of policy, strategy and tactics before offering his own refinement and its application to business and organizational decision making.

For some, his distinction between strategy and tactics is unconventional, but it follows directly from the dictionary distinction that tactics employ *available* means.

THE A TEAM

The A team was a television show in the eighties. A generation later, the A team was rebooted in the form of a feature movie.

They were a small military unit that could surely serve as an icon for the ultimate tactical team. Their adventure episodes featured such feats as turning a civilian jeep into an armored vehicle with scrap metal and a welding torch.

Whatever resources were available were re-deployed to serve the mission at hand.

In similar fashion, tactical decisions deal with available staffing, facilities and budgets.

When strategic management takes full responsibility for matching an operation's capabilities to customer expectations, and when tactical management commits to correct and consistent operation – an organization will find its peak performance.

When we fail to separate issues of customer expectations and capabilities from proper operational practices, we inevitably have failures and misplaced blame.

Respect for the principal of Division of Labor in Decision-Making creates a clear demarcation of two fundamentally different business issues. It facilitates the creation of a culture of fairness and transparency. It is a primary key to apportioning accountability properly matched with authority.

James Abbott's classes on service and manufacturing management are the definitive presentation of Division of Labor in Decision-Making. I refer you to that material for a deeper discussion and will conclude by introducing one final element.

FOUNTAINHEAD
Definition of FOUNTAINHEAD

> *1 : a spring that is the source of a stream*
> *2 : principal source : origin*
> *Source: merriam-webster.com*

Tacticians deal with particulars and risk *losing sight of the forest for the leaves on the trees*. Strategic thinking is more abstract. They know that *someone* and *somehow* will eventually be identified as a particular agent with particular means, but those particulars are set aside as they think *in principal* about how to achieve company goals.

Strategic managers weigh values and risks. Through advertising, marketing and sales, they set product expectations in the minds of customers. Through capital expenditures, they attempt to provide facilities and tools that give our operations the capability to meet and exceed those customer expectations.

Just as strategy provides a kind of guidance and structure in which tacticians can act with confidence and certainty, there is a higher level of decision-making that provides similar guidance to the strategist. *Policy* provides that guidance.

I say *objectives* and *tasks* when I discuss the tactical management of ends and means. To describe a strategy, I prefer to talk about *goals* and the *principles of action* that will achieve those goals.

Ultimately, the purpose and methods of cooperative effort must be guided by something much more concise. Every successful organization has a leader who can clearly and concisely articulate *what business we are in*. *Mission* and *Vision* are the means and ends of *Policy*.

If the Balance Sheet and the P&L are the principal responsibility of strategic and tactical decision makers, the Capital Account is the responsibility of policy makers.

POLICY DECISIONS

Reliable communications *with anyone, anytime and anywhere* – is the kind of vision that implies and guides

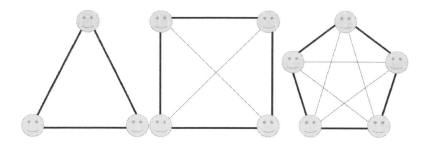

You can see that only three lines are required to connect three nodes so that each is connected to every other. Six lines are required to connect four nodes, and *ten* lines are required to connect the five. Twenty nodes would require one hundred and ninety connecting lines to connect each and every node. (*See the article on Metcalfe's Law in Wikipedia.*)

If nodes represent primary factual knowledge, consider that if we discover and identify each and every relationship of twenty facts, we have almost **ten times** as much information represented by relationships as that represented by the primary factual knowledge.

A hundred primary facts can mature with time and experience into as many as *half a million* relational facts.

Granted, not every relationship represents actionable knowledge, but many *will*.

THE MATURING PROCESS

When anyone speaks of *emotional* maturity, of maturing in one's career or of maturing in wisdom and judgment, you can see *connection-building* driving the growth process and serving as it's measure.

Improve Your Project and Process Management Skills!

How many *connections* have you made?

One is told, let's say, that it is not good to lie. From the earliest age, you may possess this factual knowledge. But, is it lying to tell a child that *"Mickey Mouse wants you to eat your peas?"* Is it lying to be cheerful on a gloomy day and say *"Great!"* when a customer asks you how you feel today?

You answer these questions from the mature *relational* knowledge gained as you connect what you know about morality, child behavior, business customs and business protocols.

WHAT CAN YOU TELL ME THAT I DON'T ALREADY KNOW?

I have taught many operations and operations management classes over the years. One new student was a generation younger than me.

He was only a few years out of school and reasonably well trained. After flipping through the training syllabus, he quickly saw words and terms familiar and fresh from college. He sized up our age difference and was certain that there would be nothing in the classroom presentation for him. His very first words were, *"What can you tell me that I don't already know?"*

A more serious attitude is commonly found in managers a decade older. Those more mature students of management had learned to prize the wisdom of relational knowledge.

Having grown to the point where *relational knowledge* represented perhaps half of their mental wealth – they were eager to seek out and add more connections. Some would

141

On Day Zero, Assets, Liabilities and Net Worth are all zero amounts. The single activity of a one thousand dollar investment makes *two* changes to the bookkeeping. A company asset of $1000 appears, and a record of the value of *ownership* is recorded.

On Day Zero, the business owner possessed $1000 in cash. On Day One, before any business takes place, the business owner owns a business that, in turn owns an asset of $1000 in cash. The *book value* of the business to its owner is $1000.

The new business owner puts on the Policy hat and answers the question – what *kind* of business am I in? His vision is a neighborhood of clean manicured lawns and he decides to make it his business mission to provide an affordable lawn care service for his neighbors.

How does one *do* that? Well, *in principle,* one must advertise a service and a price, show up at each customer's lawn with the right equipment and supplies and someone must *cut* the lawn, trim the hedges and so on.

This exercise in *strategic* thinking culminates in the need for tools and equipment, so the second financial activity is the purchase of a lawn mower.

The Balance sheet now looks like this:

ASSETS
> **Cash $800**
> **Equipment: $200**
> **Total Assets: $1000**

LIABILITIES
> **Total Liabilities: $0**

NET WORTH
> **Owner Investment: $1000**
> **Total NET WORTH: $1000**

The business has not yet made or lost any money. It still owns $1000 of assets, not all in cash, and the owner still owns a business with a book value of $1000.

There were two changes to the books. Cash was decreased by the cost of a lawn mower, and the value of the lawn mower was added as an equipment asset.

EXPENSES, PROFIT AND LOSS

Consumables such as gasoline for the mower are not typically tracked as an asset. A mower can be used to provide services for years, but gasoline is purchased and used every time work is performed.

Fifty dollars of gasoline is recorded on a second report called a *Profit and Loss statement, or P&L*. A Profit and Loss report is *not* a cumulative report. It covers a consistent period of time such as a week, a month, a quarter or a year. A simple P&L looks like this:

INCOME:
> **Total Income: $0**

EXPENSE:
> **Gasoline: $50**
> **Total Expense: $50**

Profit or Loss: -$50

The new business has spent cash and received none, so it shows a loss. Remember that every activity results in *two* changes to the company books. The second half of this financial activity in on the *Balance Sheet!* It looks like this:

ASSETS
> **Cash $750**
> **Equipment: $200**
> **Total Assets: $950**

LIABILITIES
> **Total Liabilities: $0**

NET WORTH
> **Owner Investment: $1000**
> **Current Profit/Loss: -$50**
> **Total NET WORTH: $950**

The second half of the gasoline purchase reduces the amount of cash the business owns. The adjustment to Net Worth is *not* a third bookkeeping entry – it is a *carryover* of the bottom line of the Profit and Loss Statement, and it is used to adjust the book value of the owner's investment.

The owner may have established credit at the gas station, promising to pay for the gas at a later date. Cash is retained, but the purchase still shows up on the balance sheet like this:

ASSETS
    Cash $800
    Equipment: $200
    Total Assets: $1000

LIABILITIES
    ACCOUNTS PAYABLE (Charge Card): $50
    Total Liabilities: $50

NET WORTH
    Owner Investment: $1000
    Current Profit/Loss: -$50
    Total NET WORTH: $950.

Double Entry Bookkeepers cross-check their work many ways. One rule for accurate bookkeeping is *Assets = Liabilities + Net Worth*. A total of Liabilities and Net Worth is usually added at the bottom of the balance sheet to confirm that the books are in balance.

You can see from these two examples that paying cash or buying gasoline on credit does not change the fact that our little business has lost $50, and the bookkeeping reflects this in either case.

TIME TO MAKE A PROFIT

Tactics is all about execution. With our tactics hat in place, our small businessman arrives at the customer's residence, correctly and consistently delivers the agreed service. (He cuts the grass.) Good tactical execution includes record keeping and our customer is invoiced for services at a rate of $65.

We can conclude this brief introduction to basic accounting with a positive. Our first job netted $65, leaving us with a $15 profit. Unfortunately, we must wait until the end of the month to collect our money. Our books will initially show the money owed to us as an asset called Accounts Receivable.

An asset of Accounts Receivable in your bookkeeping is an Accounts Payable on a customer's books. With double entry bookkeeping, everyone who conducts business has records that serve as a check and a balance on all of their trading partners.

It's why businesses want you to keep your receipts for cash purchases. If your cash payment on an account is lost through error or mishandling, your receipt for payment is proof that a bookkeeping entry to your credit should be in the seller's records and the corresponding cash will be conspicuously absent if the books are examined.

The P&L changes when we record $65 income, and it looks like this:

INCOME:
> **Total Income: $65**

EXPENSE:
> **Gasoline: $50**
> **Total Expense: $50**

Profit or Loss: +$15

The balance sheet also changes. An Asset is created called ACCOUNTS RECEIVABLE and the Profit and Loss number carried over from the P&L is updated to show the current accurate value, a $15 profit.

ASSETS
> **Cash $800**
> **Accounts Receivable: $65**
> **Equipment: $200**
> **Total Assets: $1065**

LIABILITIES
> **ACCOUNTS PAYABLE (Charge Card): $50**
> **Total Liabilities: $50**

NET WORTH
> **Owner Investment: $1000**
> **Current Profit/Loss: +$15**
> **Total NET WORTH: $1015**

Total LIABILITIES and NET WORTH: $1065

When the money due for services is collected, the Accounts Receivable balance decreases and the Cash Balance increases. The books stay in balance.

THE TIP OF THE ICEBERG
This much accounting is enough to at least orient the tactical manager to how financial records reflect management decisions and actual profitability.

When companies invoice large dollar amounts and fund large payrolls and facilities expenses, it is easy to be fooled into thinking that these large cash flows confirm certain and large profits. It is not necessarily so.

The financial management of an organization is a discipline in itself. *"Why must we wait until next quarter for the new equipment? Why did we turn down a particular order?"* Many strategic decisions might seem mysterious to the tactical manager who has no insight into modern accounting.

If this subject was new to you, you now have a framework of basic concepts on which to grow and organize your understanding of this important subject.

22: From Arithmetic to Algebra

Everyone who works with numbers needs to know a little algebra. If algebra did not click for you in school, this easy review may help.

Algebra is to arithmetic as strategy is to tactics. The strategic plan is full of someone, somehow and sometime. The tactical plan must say who, what, when and where.

Algebra talks about some number *X* or *Y* that will be divided, added, or multiplied. Arithmetic deals with specific numbers, like *21.25*.

In this sense, *basic* algebra is a *recipe language*. It is a shorthand for writing down arithmetic steps that we might forget. It helps us get the math right.

AVERAGES

Instead of a worked example of average, like that which appears in the preceding chapter, algebra lets us write out, *in principle*, how to average *any* set of measurements.

A formula might look like this:

$(X_1+X_2+X_3+X_4+X_5)/5 =$ *The Average* of Five Measurements

or this:

$(X_1+X_2...X_n)/N =$ *The Average* of N Measurements.

Thirty-Seven Ideas For Tactical Managers*

RECIPE SHORTCUTS

Cooking recipes can turn into disasters if you don't know the shortcuts, like the abbreviations and differences between tablespoon and teaspoon.

Algebra has common abbreviations and shortcuts that can throw a beginner. For example, the formula to *sum up* a series of numbers is typically written:

$$\sum X$$

and pronounced: *"sum of all X"*. So

$$\frac{\sum X}{N}$$

would be a reminder that the *average* formula requires that we sum all measurements (the Xs) and divide by the number of measurements (N stands for number).

Averages are a frequent ingredient to larger calculations, like standard deviation. Even the short formula for average above is to long and confusing for such a common calculation.

In algebra, an X with a *bar* across the top:

$$\bar{X}$$

is a common shortcut which means average of all the measurements.

THE FORMULA FOR STANDARD DEVIATION
The formula for standard deviation begins by calculating an average. Using this average as a reference point, the formula measures the distance from each X to the average; It subtracts every number from the average:

$$\bar{X} - X_i$$

Because these numbers are a mix of positive and negative, a simple sum of the differences would cancel out to zero. The average, after all, is the *balance point* in the midst of all these measurements.

So, the differences are squared, summed, and then a kind of *average* is calculated. The sum of the squares of the differences between measurements and their average is divided by ….*N-1.*

What a surprise! An average of five numbers involves division by five. An average of nine requires division by nine, but standard deviation calculations require a division by *N-1*!

That *other* standard deviation calculation in your spreadsheet program <u>does</u> divide by N and always produces a slightly smaller value. The difference is subtle and technical, but for our purposes in tactical management, we certainly don't want to *under* estimate variability, and we almost always use the formula below:

$$\sqrt{\left(\frac{\sum (\bar{X} - X_i)^2}{n-1}\right)}$$

As you can see, the final step in a standard deviation calculation is a Square Root. Although the intermediate result based on ounce measurement will be in units of ounces-squared, this final step completes the standard deviation calculation, and variability is measured in simple ounces – the units which were used as the original measure.

ADVANCED ALGEBRA

You may recall formulas from Algebra class that looked like this: $y=2*x$, or $y=x^2-6$. These formulas show, in principle, the *relationship* between two groups of numbers and are often illustrated by drawing a line on graph paper.

$y=x$ was the equation for a perfectly straight line. $y=x^2$ was the equation for a perfect parabola – the cone shape in a perfect head light that directs all light forward.

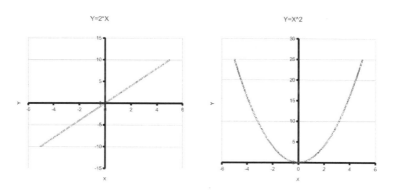

These ideal mathematical shapes from algebra have many uses. One of the more useful (and notorious) is commonly called the *bell-shaped* curve, or *normal* distribution.

A normal distribution is a picture of the *blurring* effect of random causes on measurement, when certain assumptions are carried to extreme.

The normal curve is smooth, symmetrical, and extends to x = infinity in either direction, approaching but never touching y= zero.

Normal Distribution
or
Normal Curve

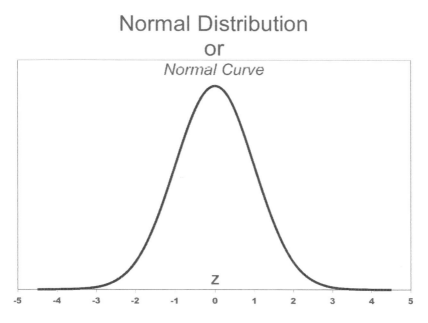

Like a perfect circle or square, the normal curve is an ideal shape because of the way that it is derived. Instead of dealing with the real world of an uncountable number of infinitesimally small unknowns, mathematicians have extended and idealized this in two ways. They assume that the uncountable approaches infinity and the infinitesimal approaches zero.

What is the combined additive effect of an *infinite* number of causes each with *zero* effect? In the real world, there is no such thing. In mathematics we can answer this question by describing what the real world *tends toward in principle*.

In a way, this is no different than the way a physicist would describe the effects of gravity on the shape of a planet. Although no planet is perfectly spherical, there is an unrelenting force that tends to pull the mass of a planet into a sphere. (*Excluding the effects of rotation.*)

Similarly, even though the distribution of measurements are never clustered in a perfect normal curve pattern around the central tendency, there is an unrelenting action on the part of *the many tiny independent unknowns -* to *blur* measurement into this characteristic pattern.

USING THE NORMAL CURVE

We all know what the proportions of a circle are as it is cut in half, thirds, or six pieces. In fact, some bakers have a template that allows them to cut a cake or pie into six equal slices.

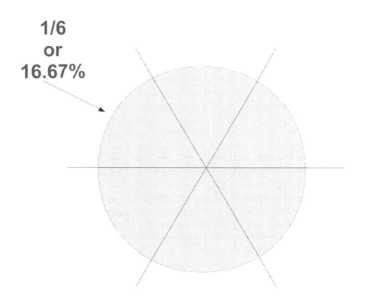

**1/6
or
16.67%**

The normal curve has well-known proportions as well. It is known, for example, that if it is divided in the middle, that 50% of the curve will be on each side of the middle, just as 50% of a round pie or cake will be on each side of a cut through the middle.

Normal Distribution
or

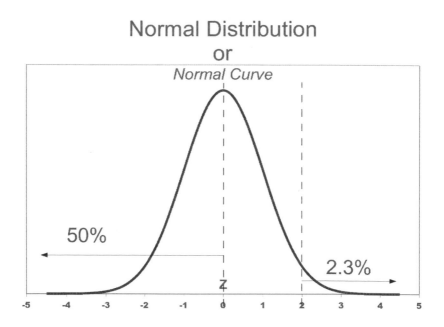

The proportions of the normal curve to the left and right of any cut are tabulated in Z-tables, like this:

Z Value	Portion Of Normal Curve
0	50.000%
1	15.866%
2	2.275%
3	0.135%

The practical use of this will be covered in detail in the next chapter. What we intend to do is use this idealized shape from advanced algebra as a kind of template to judge how much of the measurement data set is close to the average, and how far can the range of values is likely to extend.

162

23: Measuring Capability

Capability is a process management concept. However, since project and process are so interconnected, there is applicability to both.

A project manager may want to know how many sheets of drywall a crew can hang in a day, or how many screw fasteners in a plywood deck fail to attach and secure.

Correct and consistent processes with known capabilities are vital to the project manager's ability to forecast the amount and duration of work

RUSSIAN DOLLS

Russian dolls are a novelty item. The US version would be a little doll of our current President. Inside would be progressively smaller dolls representing previous administrations. Russian dolls go back at least to Lenin.

This *nesting* relationship is reminiscent to me of the relationship between processes and projects. Inside every successful project are micro-processes that must be managed to the tactical standard of correct and consistent. Their capability is the determining factor of completion times and costs.

On the other hand, the deliverable of projects is very often *facilities, methods and tools* that enable and improve business processes!

A manufacturing plant may execute an engineering project to replace a slower welding machine with one that is faster and has a greater precision.

A space designer plans and builds out square footage with a defined capability – say, call center workstations for twenty agents and two supervisors.

An IT architect plans a new eCommerce web store and chooses a platform commensurate with the anticipated usage and growth of the application.

Tactical managers need to understand *capability* from both perspectives. They must think in terms of current systems and processes and their capabilities when run correctly and consistently. They must think about capabilities as a key performance metric on project deliverables.

IT'S NOT REALLY ABOUT THE PRODUCT
Capability could describe a call center's ability to handle a certain call volume. It could describe a manufacturing operation's ability to hold a tight tolerance. We typically begin to measure and analyze capability by preparing performance chart data.

However, capability is not a description of what *has been* produced in goods and services. It is a forward looking description of what we *expect* to be able to produce. It is not about the product. It is about the process. In this sense, every product produced in a plant, every call taken in a call center is a *footprint*, an *artifact* that tells us something about the process.

A performance chart may tell us about the last one hundred customer service cases, or the last one hundred manufacturing welds. A *capability* analysis makes a prediction about process expectations for *the **next one hundred.***

GROUPING AND CAPABILITY

Production and production data must be properly grouped for an accurate capability assessment. One does not group *call handle times* of order placements with order errors and complaints. One does not group the welding performance of welding station #1 and #2 until the performance of each has been analyzed and understood separately.

Properly grouped performance results typically do not look like the badly run cable TV performance chart in our earlier chapter. When processes are correct and consistent, performance charts tend to make a bell shaped curve pattern.

When the data does *not* make this predictable pattern, there is usually a cause. The process was *not* correct and consistent across the period of time production was studied. A *consistency* chart (or *control* chart) is used as supporting documentation to confirm or disprove C&C operations.

Managers with a high degree of training in advanced statistical techniques may be tempted to use more sophisticated analytical techniques when performance data does not form a classic bell shape. Often, this is a mistake. In our later chapter (*Low Hanging Fruit*) we will discuss other causes of truncated or deformed bell shaped performance charts.

USING THE BELL CURVE AND Z-TABLES TO ESTIMATE RISK

A performance chart is transformed from a backward look at past production to a forward estimate of capability and risk by use of the bell shaped curve as a *template*.

We overlay the bell shape on top of the performance chart. *If it fits*, we can use the known proportions of the curve to estimate proportions of the total production which will fall into a given performance range.

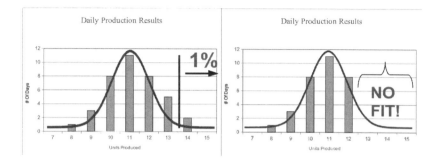

It is important to remember that capability calculations are *estimates*. The future, by definition, is unknown. Our *best* estimates of tomorrow's production will rarely be right to the penny.

On the other hand, capability assessments are essential to both strategic and tactical decision-making. To illustrate the power of this kind of process knowledge, I have repeated a discussion called **RISK** from my book, *Thirty Seven Ideas For Business Operation Improvement*.

In the excerpt on risk that follows, you can see that your capability data impacts strategic decisions regarding capital purchases of tools and equipment, and tactical decisions that can *save money* by properly deploying the right resource for a particular job.

RISK

When most people talk about 4, 5 or 6 *sigmas*, they are often talking casually about a statistical calculation known as a Z-Score. For decision-making purposes, this is typically *the next to the last step in calculating something that is actually useful*! That last step in the calculation is an estimate of risk.

Several years ago, a client asked me to predict the future! He said, "I have two welding workstations. They are each outfitted to perform the same kind of work. Each has been known to occasionally produce an improper weld. What can I expect in the future? What should I do? "

Pause, and realize that this is not the same as simply extrapolating historical performance. If you have never received a traffic ticket, does that mean we forecast 0% chance of tickets in the future? Certainly not! An estimate of *traffic ticket risk* would have to take into account many things, including how and where you drive.

Any calculation of risk is a *chain of reasoning* with critical assumptions that must be checked at each link in the chain. Failure to do so produces results that are worse than wrong; they are arbitrary! (Wrong answers can be fixed but arbitrary answers cannot!)

In this chain of calculation, the prelude to the final answer is the Z-Score (Sigma) calculation. From this answer the final answer, risk, can be determined.

Thirty-Seven Ideas For Tactical Managers*

After comprehensive research which included a visit to the welding operation, this is the kind of report that I made:

I expect that Welder#1 will fail almost 32% of the time, whereas Welder#2 will fail only 4.5% of the time. To save money immediately *without additional capital spending,* take the following actions:

1. Don't ever use Welder#1 unless you have so much demand that you have no choice.

2. If you need 1000 units welded, schedule 1048 if you use machine #2 and schedule 1465 if you use machine #1.

3. Make sure that your calculations of costs and profitability take into account the 48 (or 465) units of scrap and re-work. Modify your capital investment, product line, sales & pricing decisions accordingly.

4. *If you **do** invest in replacing or refurbishing this equipment, spend the money on #1 for increased **capacity** or on #2 for increased **precision.***

24: Measurement Capability and Quality

Repeated measurement over time of a process's metrics and the products it produces will tell us about the consistency and capability of the process, and about the expected quality of its product.

The measurement process itself can be audited for consistency, capability and quality *in exactly the same way!* Rather than measure fresh instances of production, measurement is audited by repeatedly measuring a standard.

THE COORDINATE MEASURING MACHINE

Coordinate measuring machines are computer controlled robot arms that can reach and touch the edges of objects in three dimensions.

One client had manufacturing "setup" problems. The plant would machine a sample part, and then send that part to be measured. If the measurements confirmed that the desired dimensions had been produced to customer specifications, a complete order of parts would be produced.

This, of course, is a flawed decision rule – an inappropriate way to confirm that a machining setup is correct. This was made worse by a lack of capability knowledge of the measuring machine.

We quickly identified the limitations of the machine by simply *repeating the measurement of the same part.*

Everyone assumed that because the computer displayed results to four decimal places that such precision could be trusted. An analysis of the repeated measurements indicated that the actual ability of the machine was a little more than *two* decimal places.

Our machine setup operator had been told to move and readjust their part setup again and again – not because the parts were off target, but because the variation in the measurement process was mistaken for product variation.

THOROUGH INVESTIGATIONS OF MEASUREMENT

A quick measurement experiment like this one is inexpensive, easy and often revealing. A consistency chart (control chart) of repeated measurement of a standard is always good practice to monitor a precision measurement system.

A thorough study of measurement quality is a bit more involved, and will qualify a measurement process in terms of four metrics. Those metrics are Accuracy, Precision, Stability, Linearity.

The following *quick reference* slides provide a brief explanation and visual illustration of each concept.

Accuracy

- The *Accuracy* of Measurement describes how close the *average* reading falls to the standard.

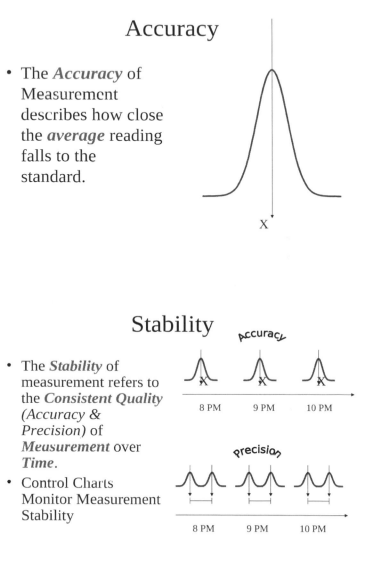

Stability

- The *Stability* of measurement refers to the *Consistent Quality (Accuracy & Precision)* of *Measurement* over *Time*.
- Control Charts Monitor Measurement Stability

171

Precision

* The *Precision* of Measurement describes smallest *differences* that can be reliably detected.

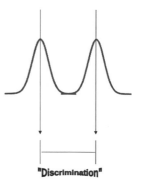

"Discrimination"

Precision

* Repeatability
  - One Gage
  - One Operator
  - One Lab
* Reproducibility
  - Multiple Gages
  - Multiple Operators
  - Multiple Labs
* Capability
  - *Sustainable* Precision
* Uncertainty
  - Capability Adjusted for uncontrolled Factors.

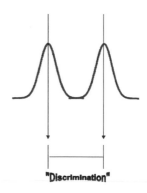

"Discrimination"

Linearity

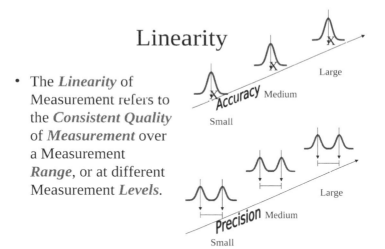

- The *Linearity* of Measurement refers to the *Consistent Quality* of *Measurement* over a Measurement *Range*, or at different Measurement *Levels*.

Overload!
Too Much Work Scheduled For a Team of Four

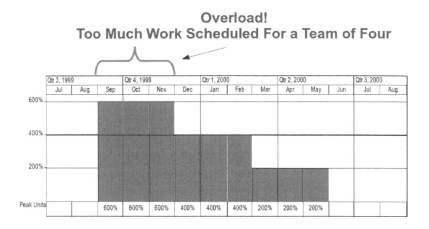

Qtr 3, 1999			Qtr 4, 1999			Qtr 1, 2000			Qtr 2, 2000			Qtr 3, 2000	
Jul	Aug	Sep	Oct	Nov	Dec	Jan	Feb	Mar	Apr	May	Jun	Jul	Aug
Peak Units		600%	600%	600%	400%	400%	400%	200%	200%	200%			

These tasks in this period of overload are in trouble. Something will not get done according to plan and the work will take longer than expected. If an overload occurs in the critical path, the entire project can be delayed.

Fixing overload problems is called *Resource Leveling.* Be careful with automatic leveling features of software packages. They will stretch durations of tasks or delay completions automatically. These kinds of changes are typically something that the tactical manager wants to control.

TASK DETAILS
We all know that packing a car trunk with small pieces of luggage generates more options and is easier than trying to stuff a couple of too large suitcases under the lid.

A proper level of task detailing works the same way. Detailed planning of sub-objectives and tasks generates tactical

176

opportunities – options for how and where resources can be deployed, and re-deployed.

On the other hand, too *much* detail can work against the planner as well. Too much detail manufactures unnecessary complexity.

Imagine that one hundred recessed lighting fixtures are to be installed in new construction. Wires must be stripped and attached. Lighting fixtures may requires some assembly, screws must be attached, and trim kits must be counted and stored for later installation.

It would create unnecessary complexity to detail every one of these tasks for every fixture. What we need, and what the tactical manager *has*, is a *process management* tool.

The project manager can create and assign a *single* task *Install One Hundred Recessed Fixtures*. Using our process management tools (dependency diagrams), the project manager can say: *"This is the process we use to install each light fixture. Go put in one hundred."*

In task areas where there is *no* process, it is often worth investing a little time to develop and prototype one.

Getting the right degree of task detail seems to be as much art as science. The tactical manager with project and process management skills possesses an advantage that will help him to keep resources deployed when and where they are needed in the face of change.

COST OF QUALITY EXAMPLE:

ACME sign company typically charges $450 for an aluminum core business sign.

A capability analysis estimates that ninety eight per cent of the time signs are cut to perfect customer dimensions. Ninety three percent of the time the color, layout and copy printed onto the sign are exactly what the customer ordered.

The combined capability of the fabrication and art department is about ninety one per cent; 98% x 93% = 91% .

A typical month's production is one hundred signs. Capability analysis estimates that 9% (9 signs) must be re-manufactured. Cost of Quality is 9 x $450. = $4050.

> *Why was Cost of Quality not computed in steps, once for the cutting process and once for the printing process? Some assumptions were made about exactly when and how defective signs are uncovered.*

Like any analytical technique, transparency in method means that the results are open to review and mistaken assumptions can be corrected.

To many businesses, COQ is a cost that remains hidden until the end of the accounting period, where it appears as an unanticipated and unplanned expense.

Simply being able to anticipate this cost *before it is* incurred generates options for the business:

- Corrective expenditures can be justified on the assumption that some of this cost will be reduced.

- Less capable equipment can be held back to accommodate peak load production requirements – favoring more capable equipment for the bulk of production.

- Product pricing and competitiveness can be re-evaluated, given a more realistic analysis of product costs that incorporates cost of quality.

27: Introduction To Earned Value

There are at least a couple of ways that *Earned Value* is used to measure the progression of projects to completion.

We start with the idea that each task has a planned expense for materials and labor, and that every task is scheduled on the calendar. Then, an earned value analysis begins by creating a *baseline* that shows by calendar day *when* the planned expenditures should occur.

As the project is tracked, credit for the value represented by each completed task is recorded and the *cumulative credited value, or earned value,* can be seen to be on, behind, or ahead of schedule.

In some reporting systems, the acronym BCWP (Budgeted Cost of Work Performed) is used instead of earned value. Assume $1000 is budgeted to install one hundred light fixtures. When three have been installed, $30 is the Budgeted Cost of Work Performed, or Earned Value.

EARNED VALUE AS A VARIANCE DETECTOR

An earned value analysis that shows the dollar value of planned deliverables is on schedule serves as a *cross check* on a review of the task plan.

This shortfall between earned value and the anticipated rate at which effort will be expended (*Planned Value*) is a warning flag to the project manager.

EARNED VALUE EXAMPLE:

This graph contrasts the rate at which planned versus actual earned value accumulates for a software development project. You can see that Earned Value (BCWP) is *lagging behind the* Planned Value (BCWS – Budgeted Cost of Work Scheduled.)

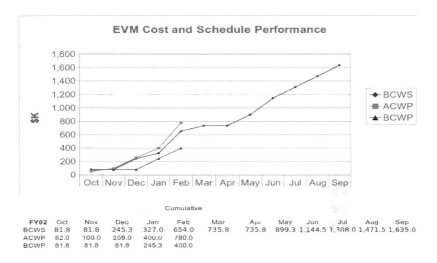

FY02	Oct	Nov	Dec	Jan	Feb	Mar	Apr	May	Jun	Jul	Aug	Sep
BCWS	81.8	81.8	245.3	327.0	654.0	735.8	735.8	899.3	1,144.5	1,308.0	1,471.5	1,635.0
ACWP	62.0	100.0	259.0	400.0	780.0							
BCWP	81.8	81.8	81.8	245.3	400.0							

There is a third line on the graph, the top line shows actual expenditures to date (ACWP – Actual Cost of Work Planned).

From this example, we can see that this project is not producing deliverables as fast as expected. Expenditures are occurring faster than expected, and costs are higher than expected.

Earned Value tracking is currently popular as a financial control in bank or government funded projects. The project manager must demonstrate an accumulation of earned value before funds are advanced to pay for work completed.

*Thirty-Seven Ideas For Tactical Managers**

As tactical managers, we continually remind ourselves that change, even significant change, is neither intrinsically good or bad. It depends on the nature of the cause. This is true whether we are monitoring a process for consistency with a time series chart, or whether we are monitoring a project via a task schedule or earned value analysis.

In my experience, earned value analysis reports like this one is a working document that conveys a high altitude view to a program manager or customer. It tends to call for strategic action. *"Do we continue the project, or quit while we are behind?"*

The tactical manager needs to focus most of their attention a level of detail lower, and on a more frequent time frame. Are people, equipment and materials *where* we need them, *when* we need them? Have tasks been left out? Have our efforts been diverted into activities that do not advance us toward the objective? Are the little processes that let us complete tasks *correct, consistent and capable?*

28: Factor tables

Years ago, a young machinist embraced the idea of dependency diagram with enthusiasm.

He made fifteen different machined parts at his workstation, and setup was a tedious process where one of four fixtures was installed at one of two positions. A different diameter hole was drilled – varying by part number.

On his first dependency diagram for part #1, he carefully recorded target values for fixture, workstation mounting position and finishing tool. Then he paused, *"How many of these pages are we going to have? Our company has* <u>hundreds</u> *of part numbers? Is this going to be manageable??"*

THE FACTOR TABLE

The process was essentially the same for each of his fifteen parts, and we showed him that fifteen dependency diagrams were not necessary. All he had to do was add the following two exhibits to the lower left of his dependency diagram:

Exhibit #1:

Fixture List	Position List	Hole Diam. List
1001	A	.375
1002	B	.500
1003		.625
1004		.750

It is easy and fast to make consistent wholesale updating of process targets such as pressures and temperatures when changes occur in aging equipment (furnaces, presses, etc).

SERVICE APPLICATIONS

Factor tables work in customer service applications too. A factor table can help a triage desk correctly handle redirects. It can facilitate the classification of a call as urgent or crisis.

You have certainly noticed that the dependency diagram is very different from a flow chart. Actions flow from prior actions and from incoming products. There are *no* branches, no decision loops.

To the extent a process must be *"flexible"*, to the extent that *"decisions must be made,"* the factor table provides a way to accommodate this in a correct and consistent manner.

Factors are facts intrinsic to the incoming product, or uncovered as the process moves forward. Factor tables are downstream. They represent the systematic organization of contingent process target values for every anticipated course the process may take.

OUT OF PROCESS

There is such a thing as a service request that a help desk is totally unprepared to handle, or a piece of raw material or an order that a manufacturing facility is totally unprepared to make.

These cases are escalated to supervisors and managers who must decide if these things should be incorporated into the process or declined.

Many times, out of process requests can be incorporated into the business by simply adding a row to one or more factor tables. This approach keeps an operation agile and permits rapid accommodation of change.

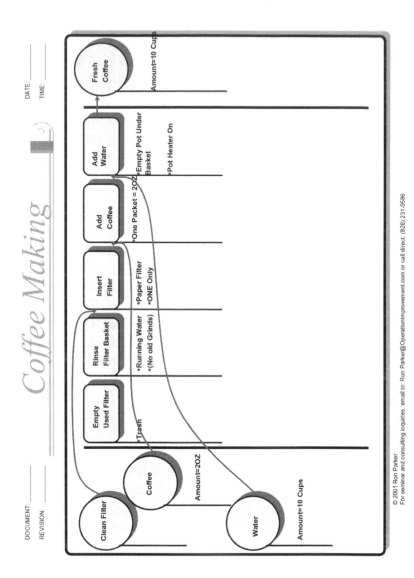

Coffee Making

DOCUMENT: _____
REVISION: _____

DATE: _____
TIME: _____

Clean Filter

Coffee
Amount=2OZ

Water
Amount=10 Cups

Empty Used Filter
•Trash

Rinse Filter Basket
•Running Water
•(No old Grinds)

Insert Filter
•Paper Filter
•ONE Only

Add Coffee
•One Packet = 2OZ

Add Water
•Empty Pot Under Basket
•Pot Heater On

Fresh Coffee
Amount=10 Cups

Improve Your Project and Process Management Skills!

Notice that this is a *process* document. It is not a *procedure* that we can mechanically follow like a computer program. We are expected to *think* as we follow the process flow.

We prefer to document the workstation in a series of *one-page/one-idea* illustrations; the same concise style we use for the dependency diagrams themselves.

Each page shows one important element of a piece of equipment, a computer screen shot, a fixture, etc. Each page communicates as clearly and rapidly as possible: *What* it is, *where* it is, and what it *does*.

Here is the visual documentation for our classroom coffee pot example:

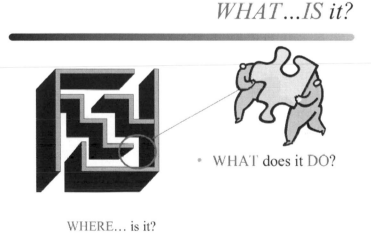

WHAT ...IS it?

• WHAT does it DO?

WHERE... is it?

Coffee Pot

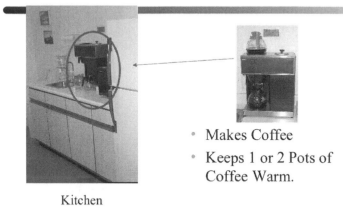

Kitchen

* Makes Coffee
* Keeps 1 or 2 Pots of Coffee Warm.

Filter Basket

Coffee Pot

* Holds Coffee Filter & Coffee
* Drips Fresh Coffee directly into Pot

Water Tank & Cover

Coffee Pot

* Heats Clean Water for –1-
  Pot of Coffee.
* (Adding 1 Pot of Water
  Forces Hot Water in Tank
  Through Coffee Filter,
  into the pot.)

Pot Warmer

Coffee Pot

* Keeps Coffee Pot
  Warm
* CAUTION: HOT
  SURFACE!

Pot Warmer Power Switch

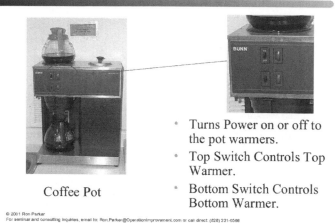

* Turns Power on or off to the pot warmers.
* Top Switch Controls Top Warmer.
* Bottom Switch Controls Bottom Warmer.

Coffee Pot

Pot Warmer Indicator Light

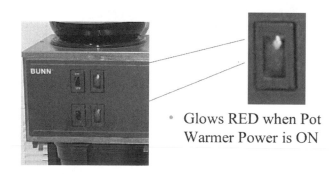

* Glows RED when Pot Warmer Power is ON

Pot Warmer Power Switch

WORK CENTERS

Once you are comfortable thinking in terms of workstations, you will find it helpful to think of Work Centers as a broader concept in the management of your facilities. If a call center agent is assigned a workstation, a work center might be a group of four to six agents who handle Spanish language calls.

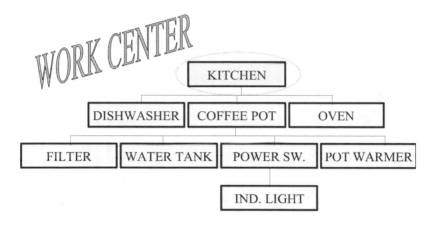

Just as a coffee maker is to a kitchen, a workstation is to a work center. In manufacturing, a work center could be a machine as long as a football field with workstations at one end to feed raw materials and workstations at the opposite end to collect and route finished goods.

SUPERVISION AND MANAGEMENT

Businesses need properly positioned lead workers, supervisors and managers throughout the organization. A proper partitioning of work and responsibilities facilitates communication. It helps to insure that information is in the hands of those closest to the points of control.

Structuring an operation into departments, work centers and workstations highlights how and where to position people for leadership duties.

WORKSTATIONS HELP MANAGE CHANGE

Tools such as desktop computers need a refresh every two years or so, but they are too expensive to totally replace that often.

It is typical to find that needs vary within the company. Some need basic email services. Others need to write letters and do simple figure work. Power users may require state of the art speed and performance.

When these different needs are organized as three classes of *workstations*, an entry level, middle, and power user class, change can be more easily managed. Every two years, power user workstations can be rebuilt with the latest technology. Their older equipment can be refurbished and refreshed – redeployed to mid-level users, and so on.

Technology can get out of control quickly if it is not managed. Printer supplies, power cords, spare and repair parts and accessories are all more easily managed in a wholesale fashion, than on a case by case basis.

30: When Leaders Must Follow

Technology has made it possible to speak to a billion people at a single time. No real or imagined technology can make it possible to *listen* to more than a few.

It is the distinguishing difference between the small and the large business. A small business leader has the ability and responsibility to speak and listen to every individual employee and potentially, every customer.

Once a business reaches a certain size, it is *organization* that makes communication possible. *Listening* is a responsibility *distributed* throughout the company.

Everyone is charged with paying attention to customers, co-workers and their direct reports. Managers are responsible for accurately identifying information that should be shared up and across the organization.

Used properly, ticketing systems, knowledge bases and other communications technology can facilitate the dissemination of timely data.

Unbridled technology tools that *tweet* every hiccup to everyone do not, in fact, facilitate information flow; they bury critical information under a pile of unstructured junk.

Thirty-Seven Ideas For Tactical Managers*

Even in freely changing *matrix* style organizations, there are islands of responsibility where someone is in charge and there is a chain of command.

"In here, within this circle of context, I am in charge."

Within any organization structure, it is important to let the designated individual *lead.*

A Vice President does not take over a manager's staff meeting, dictate an agenda and call the question. An experienced call center supervisor does not cherry-pick the calls he prefers from agents just because he thinks he can handle this one or that one a little better.

A store manager does not elbow a cashier out of the way and say *let me do it.* To do so implies that the subordinate has committed some unnamed error. To do so is criticism in deed if not word, and will always be perceived as an unfair judgment.

Some leaders pride themselves on being able to do any job their subordinate can do. Our goal should be to hire people who, with experience, can *outperform* us at delegated tasks.

It is admirable that leaders are *willing* to take on any job. It conveys the spirit that no job is unimportant; but, so does *letting* people do their job.

This goes to the essence of what people call *micro-managing.* It is not micro-management to provide good tools and equipment, to establish processes and to insist on a commitment to a correct and consistent operation.

200

It *is* micro-management to meddle in subordinates' work to the extent that they cannot learn from their own mistakes. As tactical managers, we want to coach, to prevent catastrophe, to handle *out of process escalations*, and perhaps to *spot* a worker – the way one weight lifter or gymnast helps another in a complex or risky exercise.

More than anything, we want to give people the elbow room and support that they need to grow in their job. This is as important to them as it is to us.

31: Time And Value

Imagine that it is 2013 and you have won a grand prize. You are the millionth customer of ACME groceries and you have won....*a brand new car!*

Yes! You have won a brand new 2013 Mercedes Benz sports car. Direct from the showroom, this silver beauty has only 13 miles on the odometer.

You can claim your imaginary prize by presenting an acceptable form of ID at the factory in Germany. Now, if that is an inconvenient location for you, I suspect that you are figuring the *hidden costs.* Travel to and from the factory, transportation of the vehicle, time off from work – these hidden costs cause you to adjust the true net value of your prize.

THE CATCH
There is a second catch. You must take delivery exactly *thirty years* from today! Since you are now further discounting the value of your prize, I know you already understand in some form the idea of the **Time Value of Money**.

If we figured our prize to be initially worth a hundred thousand dollars, we now must take into account the thirty years of lost opportunity. We must *discount* the *future value* of the car to an equivalent *present value.*

I call this the *bird in hand/bird in bush ratio* because of the old saying: *"A bird in the hand is worth two in the bush."*

As we are about to do a little math, let's change our story a bit and change our fantasy prize to cash, one hundred thousand dollars in cash – to be received by you exactly 30 years from today.

Of course, people disagree on exactly how much to discount value over thirty years. Just as people have differing opinions of a fair price for peaches, folks will disagree as to what is a fair price for money. The *market* price is that price where two parties come together for a successful transaction.

THE BIRD IN HAND RATIO

Would you take ten grand *immediately* as an alternative to one hundred thousand in that far distant future of thirty years? Would that balance the scales of value?

Most TVM calculations are standardized as annual *percentage rates* (APR), and are not usually expressed as a discount rate over the entire term. Mathematically though, one can be calculated from the other.

Take a simple example. A dollar today is worth *how much* n one year?

An annual percentage rate of 8% gives the future value of $1.08. A lender might lend a dollar today in return for $1.08 in a year if the lender and borrower agreed that 8% was a reasonable price for the cost of money. The annual *discount rate,* **(.08/1.08)*100,** is just a tad over 7.4%. Subtract 7.4% from $1.08 and the result is the present value: *one dollar.*

To move from present value to an *equivalent* future value, we add on a percentage amount. To back into a present value from a future value we subtract a (smaller) discount amount.

For multiple year calculations, the calculations are repeated. One Dollar x 1.08 x 1.08 gives a 2 year future value of 1.164. Subtracting 7.4% from this future value, and then repeating – subtracting 7.4% from *that* value discounts two years of value from $1.1664.

The *compounding* effect of discounting future values, or accruing an annual percentage interest can produce startling results. Our 8% APR compounded over thirty years increases a present value by about a factor of ten!

The reverse is true. An annual discounting of value by just 7.4% reduces our $100,000 future fantasy prize to an equivalent value of less than $10,000 cash in hand today.

Time Value of money mathematics is like looking though the wrong end of a telescope at a future dollar amount. The TVM calculation objectively shrinks a future measure of value into an exact equivalent value today by compensating for the *hidden cost* of lost opportunity.

There is only one variable, one knob to tweak in TVM math, and that is the APR.

CASH FLOWS

Present and future values can also be converted into periodic payments, or cash flows. A ten thousand dollar present value is exactly equivalent to $882.74 in annual payments over thirty years.

Notice that this amount times 30 years is about $26,500. That is *more than* the present value of Ten grand, and *less than* the future value of one hundred thousand dollars.

This makes common sense. The recipient of value does not have to wait a full thirty years to receive and enjoy the opportunities that cash provides. There is *some* delayed gratification, so the sum of payments as a dollar amount is a number between the present and future values.

UNCONVENTIONAL TVM EXAMPLES

Tactical managers need a basic understanding of Time and Money mathematics. In a project, the decision to rent versus buy, the decision to spend ASAP or ALAP (as <u>late</u> as possible) may have a sizable impact on project costs if large dollar amounts and long time frames are involved.

However, it is not just cash that has a Time-Value relationship in the eyes of the beholder. *Any* value will have some kind of mathematical Time-Value relationship. It may be inconsequential to management decision-making, or it may mean the difference between success and failure.

Imagine that as a tactical manager you are assigned a project to plan and coordinate a major event such as a wedding. What is the value of a wedding cake that is only *one day late?* What is its value if it is two months early?

Customer deliverables do not have the simple relationships that one sees in *cost of money* calculations. For most deliverables, there is an *optimum* time, a point where the value is maximized. This is analogous to picking fruit when ripe.

A wedding cake and a load of concrete can neither be delivered too early or too late. The value of many deliverables is so totally negated by missing the target that customers have been known to say, *"if I had known that we couldn't meet the schedule, I would not have commissioned the project at all!"*

This is a difficult concept for many managers to grasp. They think their deliverables have an innate or intrinsic value. "Of *course* it will have at least *some* value, *even if it is late"*.

Confusion also arises by failing to mentally separate cost from value. A successful project is one where the value produced exceeds the cost. A successful business product may have many times the value over the costs to produce it - thus wealth is created. Never forget that *value and price* is totally different from *cost.*

You see this in software projects. A deliverable is delayed by months or years. By the time the software system is delivered, the business has changed or the enabling technology is already obsolete. The developers attempt to defend the value of the system by its cost.

You sometimes see blindness to time-value in service. Customer service sometimes fails to assign a dollar value to the customer's time. In the name of efficiency, they run utilizations high and make customers wait. Hours of customer wait time mis-priced at a cost of *zero* yields an erroneous analysis.

If we inject a huge hidden cost into the price of our goods and services by making customers wait, we can expect at least some to say, *"If I had known how long I would have to wait for service and support, I would not have bought the product at all."*

TIME-VALUE CURVES

Unconventional relationships between time and value can at least be qualitatively described in a graphical picture, like this:

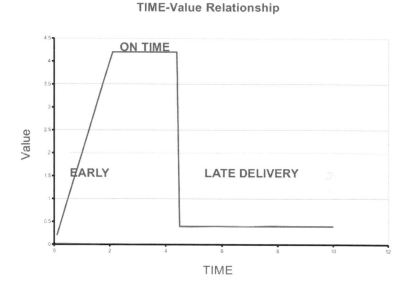

An illustration like this reminds us that there is a time when the deliverable is *ripe* – that maximum value is attained by meeting a target.

In this example, we show that early delivery carries a decreasing penalty, but a day late is *too* late.

32: Dealing With Technology

Technology is more than *Information* Technology. It is electroplating, electrolysis, conveyor systems, access control and security systems, radio technology, and more.

Information technology *does* touch all of these other resources. It is the strong force that interconnects technology and places a lever in the hand of a human.

Never forget that a human being *always* does the work. Man is never replaced by machines – our abilities are *amplified by them.*

Along with the growth in technology's use and complexity, our modern era has given rise to a new kind of customer service: *The Help Desk.*

THE HELP DESK

The help desk is sometimes called *Tier I* support. They are purely tactical in that they cannot make engineering modifications to the systems. They can *"unstop a pipe"* but are not typically authorized to make changes to the plumbing.

A fast food restaurant would not simply shove meals out and customer cash into a bag. No matter how busy, the paperwork must be done for every individual customer. There must always be a receipt. It is essential if the operation is to be managed *at all.*

Similarly, a help desk needs a kind of receipt, or record, for each service inquiry received. Service work becomes invisible, unappreciated and therefore dispensable if there is no audit trail. Without a *ticketing system*, a help desk manager has nothing tangible to show for hard work and jobs well done.

Every ticketing system has its critics, and salesmen will seize on every complaint about a competitor to promote their own brand.

In my experience, it is the *implementation*, and not the ticketing system itself, that causes frustration and grief at the Help Desk.

I know of organizations that have had wonderful experiences and others that have had awful experiences with commercial ticketing systems like Remedy and its successors. The same is true of those who saved a little money and implemented an open source solution such as RT.

Successes start with well defined operations processes that dictate how the ticketing system will be implemented. Failures expect the ticketing system and its implementers to impose order on chaos.

HELP DESK PROCESSES

Driven by their interpretations of customer surveys, some help desk managers seek high one call/one agent metrics as their ultimate measure of performance.

It is true that nothing is more frustrating than fruitless phone transfers that leave the caller feeling like they are back at square one. On the other hand, if call transfers rapidly advance a caller to the right agent and a competent solution, a warm transfer or two can be well worth it.

The first process in a well-run help desk **creates a service ticket** and is sometimes called the triage function.

TICKET CREATION

If properly scoped, the processing time to handle any individual call should be very close to the *average* processing time.

This low variability in triage gives us the ability to run this process at a higher utilization. Agents on this front desk will have less idle time between cases than other agents that are handling case details, while wait times for callers will be kept to a reasonable duration.

The triage desk cannot diagnose problems. Our ticketing system, at this stage of help, should be oriented to capturing *symptoms*. Like an ER nurse, we want to know *"Where does it hurt?"*

We want to be on the lookout for symptoms that may indicate major problems or a crisis, and route those callers differently. But, we must remember that at each stage of a process, there are things we know and things we do not know.

If a caller cannot send and receive email, one does *not* document this as an email failure. It is the *symptom*, what we see and hear, that builds an accurate picture for service resolution.

Some triage desk calls are simply a request for a re-direct. Others are requests for quick information. As long as these requests can be handled *without adding* significant variation to the process, the triage desk can simply create a ticket, handle the caller request, and close the ticket in one step.

TICKET ASSIGNMENT

One call center expected all one hundred agents to answer any question on any one of one hundred different software applications. Their success rate was dismal.

We calculated that the call volume for a single critical application could be handled with four or five agents and we created a team to specialize just in that application. They surprised everyone by becoming the Tier I experts in this application in just a week.

Previously, they might need to research an obscure hiccup in this critical system once a month. By specializing in this one system, they gained an *intensive* knowledge *just by repeatedly applying their general technical expertise to this one system.*

The secret to this kind of rapid success is not simple specialization. It is specialization *in the right things*. This means the incoming work load must be properly grouped or *factored*.

What constitutes a batch of similar work in a help desk is a difficult question. Ticketing systems attempt to tag and group requests hierarchically by category, type and item.

Unfortunately, this is usually implemented as an unmanaged sprawling mess of too many conflicting and duplicate classification codes. It is *the root cause* of inefficiency, and frustration with ticketing systems. It is the principal cause as to why cases fall through the cracks.

I have fixed these kinds of problems before, and I have found that, once again, a dependency diagram is a useful tool in creating logical groupings for help desk tickets.

DEPENDENCY DIAGRAMS AND TECH ANATOMY

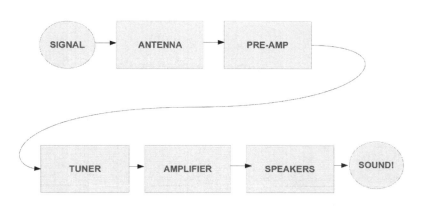

Old School radio technicians relied heavily on dependency diagrams like the one above to learn, teach, and diagnose radio receiving systems.

In the electronics field, these pictures were called *functional block diagrams*. They separated out system components of like kind to expose *test points* between each block.

Instead of laboriously diagnosing a problem by starting at one end and checking each component, a technician would start in the middle. If a signal could be heard at this mid-point, one half of the system was eliminated as a cause of failure.

Contrast that approach with today's computer help desk that begins by having you unplug and reboot computers, reinstall software packages, and so on. The slow process of elimination via the modern support script is suffering from a profound lack of understanding at the Tier I desk as to how systems work.

Before I create ticket categories, I like to create a dependency diagram to organize what is known about the technology system we are trying to sustain. The diagram for a client/server database system is different from that of a local stand-alone application. Thin Clients and Cloud Applications are different from traditional *fat* desktop configurations.

This analysis by diagram not only allows me to create useful areas of specialization for support teams, it creates a tool that helps the triage desk more effectively classify a symptom to a technology subsystem.

Just as an ER nurse wants to quickly relate symptoms to a major system of the body (respiration, nervous system, heart and circulation), we want our first placement of a service request with a specialist to have a high probability of success.

TICKET BACKLOG

What does it mean if a ticket doesn't move? If its status is indefinitely *"pending"*?

It could be a failure of *correct and consistent* process, or it could be *out of process* – a case for which we have no plan.

213

Monitoring of the open ticket backlog is one of the most important tasks of the front line tactical manager at a help desk.

Help desk workers today function in two roles; they *wear two hats*. They speak to customers as *representatives* of the company – providing service and communicating policy on the company's behalf. Under certain conditions, they also function as *agents* for the customer.

The internals of help desk processes should neither be seen nor heard by the customer. They should be self-evident, simple, fast, frictionless and reliable - like a perfect vending machine.

Customers need only be concerned with the product. If a customer doesn't "*follow our process*", that's -our- problem.

ONE CALL RESOLUTION

When tickets begin to grow stale in our system, we don't wait for the caller to inquire about the delay. We don't advise them that they *should have* called a different department.

We switch roles and make the inquiries, move the case forward *on behalf* of the caller. We take responsibility for our own processes and systems.

This is the true spirit of *one call* resolution. The caller makes one call and need not worry if their request will die somewhere within the support system. They know that their service request will be handled as quickly and as professionally as possible.

33: Break-Even Analysis

Imagine that your product sells for $100/each. A product would require raw materials– let's say the cost is twenty dollars for each unit of production.

You now envision tremendous profits of **eighty dollars** on each sale, right? What are we forgetting? *Fixed Costs!*

VARIABLE AND FIXED COSTS

Variable costs are things like the hour of labor to produce an hour of service, or the raw materials required to produce quantity -1- of a product. It is a cost that can be calculated by multiplying product or service volume by a dollar amount.

Simple, right? So what about the fixed cost? Fixed cost is *everything else*. It is the facilities, tools, machinery, computer systems, monthly utility bills, accounting and administrative overhead, and so on.

While variable cost is computed as a cost per item, fixed costs are computed as a cost per *time period*, whether there is production and sales or not.

BREAK-EVEN ANALYSIS

If monthly fixed costs are $1000, and sales are one unit per month, business is dismal. The eighty dollars income over and above the variable costs of twenty dollars is the proverbial drop in the bucket – totally inadequate to cover fixed costs.

Sales of a dozen units per month with proceeds after variable costs brings in $960, and sales at a *rate* of thirteen per month represents *Break-Even*.

The key concept here is the *rate* at which products or services can be sold. Break-Even analysis is typically shown graphically. The Y axis shows dollars, and the X axis show rates of sale, 0, 10, 20 units per month...and so on.

A line on the graph (ideally *red*) shows how costs increase as the *rate* of sales increases from zero to larger and larger numbers. A second line (ideally *green)* shows total income at each *rate* of sales.

What Is Our Break-Even?

Thirteen Units Sold PER MONTH!

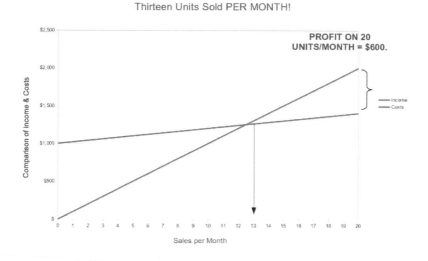

The cross-over point is called the *break-even* rate of sales. Orders for goods and services must be coming in at a faster rate than this break-even rate for a business to be profitable.

216

STRATEGIC OPTIONS

A strategic decision maker can often *move* the break-even point. They may want to move it *higher* -or- lower.

In *good* times, strategic decision makers often take on additional fixed costs. They buy new equipment, invest in training, etc. The expectation is that these business improvements will *lower* the variable costs.

Good times means *great* sales expectations. Even though the break-even rate of sales will *go up* with capital expenditures, the rate at which dollars are brought in is expected to more than make up for the increased monthly cost.

In *lean* times, strategic decision-makers prepare for the rate of sales to decline. They look for ways to *reduce* fixed costs even if variable costs increase. They may eliminate an in-house capability and outsource it to a contractor at a higher *unit cost*.

Their hope is to reduce fixed costs to the point where the business can survive the lean times on a smaller number of less profitable sales.

What Is Our Break-Even?

Ten Units Sold PER MONTH!

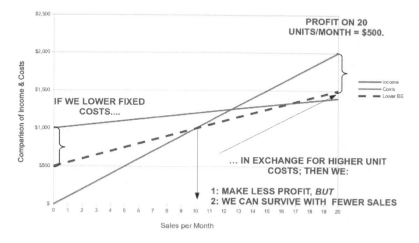

TACTICAL OPTIONS

What many businesses overlook are the tactical options – the things that can be done with *available means* to improve profitability in lean times as well as good.

Some of these tactical options will be introduced in the next chapter, an introduction to *low hanging fruit*.

34: Low Hanging Fruit

Every organization has *low hanging fruit – opportunities* for improvement that are in reach to be seized if they can be recognized.

There are three common kinds of easy pickings for improvement: 1) Non-obvious constraints that, once recognized, are easily removed. 2) Hidden scrap and inefficiencies due to poor First Pass Yields. 3) Trial and Error Decision-Making.

HIDDEN CONSTRAINTS

Our client had always seemed to fall short of its production goals. On a typical day, they produced twenty units – sometimes more, sometimes less.

That should equate, they thought, to a hundred a week, and four hundred per month. Yet, they always seemed to fall short.

They brainstormed. They analyzed and over-analyzed those days when production was below twenty. *"What can we do to avoid those low production days?"* they asked.

TRUNCATED DISTRIBUTIONS

I created a performance chart of their data that looked like this, a badly deformed bell shape:

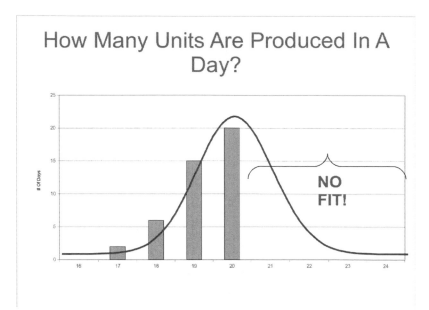

How Many Units Are Produced In A Day?

Data that tends to be a bell shape is sometimes truncated or folded – distorted from the typical symmetrical form. An analyst volunteered, *"I have a program that analyzes data that does not conform to a standard normal curve."*

"I don't think we will need it." I said. *"Let's ask ourselves a different question. First, forget about the low production days for a moment. Everyone expects days that are better than typical and those that are <u>worse</u>.* **What happened to your <u>great</u> days?"**

In fact, there were *no* spectacular days of production to offset the occasional weak days. The result was that the *average* production was far below the *typical* day. The result was that forecasts made on a typical day of production would always be too rosy.

We were looking for a constraint and we found it in the loading bay. There was just enough room for a little more than twenty finished units on the shipping dock. Production was moved out by freight once per day, and the lack of room for additional production kept the facility from meeting their monthly quota.

Better shipping bay space planning and an investigation into the *cause* of production variation helped this facility to meet its production targets. The cause of variation is not typically found by examining the *worst day*, but by examining our time series records for *change* (Chapter 16).

"WE CAN FIX THAT LATER"

It took a week, but I had made dependency diagrams for an entire plant of four hundred. I followed work in process from station to station, and developed a one page dependency diagram of each operation, along with an initial set of metrics.

Dependency diagrams can be assembled such that outgoing products are connected as incoming products to other processes.

One of the supervisors created what he called a *war room*. He papered the walls with the connected dependency diagrams and an interesting fact emerged.

Every unit of production passed routinely through *two* workstations, one of which was *final inspection*. The other common station was called *rework*.

They were a little shocked when they realized that *every* piece produced visited the rework station at some point in its journey through the plant.

Although the scrap production rate for the plant was low, this *hidden* waste was costing them money on every piece produced. To combat this, we instituted a metric on every process known as *First Pass Yield.*

Initially, the FPY scores were awful. No one, it seems, was able to complete a total unit assembly without at least one defect that required rework. But, FPY monitoring helped operators to catch errors in component parts *before* they went to assembly. As FPY scores rose, rework became the exception rather than the rule.

TRIAL AND ERROR

(Reprinted from my book, *Thirty Seven Ideas For Business Operation Improvement).*

The *trade secret* of rapid improvement is this:

> *Look for indecision, uncertainty, and trial & error behavior.*

THE STORY OF THE EIGHT STATION

The plant had everything from low end computer controlled cutting equipment (CNC machines) to high end finishing equipment designed for better than 100 millionths of an inch tolerances.

The natural interest of the engineers was the complex CNC devices, and the high precision finishing tools, but in this facility there was a *big payoff* opportunity that had not been discovered.

An inexpensive series of low tech workstations prepared every single metal casting before they went into the CNC or finish-work processes. The centerpiece of this line was called the *eight station.* Designed for low cost and maximum throughput, the heart of this workstation was a turntable on which eight un-worked metal castings were placed at forty-five degree intervals.

The table would make a 1/8th turn, and each of seven machining stations would simultaneously make their specific cuts. Station #8 was for the operator who loaded and unloaded parts.

It was soon obvious to me that this particular operation was a den of confusion. The operators called it, *the machine from hell. "Only Johnny can set it up, and it takes hours."* they said.

As I watched, I quickly saw why the machine was so difficult to set up. Eight fixtures for holding parts must be bolted onto the turntable. They could be placed too close or too far from the center of the table. They could be placed too far to the left or to the right. Two degrees of freedom times eight fixtures equals sixteen different adjustments that must be exactly right.

There was more. The operators had to unbolt and lever the machining stations into position. Seven movable machining stations meant fourteen more dimensions to the problem. There were a grand total of 30 independent but interrelated dimensional adjustments that had to be brought into harmony before the machine was set correctly.

I watched as Johnny, the best operator in the house, struggled for hours to get all the pieces of this machine into position. Tweaking the setup by trial and error, one adjustment always led to a dozen re-adjustments.

A trial run meant wasting raw material by making sample cuts that were sent to the measurement lab for evaluation. It was usually fatigue and an urgent demand for production that forced him to surrender the cause and actually attempt to produce a product.

THE SOLUTION

I took a little time to think about the problem. How should the setup of this machine be handled? When I thought I had the answer, I went back to Johnny.

"Tell me," I asked. "Is there anything on this machine you won´t move to make a correct setup?"

Johnny answered, "Well, the engineers told me that I should try not to move the stations on the left and right of the operator position. They didn't know why. I tried to leave them alone but I´ve had to move them anyhow."

His answer confirmed my suspicions. The machine's designer had intended that two of the workstations, together with the center of the turntable, form a perfect ninety-degree angle.

Those three points would establish the absolute reference frame from which every component could easily and systematically be placed in its one and only one correct position.

Once this *carpenter's square* had been broken, the machine could no longer be set up with certainty. There was no longer one and only one place to position any component.

The solution was:

1. Re-establish the permanent location of the two stations on either side of the operator by precision measurement.

2. Teach the operators that the setup process must be remembered as an ABC sequence that must be followed carefully and in order.

   a) The built-in 90-degree reference angle must never be altered. It shows *where to exactly place fixtures*.

   b) Fixtures are systematically placed on the turntable underneath the two workstations on either side of the operator. The table is turned, and then all fixtures determine the *one and only one place* for the remaining five workstations.

   c) The remaining five workstations are positioned last, after every fixture has been placed on the table and carefully aligned with the immovable workstations on either side of the operator.

There were some optional elements to this improved setup, but it was no longer trial and error. Instead, it was now a consistent process with a predictable duration and a certain outcome.

35: Sub-Optimization

The best tacticians sometimes fall into the trap of *sub-optimization*. It is an approach that creates a *local* efficiency or solution at the expense of the whole.

Some outside trouble-shooters and problem solvers for hire make this mistake too. They push a problem from the P&L to the Balance Sheet, from current period sales to future period warranty claims, from the plant that *made* a faulty product to the end of year *charge backs* assessed upon all facilities.

WATER

It is ironic that fresh water is scarce in certain places on a planet that is 70% covered by ocean. Of course, for most of human history, people have migrated to where drinkable water was plentiful and almost free.

Today, the choice to build and live in a certain place is driven by other concerns. Unlike food or most other necessities of life, it is taken for granted that government, typically a city or a state, will take care of an intensive need for water.

For years now, sporadic and seasonal water shortages have troubled metropolitan zones. Although true strategic solutions are possible, these are often mired in politics and muddied by jurisdictional and property rights issues.

Years ago in my neighborhood, school children were sent home with bricks and good intentions. The brick was to go in the bathroom toilet tank. The theory was that a brick would displace water, reduce the capacity of the tank and promote conservation. Each push of that little lever was expected to make our troubles go away with a quart less water than before.

The problem was that one flush was often no longer enough. The tactical solution reduced the amount of water *per use*, but increased the number of uses!

Before plumbing design could catch up with policy, governments began to mandate smaller tanks and *every new and renovated bathroom* was saddled with under-performing plumbing.

The culmination of this era was the Seinfeld TV series satire where Kramer was running contraband high capacity toilets under the law and across state lines to satisfy people's desperate need for plumbing that actually worked.

It's a somewhat funny story in hindsight, but it is one of my first memories of well-intentioned tactics with unintended consequences.

AIR

All home construction produces a boxed interior that *leaks* air. Traditional construction relies on this so that a structure can *"breathe"* a bit. The air inside the structure exchanges with the outside air and remains clean and healthy.

When energy prices began to rise, builders pushed to seal up houses. Lost air is lost *conditioned* air. In the summer, this represents an extra cooling load. In the winter, lost air increases heating bills.

I built a house with a construction technique that minimizes the loss of conditioned air. To keep the house healthy, we had to install two constantly running commercial fans to insure that a consistent and controlled amount of air was exchanged with the outdoors.

The strategic solution was a reasonable trade; we sealed the house and installed circulating fans so we could *manage* the air exchange.

The electrician installed these fans on switches per our local code. Unfortunately these switches are *too* convenient for guests, who continually turn them off and chide us for *wasting energy*.

While they are trying to save us pennies on our electric bill, we have already saved *dollars* in heating and cooling because of our construction design. It's another example of *sub-optimization,* attempting to create a local efficiency that does not contribute to the total picture.

VACUUM

Half a dozen machines filled the manufacturing floor. They represented tens of millions of dollars in capital investment – but they were worth it.

When those machines ran, their production rate was many thousands of units per minute. When the machines stopped, thousands of dollars were *lost* each minute.

Fed by electricity and compressed air, vacuum lines completed the pneumatic circuit. The original engineers had designed what amounted to a *shock absorber,* a valve assembly on each machine that connected it to the common vacuum line.

When the machines were new, life was good, but the valve assemblies were relatively high maintenance. A well intentioned efficiency study found that vacuum valve maintenance was a common work order request.

To save on maintenance dollars, maintenance *removed* the original engineering designed valve system and *straight-piped* every machine into the vacuum system. Maintenance savings on that sub-system were immediate.

However, in the weeks and months that followed, operations began to notice that total production was *dropping*. Operations personnel began to be hammered by upper management. *"Why can't you keep those machines running?"*

When the manufacturing floor was studied *as a whole*, an interesting new pattern was uncovered. When one machine stopped production, its nearest neighbors stopped, and then more machines stopped. Like falling dominoes, a work stoppage on one machine spread to its peers, most likely stumbling over pressure fluctuations in the vacuum lines.

Although the maintenance tactic was well-intentioned, this and every instance of *sub-optimization* violates the tactical manager's directive: to run an operation *correctly and consistently*.

LOW COST BIDDER

An inflexible *low cost bidder* approach to product and vendor selections can sometimes result in sub-optimal solutions. This is more typically the mistake of a strategic decision maker who falls back to tactical decision rules – unable or unwilling to make judgments of value and risk.

36: Capacity, Utilization & Duty Cycle

You will often find the usage of these five classic concepts to be casual and imprecise. Each is worth a few words to sharpen their meaning and usefulness. They are: Capacity, Utilization, Efficiency, Effectiveness & Duty Cycle.

CAPACITY

Capacity refers to the maximum sustainable rate of output. It is always greater or equal to the actual output under any possible circumstances.

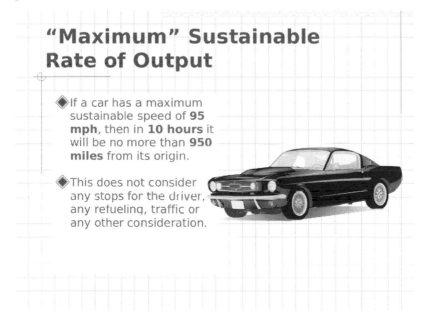

"Maximum" Sustainable Rate of Output

- If a car has a maximum sustainable speed of **95 mph**, then in **10 hours** it will be no more than **950 miles** from its origin.

- This does not consider any stops for the driver, any refueling, traffic or any other consideration.

Strategic decision makers have a major impact on Capacity. A Strategic decision maker could decide that we buy planes rather than automobiles.

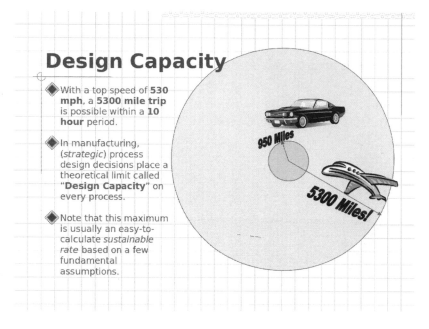

Design Capacity

◆ With a top speed of **530 mph**, a **5300 mile trip** is possible within a **10 hour** period.

◆ In manufacturing, (*strategic*) process design decisions place a theoretical limit called "**Design Capacity**" on every process.

◆ Note that this maximum is usually an easy-to-calculate *sustainable rate* based on a few fundamental assumptions.

950 Miles

5300 Miles!

If an airplane has a top speed of 530 mph, a 5300 mile trip is possible within a 10 hour period. Strategic process design decisions place a theoretical limit called "Design Capacity" on every process. Note that this maximum is usually an easy-to-calculate sustainable rate based on a few fundamental assumptions.

UTILIZATION

Unless the assumptions underlying "Design Capacity" change are wrong, actual rates of production are always less than design maximum.

232

Assume that the design capacity of a painting station allows a maximum of 1000 units to be painted per week. If the yield of correctly painted units is 730 per week, then the paint station utilization rate is 73% . *Don't forget to adjust utilization calculations for scrap and rework!*

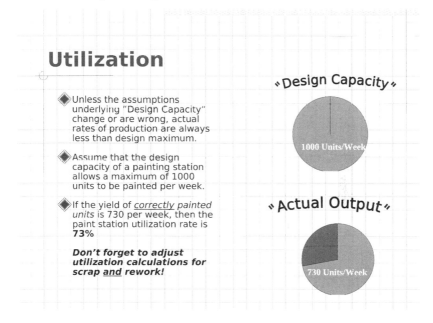

Utilization

◆ Unless the assumptions underlying "Design Capacity" change or are wrong, actual rates of production are always less than design maximum.

◆ Assume that the design capacity of a painting station allows a maximum of 1000 units to be painted per week.

◆ If the yield of *correctly* painted *units* is 730 per week, then the paint station utilization rate is **73%**

Don't forget to adjust utilization calculations for scrap and rework!

"Design Capacity"

1000 Units/Week

"Actual Output"

730 Units/Week

EFFICIENCY & EFFECTIVENESS

I often use the term efficiency to refer to performance measures that are assessed *independently* of the end, the goal or the objective. One talks about the efficiency of car in miles per gallon. Or, sometimes people describe the efficiency of transportation in terms of passenger miles per dollar.

In this usage, efficiency measures how hard a dollar is working to move machinery, people, and so on. It is a *cost accountant's* view of a well run business.

DUTY CYCLE

Did you know that many mechanical systems are *not* designed to run 24x7? A *resting* period, or a pattern of light consistent use, is required of many devices.

A braking system, for example, might be designed to break for fifteen seconds every minute. The engineers may have planned for that idle time to allow the brake to cool. The heat of prolonged and extended braking could reduce the useful life of the brakes from months to days.

Strategic concerns can override duty cycle. How many times have we heard that *"The ship can't take warp 8!"* on that TV show – whereupon a command decision is made to push the engines past their duty cycle. In an emergency, it is a decision that weighs values and risk.

EMPLOYEES AND DUTY CYCLE

The point will be made in the next and final chapter that one cannot treat employees as expendable commodities. From the perspective of *duty cycle,* we simply have to realize that human bodies and human attention must focus and then rest, if they are to sustain maximum productivity.

37: The Things Money Cannot Buy

You may have carried a *coffee* card from Starbucks or another popular cafe. It's good at that store for coffee and little else. It can't be used to pay taxes or to shop on Amazon. There are things a coffee card cannot buy.

Cash, on the other hand, is more widely accepted. In the fifty United States and in many foreign countries, dollars will buy coffee, donuts, room and board, clothing and cars, and more.

Still, there are some places where the dollar is as suspect for payment as a coffee card. In every society, one can trade down to the local currency from gold. Gold, it is often said, is the *standard* of money.

TIME MANAGEMENT

Behind dollars and gold there is higher value that is best saved for the things money cannot buy. Dollars can substitute for a coffee IOU, but the reverse is not too likely. So it is with money and *time*. Time is the opportunity for action.

Money can be a proxy for time. In some sense it can be said that money *is* time, but only time is to be invested in the things money cannot buy.

If you are having trouble creating a list, I will give you a couple to start. Consider the waste if you paid someone to take a nap or a vacation for you. Can you hire someone to take your dentist appointment, or to see a your child's first baseball game? Such are the kinds of things paid for with *your* time and *only* your time.

These philosophical thoughts are intended to remind you and me that although working and earning is a central and valued aspect of modern life, it is not *everything*.

As a manager, we must not forget that the people who work with us are interested in more than making a living – they are *making a life*.

Your most loyal worker will have an immediate adjustment in their priorities if someone they love is in crisis. You must understand and respect that.

A soldier on deployment, a firefighter in an emergency, or a doctor in the middle of surgery knows that their occupation calls for them to set aside almost every personal concern until their time of duty is over and lives are no longer at stake. The rest of us have a little more leeway in our commitment to work.

We all expect to be able to take vacation in more than twenty-four hour increments. We expect some accommodation for the rare occasions when a loved one is suddenly ill.

We all appreciate a little acknowledgement that we have a life outside of work. It is respectful to inquire *"How was your vacation? How is your mother?"* It is a common courtesy to send a thoughtful card or flowers.

"I don't care about their vacation", some say. *"It will make you a better manager if you learn to care"*, I advise.

It is also wise to let someone leave with your best wishes if they feel they have found a better position, or if they feel that because of personal circumstances they can no longer commit to their job.

"*Why are they leaving, after all I have done for them?*", managers may grumble. "*Because they must do what is best for them*", I remind.

Think of this coldly if you must, as a form of risk management. Being aware and respectful of your coworkers as individuals who have a life, who are *making* a life outside of the workplace keeps *attitude* inside the workplace positive. It diffuses defensiveness and encourages associates to open up and contribute in mind as well as body, and its keeps your expectations in line with *human* capabilities.

People can "*suck it up*" only so much. They can "*play while injured*" for only so long. They can pass up better opportunities only so many times.

To ask for more is to ask too much. There is a reason for the popularity of that country music song, *Take this job and shove it...* Too many managers have not taken these last ideas to heart.

If you project an attitude that your direct reports are expendable "*wage slaves*", your lack of respect toward them will be reflected back in their attitude to you.

Remember that everyone has a personal hierarchy of values. You can fight it, or you can learn to integrate this fact of human nature into your management skill set.

Where To Go From Here

If you have studied Time Management, Process and Project Management, or any of the many technical topics touched on in this book, I hope that these *background* concepts have clarified questions that you may have had from previous studies.

If you have yet to take an advanced class that digs deeper into the technical aspects of accounting, statistics, workforce and resource loading, etc – I hope you find that these *Thirty Seven Ideas* have prepared you to learn more about these subjects.

For the definitive book on Time Management, you should read *Time Power* by Dr. Charles R. Hobbs. See:

http://CharlesRHobbs.com

For James Abbott's contact information and details on an extensive array of services and resources for call centers and customer service, see:

http://EffectiveCallCenters.com

A deeper investigation into any of these topics is available to your organization in the form of private workshops and operations turnaround consultation. See:

http://OperationImprovement.com

Our Management Philosophy

FIRST: THINK & COMMUNICATE CLEARLY

Practice and encourage the policy of only using words and acronyms you are prepared to define. You needn't be a surgeon to discuss *brain surgery*, but you should to be able to define *brain* and *surgery*. If it is true that you can´t effectively manage without measuring, then you surely can´t manage what you cannot define.

SECOND: BE DECISIVE

The time for action and the decision to act are two different things. The difference between Decisiveness and Impulsiveness is patient and prudent timing of action. Decisiveness is the ability to mentally adjudicate a matter so that it no longer consumes your most precious resource - your focus.

THIRD: DON'T BE A "BOTTLENECK"

Successful follow-through takes a network of key individuals and massively parallel and well organized activity. If you try to do everything yourself, then you will limit managed work to your personal ability to process information and make decisions.

FOURTH: HOLD PEOPLE ACCOUNTABLE FOR THINGS THEY CAN CONTROL

Properly apportion work and responsibility. An objective division of labor is based on product, process, decision-role and human factors. Holding people accountable for the wrong things is self-deceiving, self-defeating and the biggest destroyer of productivity and morale. Make sure you understand the difference between accountability and blame.

FIFTH: BUILD REAL PROCESSES

Processes are intentional methods of achieving repeatable results at a predictable cost. Many operations claim to have processes, but upon examination, they obviously don´t. If every undertaking is approached as a first-time initiative, then a company only achieves a fraction of its potential for productivity.

SIXTH: PAY ATTENTION, AND MAKE EVERY DAY A REAL DAY OF JOB EXPERIENCE

When we were young, we were told to "*pay attention in school*". However, at any skill level, the essence of work is attention. Learn and encourage the policy of learning something new every day. Evaluate what you learn. Call a bad theory just that; not a "*good theory that doesn't work in practice*".

Made in the USA
San Bernardino, CA
31 August 2014

73617367R00123

Made in the USA
Lexington, KY
10 December 2017

ABOUT THE AUTHOR

JT Lawrence is an author, playwright
& bookdealer. She lives in Parkhurst, Johannesburg,
in a house with a red front door.

❀

STAY IN TOUCH

If you'd like to be notified of giveaways
& new releases, sign up for JT Lawrence's mailing list
via Facebook or on her author platform at
https://pulpbooks.wordpress.com/

ALSO BY JT LAWRENCE

The Memory of Water (2011)

Why You Were Taken (2015)

The Underachieving Ovary (2016)

Grey Magic (2016)

How We Found You (2017)

ACKNOWLEDGMENTS

Thanks go to my father, Keith Thiele,
and his better half, Gillian,
for proofreading every story I write.

Thanks to my beta readers: Priscilla Fick;
Roulon du Toit; Jestine Voges; Shirley Goodrum;
Angelique Pacheco and Janice Leibowitz.

Thanks to my husband, Mike, who literally
tag-teamed with me to get this book together on time:
beta reading, tweaking the cover design,
and holding our new baby, Alexandra, late into the night.
I know how lucky I am to have you.

Cover photography courtesy of Canva.com

1 / BRIDGE GATE

Dear Dad

Mom said it would be okay to write you a letter. I asked her when I'd see you again and she said she wasn't sure. I said I wanted to call you but she said you're not taking calls at the moment. She said you might not answer the letter, either, but that I could try.

The address is to 'Bridge Gate' but I don't know what that is. It sounds like some kind of B&B. Are you staying at a B&B?

The problem with a letter is that I don't really know what to write. If we could talk then I think I would know what to say but a letter is different. It's like talking to an empty room.

Mom said to tell you about school. School is fine. I like English but I hate geography. In English we are reading some Shakespeare and it's difficult to understand but I like it anyway, especially Macbeth. Next year we will study Romeo & Juliet which I am looking forward to.

Me and Sarah-Jayne (she is my best friend) cut off all our hair the other day! Mom was cross but I think it's my hair and I can do what I want with it? I'm 11 now so it's not like I'm a little kid anymore. Anyway it didn't look THAT nice so S-J's mom took us to her hairdresser to tidy it up and it looks better now. Mom was happy. S-J's mom says I am a bad influence on S-J but Mom says it's the other way around. That's mother's for you! The hairdresser said I look more cheeky elvin now than keemo chic but I don't know what that means. I don't know what elvin or keemo is.

I'm going to stop writing and post this letter now. I hope you get it. I hope you reply. It's weird knowing that you have a dad out there somewhere but you don't get to see him. It's a little bit like you died.

Please write back!

Love from Em.

Dear Emily

I have included the letter that you sent me in this envelope. You will see I have made corrections where your spelling or grammar was incorrect. I hope you will study it thoroughly. Specifically I would like to point out your usage of "me and Sarah-Jayne" where it should have been "Sarah-Jayne and I". Also remember that contractions are signalled with apostrophes but plurals are not. Instead of writing "That's mother's for you" with an apostrophe, it

should have been "mothers" (plural), without the apostrophe. Also, you use too many exclamation marks. Like insults, exclamation marks shouldn't be employed unless they are absolutely necessary.

By "elvin" I assume you meant "elfin" which means like an elf.

By "keemo" I assume you meant "chemo" as in "chemotherapy" which is a cancer treatment that can make your hair fall out (and is not to be made light of, especially by a hairdresser).

I hope this is clear.

Sincerely,

Your Father.

Dear Dad

I was so happy to get your letter, thank you!! I read the corrections you made and I will try not to make the same mistakes again. I like your red pen. Where did you get it? I have one that is similar but it is pink and it smells nice and when you shake it the glitter inside sparkles.

Sarah-Jayne and I had a fight about who is a better dancer (between us) but we are friends again. Her mom was so happy when we weren't speaking to each other and now she's not because we ARE speaking to each other again!. We're back to being best friends. S-J's mother pulls a funny

face now when I'm over there. Like an old dog without teeth who tries to smile but can't. It's better to be at our house, anyway‡ Mom's always at work so we get to do whatever we want. We watch American Idols and eat popcorn or cereal for dinner. Grilled cheese if we feel like cooking. There's not always that much food in the fridge but there is always cheese and bread.

What do you have for dinner there, where you are staying?

Love from Em.

PS. Sorry about all the crossing out. I keep using exclamation marks and then I remember what you said about them and then I take them out.

Dear Emily

I have again included your most recent letter to me, in this envelope. I see your spelling is improving. Your sentence structure can do with some work. You should not write "and then and then and then" but instead use the correct punctuation and conjunctions. In this instance, I would recommend thus: "I keep using exclamation marks, but then remember what you said about them, and take them out."

This is the written word, which should be clear and

eloquent; not some reality TV marathon dance-off that leaves you out of breath.

Dinner this evening was pork sausages and mashed potato. There were some peas, too, but they were grey and best left alone.

Sincerely,

Your Father

Dear Dad

I can't remember the last time we had bangers and mash! Yum! You're lucky. I miss mom's cooking. I don't remember your cooking. Did you ever cook? Maybe you were the best cook ever but I was too small to realise. Or it was too long ago to remember. Anyway, I know that Mom has to work all the time to keep the wolf away. At least she's still living in the house, kind of. I mean she's not home most of the time but when she is, it feels like she is far away. Like she's here, but she's not really here. Like she thinks herself into another room, or another house.

Sarah-Jayne's mother is worse than ever. S-J's father went away for a while (like you) but then he came back again. According to S-J's mother he's a loser and a Miss Cree-ant. No idea what a Miss Cree-ant is but she let him move back in and now she walks around all dog-face again.

I wish you'd come back. When I ask Mom if it will ever

happen she just gives me the Death Stare. The Death Stare is when you look at someone with evil eyes and a cross face until they get the message that whatever they have done is NOT O.K.

I'm turning 12 on Saturday which means I'm almost a grown up. Mom wants to have a party at our house but I said that parties are for babies and that I just want to go ice-skating with S-J and Murray and then go for waffles afterwards at Milky Lane.

Do you ever go ice-skating at the B&B?

Love from Em

Dear Emily

Please find your most recent letter enclosed as usual.

A miscreant is a reprobate, a rogue, a rascal.

The saying is "to keep the wolf from the door," not "to keep the wolf away."

Your sentence structure is much improved, but I'm afraid your spelling has taken a turn for the worse. Perhaps a dictionary would come in handy? I used to have one in my office at home but I am assuming that my office is no longer. Perhaps your mother will know where it is. Ask her if you like; if you are not too afraid of getting another Death Stare.

We don't have waffles or ice-skating here. I miss neither.

Who is Murray?

Sincerely,

Father

Dear Dad

I asked Mom for your dictionary but she just stormed out of the room as if I said something wrong. She says I have an attitude problem but really I think she's the one with anger management issues. Anger management is when you get really really cross but then you just swallow it until later and then get it out in a constructive way like kickboxing or pigeon shooting or something like that. She says ever since I turned 13 I've been a 'nightmare.' I didn't think that was a very nice thing to say.

Murray and Sarah-Jayne and I are best friends now. We do everything together. S-J borrows me nail polish and earrings (did I tell you I got my ears pierced?) and Murray borrows me books. Really interesting books that open my mind.

Anyway I looked everywhere for your dictionary and I found some pictures of you and mom when you were younger. I didn't know you were ever so happy. It felt weird to look at them — they made me happy and sad at

the same time. I didn't say anything to Mom. I don't like to see her cry, even when she's being mean. I can't help thinking that you went away because of me.

What is it like where you are, Dad? What do you do all day at the B&B? It's hard to picture you there because I don't know anything about it.

Love from Em

Dear Emily

Recent letter enclosed. Please study it carefully. The correct way to use the term 'borrow' is 'lend to, borrow from,' and not the other way around. In other words, Sarah-Jayne lends you her nail polish and Murray lends you his books. You borrow nail polish and books from your friends.

Look again for the dictionary. It must be there somewhere.

What do I do here? I study and garden and try to stay alive. That's about it.

Sincerely,

Father

PS. I didn't leave because of you.

Dear Dad

I'm in love with Murray. I can't stop thinking about him and I spend geography class writing my name and his surname as if we were married. I think up names for the babies we will have one day. I know I'm only 14 but I wish we could get married. If we lived in Romeo and Juliet's time then we would be able to. My English teacher said so.

I was looking for your dictionary AGAIN the other day (it's just something I do sometimes when I wander around the house) and Mom just exploded (clearly her anger management is not going very well) and admitted that she packed up most of your things after you moved away and donated them to Hospice. I couldn't believe it! I hope you are not too upset. I have chosen a few of your things (what is left of your things, anyway) and have hidden them away in my bedroom so that she can't give those away, too. I know that she snoops through my things though so I can't promise I'll keep them forever.

What kind of gardening do you do at the B&B?

Love from Em

Dear Emily

You use too many parentheses in your writing. It's a bad habit. Try to stop it now before it's too late.

Don't be too hard on your mom. I'm sure she's trying her best. It's not easy for her.

I am in the middle of planting out a rose garden. It involves a great deal of digging and my hands are almost always lacerated by the thorns. They would sting in the shower if we ever got hot water here. The Bridge Gate is not a B&B.

Regarding Romeo & Juliet: try not to rush into anything. Keep in mind how that particular story turns out. We have a Shakespearean story (of sorts) playing out here. Instead of the Montagues and the Capulets, however, we have the BlackJacks and the White Collars. Although I disapprove of the division and don't want to be involved, I am seen as a White Collar. I try to mind my own business and tend to the important things, like the roses. In my experience nothing ever good comes from choosing sides.

Don't worry about my things. I have everything I need here. Keep what you want for yourself and throw the rest away.

Smith always says that the more possessions you have, the less energy you have because owning material things costs you energy. Less is almost always more. Sometimes I think Smith is full of it — he reads too much — but I think this is true, even though Smith collects bananas and keeps them under his pillow. For some reason he doesn't think the rule applies to bananas.

Sincerely,

Your Father

Dear Dad

I hate Murray and Sarah-Jayne. Do you see these watermarks on the page? They are tears. My heart is in a million pieces. I tried to talk to Mom but all she says is 'good riddance' as if she doesn't care about my broken heart at all. I hate her. And I hate Sarah-Jayne. I wish I could hate Murray but when I think about him my chest just crumples inside. I need you, Dad. Can you please come and visit? You can sleep in my room and I will sleep in the lounge on the lumpy couch. I don't care.

Love from Em

PS. What are parentheses??

Dear Emily

Youth is full of excitement and heartache, and you should ride the waves while you can. At least that is what Perkins says. He is a philosopher, so he is probably right. On the other hand, sometimes he sings *La Traviata* (Italian opera) at the top of his voice and forgets to wear his pants, so perhaps we should take what he says with a pinch of salt.

There weren't any errors in your previous letter.

'Parentheses' are commonly known as 'brackets.'

I'm sorry I can't visit you. The rose garden is at its most vulnerable and needs daily attention.

Sincerely,

Father

Dear Dad

Mom is acting weird. I'm the one with the broken heart so you'd think that I'd be the one eating an entire litre of tin roof ice-cream in the lounge with the curtains drawn and watching *Come Dine With Me* reruns, but she has been hogging it instead. Sometimes when I get home from school she is just sitting there, and the phone is ringing. She acts as if she doesn't hear it. I know I was always complaining about her never being home but this is worse.

I don't like being at home anymore, but I don't like school either. Murray is there. I hate Murray. He is an asshole.

If you can't visit me here, maybe I can come visit you there at the B&B? I'd love to see the roses.

Love from Em

Dear Emily

Please refrain from using curse words in your letters to me and your writing in general. Curse words are for commoners and for people who lack a good vocabulary. Nothing good comes of swearing. It's a filthy habit, like smoking.

That said, if you must use the term 'asshole' please spell it correctly. We are not referring to a donkey. Hence: "arsehole" is the correct spelling.

I am not allowed visitors. Bridge Gate is not a B&B. Even if you were to come, the rose garden isn't blooming yet. You'd be disappointed.

Sincerely,

Your Father

Dear Dad

I can't believe Mom told you about the smoking! It was just once, and getting caught was just bad luck. It's not like I'm addicted or anything. The teacher that suspended me has never liked me and was SO happy to catch me doing something wrong. It didn't mean anything. I was just doing it to get back at Murray. He and S-J go around like life is so bloody wonderful (when it's NOT) and so when Vince asked me if I wanted to go share a cigarette with him in the boys' locker room (Vince always wears black and he listens

to cool music and talks about deep stuff that I don't understand) of course I said YES.

Please don't be cross with me. Everyone else is cross enough.

Love from Em

Dear Emily

At least you spelt 'bloody' correctly.

Smith (he was talking about us, not about you) says that saints are just sinners who keep trying. I think it's true. So I'll keep trying, and you must, too.

One cigarette is not the end of the world. It's the boy you should be cautious of. Don't let your broken heart lead you down a barbed path you can't reverse out of. Murray is not worth it, and Sarah-Jayne is certainly not worth it. Besides, the best revenge is to be successful. You won't be successful if you keep skipping class to smoke with a boy, no matter how interesting he is.

Perkins says that our poor life choices are like tattoos — you can try to get rid of them but they'll always be there, under the skin. Best not to get a tattoo in the first place.

Sincerely,

Your Father

Dear Dad

Okay, okay, I won't get the tattoo. How did you know about it, anyway? Mom swears she hasn't spoken to you in years so I don't know where you're getting your intel from. 'Intel' means intelligence, as in information. I learnt it from the TV. I've been watching a lot of TV lately because what else am I supposed to do when I'm suspended from school? Mom has forbidden me from seeing Vince. I think everyone is overreacting. (Although I am glad that Mom is off the couch and in the land of the living again, even if it is just to shout at me).

Thank God that I'll be 16 soon. 16 is pretty much an adult. Sweet 16! Ha! More like the opposite. I don't want a party if you can't come. Maybe I can write a letter to someone there and ask nicely to let you come out just for a weekend? I am getting good at writing letters!

Love from Em

Dear Emily

I'm afraid a letter from you, no matter how well-written it is, will not secure an exit pass for me for the weekend. Besides, things are very busy here and I can't leave Smith. He has a cracked skull and some broken ribs. He was in the

hospital wing for a few days but now he's back and I need to look after him. He is not to be left alone.

Sincerely,

Your Father.

~~Holy Shit~~ Dad

What happened to Smith??

Em

Dear Emily

There is no need to use two question marks after your questions. One will suffice.

Smith got himself into a spot of bother with another resident. A BlackJack, as you have probably guessed. Next time he will know better. We live and learn, as Pant-less Perkins says.

Sincerely,

Your Father

Dear Dad

Did they get into a fight? What were they fighting about?

I got into a fight with S-J last week (who else?!) but there were no broken ribs exchanged, just horrible words.

I have always pictured Smith as a respectable accountant type of person. Not someone who gets into fights! Perkins, too. Are they not?

I am secretly dating Vince now, despite (or maybe because of) everyone's pressure not to. I don't know why people think they can just tell me what to do as if I'm some kind of sheep. Mom bought me some colourful tops the other day because she's tired of me wearing black all the time and because she felt bad that we are always fighting. If she could stop telling me what to do we'd probably get on better. I'm not some kid she can just boss around. She keeps searching my room for drugs but I told her I'm 16, not stupid. (The smokes she found were Vince's, not mine).

Love from Emily

Dear Emily

The altercation concerned a pack of cigarettes, I believe. Not dissimilar to your argument with your mother.

Smith is neither respectable nor an accountant. Perkins is even worse, but it's not his fault.

Despite their shortcomings, they have many redeeming qualities. Smith is kind and shares his paper with me so that I can write to you. Perkins ... well, Perkins tries his best but he has had a difficult life.

We had bangers and mash for dinner this evening and it made me think of you. We also had carrots cut into coins that had all the goodness boiled out of them. A bit like Perkins.

Sincerely,

Your Father

Dear Dad

I need help. I feel like life is not worth living. I know it's a cliché but I don't care. I don't care about anything. Now I am the one sitting in the dark lounge and not talking to anybody. How do you get the goodness back into the carrot coins? There must be a way. I have given mine away and now I regret it. I feel used and soul-shrivelled. I need my carroty-ness back.

Love from Em

Dear Emily

Your writing has come along so well. I am proud of you.

I'm afraid once the carroty-ness is gone it is gone forever. But don't despair. Your carroty-ness is not the only thing you have going for you. There are other parts of you that are in full bloom that you must be proud of.

Love, Dad.

Dear Dad

You have no idea how your previous letter saved my life. Thank you. I love you.

Em

Dear Dad

I'm much better. I'm back in school. Vince is history. Mom and I are talking. My marks are improving.

I haven't heard from you in a while. How are the roses? Are you okay?

Love from Em

Dad

Are you okay??

Em

To my dearest Em

Smith has been killed. He was in another fight and a man named Axxe drove a shiv into his stomach. Talk about nominative determinism.

Nominative Determinism is when you live up to your name. For example, a plumber named Piper, or a chef named Cook. Perkins said my name would also make a good example, being Locklear, and being held here. You'd better not live up to your name. Maybe you SHOULD get married early after all, to a Bond or a Gold, or, even better: a Joy.

Try to forgive S-J and Murray, even if they don't deserve it. Hate is a destructive emotion: like drinking poison and expecting the other person to die.

When I found Smith in the library he was still alive but there was too much blood lost. We had a small ceremony yesterday where we all said a few words. It's not the same without him. No more stockpiled bananas, for one. Perkins (wearing pants, for a change) said that if he had to choose

between feeling grief and feeling nothing, he'd take grief. I'm not too sure about that.

Someone from our side (a White Collar) witnessed the thing and Axxe has been thrown in solitary confinement. We won't tell them who the witness is, despite their threats. He did the right thing, and now we need to protect him. I don't want you to worry.

I am writing especially to let you know that the rose garden is flourishing. I also wanted to let you know that every rose I planted was for you. Every time I received a letter from you, I planted a new rose. There are 15 now and they look beautiful.

Don't be afraid of wearing some colour. There is a time for wearing black.

Tell your mom that I love her; that I never stopped loving her.

I never stopped loving you. I'm not a man for regrets but I'll always be sorry for how things turned out between you and Mom and I.

The wonderful thing about having children is that they can fix what you have broken. You are my upgrade, Em. Keep trying. Do better.

Love from Dad

Dear Dad

I found your dictionary!!! At last. And I'm coming to

visit. Mom will bring me. She said she loves you, too. That's why it's so hard for her.

Love from Em

Dear Susan and Emily Locklear

It is with deep regret that I write to inform you of the passing away of your husband and father, Michael Locklear.

Mr Locklear was involved in an altercation. We don't believe there was much pain.

The men responsible have been transferred to the maximum security wing pending their trial, the details of which we will furnish in subsequent communication.

Mr Locklear was always a polite and generous man, and he transformed the gardens in the years he spent here. We are grateful for his work. In his studies, he completed various degrees and tutored others. His positive attitude and hard work are some of the qualities the parole board took into account when they granted his early parole yesterday, unaware of the fact that he had just passed away.

Please find the attached box of flowers that a fellow prisoner, Perkins, insisted you have. Inside is a bloom cut from each of the roses he had worked on every day for the past 6 years. My thoughts are with you in this difficult time.

With my sincerest condolences —

Frederick Collis

Director at Bridge Gate Prison

Department of Correctional Services

2 / THE ITCH

It starts as a tickle. A pin prickle. As if there is an insect on her scalp. It wakes her up. It isn't difficult to interrupt Sam's sleep. She hears everything at night: every serrated cat fight, every wail of house alarm, every empty midnight argument within a two block radius. It isn't a sudden alertness, like when a car backfires and sends her heart sprinting; sends her mind wandering into fantasies of hot guns and wasted bullets.

No. It's a slow surfacing; an un-rushed floating up from the warm depths of slumber. If she opened her eyes she would see the very first drafts of light spilling like smoke from behind the blinds.

Certain it's her imagination pulling at her follicles, Sam ignores the urge to swat away the phantom beetle. She tries to drift back down into the still murk but it has been disturbed; dredged from dark into colour.

One day, she says to herself, swinging her legs off the bed. One day I won't wake up exhausted.

One day you won't wake up at all, says a voice that sounds like her own.

At least, then, she says, I won't be exhausted.

Well, that's one way to look at it, says the voice. Only you would think Death has a silver lining.

Ha, says Sam.

What's wrong with you? the voice asks. You used to be a pessimist.

I don't have the energy to be a pessimist anymore.

She rubs her feet together, knits her fingers, stretches.

Is it normal, do you think, says Sam, to have conversations with yourself?

What do you mean, 'normal'?

Well, do other people do it?

Would that make it 'normal'? Anyway, why does it matter?

Sam sighs. She knows better than to get into a philosophical debate with herself so early in the morning. She yawns and knuckle-scrubs her swollen eyes. She thinks the itch is gone.

'You're early!' Pete from Accounting says.

Why does he always act surprised that you're early?

says the voice. Besides, he's always here before you, so that makes him even earlier.

It's just something to say, that's all. He doesn't mean anything by it.

'Hi, Pete,' says Sam. 'Good weekend?'

'Yip, yip,' he says, 'Yip, it was a good one.'

She can tell by the way his eyes move upwards that he is searching for something interesting to say. Sam lifts her laptop bag as a signal that she should be working, and he gives up and lets her go. As she passes him she gets a faint whiff of wool and cologne. It smells wrong. Plain soap would suit him better.

She reaches her office and sighs down into her swivel chair. Switches on her machine. Starts her regular morning ritual of clearing her desktop of the previous day's chaos. Her stomach snarls.

Should have had breakfast, says the voice.

Yes, says Sam.

You had the time.

Yes.

Pete's rosy cheeks appear in her doorframe. He waits for her nod before crossing the threshold, and places a steaming cup of coffee on her desk with exaggerated care.

Ah, look, it's your favourite mug, says the voice.

'It's your favourite mug,' says Pete. 'Half a sugar, dash of milk.'

'You know me so well, Pete,' says Sam. 'You're a saint.'

'No,' blushes Pete.

'Saint Peter,' she smiles. He smiles back.

They crucified him upside-down, you know, says the voice. Caesar's lot. That's really nothing to smile about.

At her lunch hour (Emmentaler and ham on rye) Sam wonders if she should phone the boys; see what they're up to on their school holidays. She always has to weigh up the consequences of hearing Barry's disapproving tone, like ice water, versus the warm buoyancy she gets when she hears the animation in her sons' voices.

Bugger him, says the voice. They're your kids too.

I lost them, says Sam.

They're not lost, says the voice.

She's about to dial when there is another barely-there prickle on her scalp: a bright green caterpillar; a fruit bug; a hornet. Her fingers fly up to inspect the spot: half expecting nothing; half expecting the shock of a small interloper. She scratches the vacant patch. There is temporary relief, but then it returns with double the intensity. She shoots up, sending the chair coasting backwards and crashing into the wall. She turns her head upside down and rubs her whole scalp frantically, trying to dislodge the itch.

What is it? asks the voice. What is that feeling?

Sam is too busy shaking her hair out to answer.

She's certain that if there ever was an insect, it's now gone, but the itch remains. She walks down the corridor to the restroom, where she parts her hair, leans over the basin, inspects the skin under the downlight.

There's nothing there, says the voice.

There must be something, says Sam. A mosquito bite. A hive. A blister.

There's nothing there.

It's itching like … like … I don't know, I've never had an itch as … ferocious as this before.

Don't scratch it.

I have to!

Don't scratch it! It's making it worse.

I don't care. I can't help it.

We need to get to a doctor.

A doctor? laughs Sam. It's an itch!

It could be something bad.

Oh please. Like what?

Shingles.

Shingles! I'm not an old man!

Your immune system is compromised.

No it is not! ... Besides, shingles is more of a pain, isn't it? This is an itch.

It could be anything. Let's just pop in at the medical suites on our way home. See Doctor Callie.

Stop being such a hypochondriac.

Chicken pox!

It's not chicken pox. I had chicken pox when I was five. Still have the scars on my stomach where I could scratch without my mother seeing.

I know.

You know?

I was there.

I need to get back to work.

No you don't. You're days ahead. Take the rest of the day off. Maybe you just need some down time.

I can't just leave the office halfway through the day!

You used to.

That was another time. Another life. I'm not the same person.

Sam still finds herself shocked by how quickly an

ordinary life can be derailed by just a couple of bad choices. She won't make the same mistakes again.

Stop scratching, Samantha, for God's sake.

I hate it when you call me 'Samantha.'

The parking lot is still full of cars when Sam reverses out. The security guard looks surprised that she is leaving early. She winds down her window.

'I'm just off to the doctor,' she says, to ease the guilty edges of her thoughts. Brown, foxed, like the pages of a well-read book. 'I'll be back soon.'

'Hope it's nothing serious,' the guard says.

She wants to say 'it's nothing' but then her excuse will be blown. She scratches her head.

'I'll be okay,' she says.

So we *are* going to the doctor? asks the voice.

May as well, says Sam. It's Monday afternoon and the sun is shining. What else do we have to do?

Doctor Callie surveys Sam's scalp.

'I can't see anything,' she says. Cheerful.

Is she blind? asks the voice.

What?

She just said she can't see anything.

She meant that she can't see anything *wrong*, says Sam. Anything *unusual*.

'I mean, it's a bit red, maybe from you scratching it?' says the doctor.

'I've been trying not to, but it's so ... the itch is so intense.'

'Well,' she says, 'I can give you some topical steroids. That should help.'

We could have bought cortisone cream over the counter! What a waste of time.

You're the one who insisted we come here.

Do I hear a duck in here?

What?

Quack!

What else can she do? Sam asks the voice. She can't diagnose something she can't see.

Doctor Callie types the script up on an old school typewriter on her desk. Sam studies the antique.

'Yes,' she says, mid-type. 'I'm a walking cliché. My handwriting is *that* bad.'

Sam balls up her fists, denies the beckoning itch.

'It's extra strength. Schedule 4,' Callie says, pulling it out of the machine and handing it to Sam. 'Use it sparingly.'

Oh. Okay. Extra strength. That sounds good.

'Come back if any more symptoms develop.'

The bald pharmacist passes her the tube of ointment. Sam inspects his shiny scalp.

'Apply to the rash as needed,' he shouts for the whole pharmacy to hear.

Sam's cheeks flare.

'It's not a rash,' she says.

'Huh?' his eyebrows are like climbing ants.

'Never mind.'

It's not a venereal disease, she wants to tell everyone. It's not herpes or syphilis.

— As far as you know — says the voice.

It's not contagious, she wants to say.

As far as you know, says the voice.

Sam doesn't wait to get home before puncturing the tin tube and rubbing the ointment into the offending skin. She sits in her car, waiting for the relief. She taps her steering

wheel.

Do you feel like driving somewhere? asks the voice.

Not particularly, says Sam. Unless you mean home. I would like to be at home.

I mean … maybe the itch is psychosomatic.

It's not. The itch is real.

Psychosomatic doesn't mean it's not real. It means it's caused by your mind.

If it's caused by my mind then I should be able to stop it with my mind and believe me, I can't.

Have you tried?

Yes.

Try again.

Well, I've got the cream on now. The cream should work. How will I know if I cured myself with my amazing mental self-healing powers or if it was the cortisone?

Let's go home.

Yes. Let's.

Sam closes the front door behind her, hangs up her keys and her jacket. Sits on the creaking couch in her lounge holding the ointment in both hands like prayer beads. Kicks off her pumps, lies down with a throw pillow under her

head and another under the backs of her knees. Comforting. The itch has definitely receded. She can still feel it nagging, but it seems further away. As if it's in the next room.

What shall we do now? asks the voice.

Why do you always want to *do* something?

What do you mean?

What is wrong with lying here?

Just lying here?

Yes. Just lying here for a moment. What is wrong with that?

It won't just be a moment. That's the thing. Besides, life is about doing things, isn't it? Doing one thing after another. A string of events. Lying on your couch is not an event.

I'm tired.

You're always tired.

You make me tired.

Maybe if you did something you wouldn't be as tired.

Maybe if you gave me a break I wouldn't be as tired.

Sam lies there for a while in the quiet cool of the room. There is no sound apart from the hum of the refrigerator and the occasional car passing outside. An hour passes in peace.

Sam waits for the voice to nag her, but it doesn't.

You know that things are bad, she thinks, when you give yourself the silent treatment.

It's itchy again, says Sam, but no one answers her. It's itchy! Damn it! Aren't you going to say something?

What do you want me to say? says the voice. I thought you wanted me to keep quiet.

Don't be petulant. It doesn't suit you.

Alright.

Alright?

Put some cream on. It definitely helped last time.

I have.

When?

Earlier, when you weren't talking to me.

Put some more on.

The doctor said to not use too much, says Sam.

She doesn't know how itchy it is.

True.

Desperate times call for desperate measures.

Yes. I'll put some more on.

Sam squeezes more ointment out, applies it liberally to the irritated patch.

There. You'll feel better now.

What if I don't?

Let's worry about that later.

I'm not going to be able to sleep tonight.

It won't be the first time.

True.

You'll live.

Yes, Sam sighs, yes, I suppose I will.

It's not working, says Sam. It's even worse than before.

Give it some time, says the voice.

I've given it time. I'm going to put some more on.

Are you sure?

It's just cream. What's the worst that can happen?

You shouldn't tempt fate.

I don't believe in fate.

Yes, you do.

You've been lying here for ages. Let's get up. Make some dinner.

There's nothing in the fridge.

Crackers, then. Cheese. I think there might be an old apple lurking in the fruit bowl. You have to eat something.

An old apple, says Sam. That sounds appealing.

She gets up slowly, rolls her head around on her neck. Finds a rind of cheddar but no crackers. No apple, old or otherwise. Puts on the kettle to have tea instead.

Maybe we can go grocery shopping tomorrow. Just to get a few things. You know, if you're feeling up to it.

Stop scratching!

What?

You're scratching like a rabid cat. Stop it.

Hey, I was sleeping!

Yes, well, maybe sleeping isn't such a great idea if it means you're going to scratch your head open.

I can't believe you woke me up. You know how difficult it is for me to —

Sam stops talking when she notices the sticky feeling on her fingers, the smell of copper. She switches on her bedside lamp. A bright halo jumps out of the bulb. Her

fingers are bloody. Sam's confused. Where is the blood coming from?

I *told* you, says the voice.

Bright blood all over her pillow.

Oh my God.

Sam feels as though she has been attacked. As if a man dressed in a black balaclava had come through the window and battered her.

Why does it always have to be a man? asks the voice.

What are you talking about?

Your imaginary intruder.

Because they almost always *are* men, says Sam. Men are the ones that harm. Mostly.

Have I ever hurt you? asks the voice.

No. I don't think so.

You don't *think* so?

No, you haven't. Now can we get back to this ... massacre ... on my pillow?

What is there to say?

It's still itchy, for one. Shall I put more steroid cream on?

Er, I don't think you realise —

What?

— How much damage you've done.

Sam gets out of bed, pads into the en suite. Gasps at the spectre in the mirror. Matted hair dyed red. As if perfectly choreographed, a fresh rivulet spills down her forehead.

Is this real? she asks. Is this really happening? It feels like a scene from a horror movie.

Stephen King, says the voice. Carrie. The sad girl with magic powers. Pig's blood. Everyone dies in the end.

You're not helping.

Sorry.

Sam leans forward to get a closer look. She is both repulsed and fascinated by the dark gash in her scalp.

Emergency room? says the voice.

At 3AM? It's not that bad.

It needs stitches.

No it doesn't. It needs a plaster. A shower and a plaster.

You can't be serious.

What do you know? demands Sam.

She turns on the hot water. Strips off her bloodied sleep shirt and kicks it towards the laundry bin. The steam billows, filling up the bathroom with its soothing mist. Sam steps into the smoky cube, tentatively moving her head

underneath the rose. The water drums down on her lacerated scalp. It stings with a white light.

Sweet Jesus it stings!

Of course it bloody well stings, says the voice. It's an open wound!

Tinted water rushes down her body. She massages her hair, scrapes the dried blood from underneath her nails. The hot water hurts, but it takes away the itch. Pain. Relief. Pain. She stands there until the water runs clear and cold. Wraps herself up in a clean towel, shivers at her new reflection. Washed out. The only plasters she has in the house are five years old and have Mickey Mouse on them.

Why did I keep these? she asks herself, but there is no answer. She tears the paper off with her teeth. Uses three to cover the abraded area. Cuts her nails as short as they will go. Puts on some warm clothes. Casual. She won't be going in to work today, not with Disney plasters on her head.

Sam sits on the chair in the dawn-dark bedroom, waiting for the day to begin.

You could try to sleep, says the voice.

Ha, says Sam. Sometimes it's like you don't know me at all.

Ha, says the voice.

Sam waits. She taps her toes. Sighs.

Still itchy.

Yes.

That's surprising. I would have thought you had scratched all the nerve endings to death.

I wish I had.

This isn't healthy. Sitting here in the gloom.

Let me guess. You want to do something.

You don't actually have to *do* something. You just need a distraction. You could just put something on. The TV. Read a book.

That's a good idea, she says, but she doesn't move.

I know what you're thinking, says the voice. Stop. Just stop. You're just making it harder.

I can't help it.

Yes, you can. You know how.

I'm too tired. That's the problem. Worn down. How can I hang on to willpower when I feel this way?

You'll feel better soon. You just need to get through this … whatever this is.

I need a drink.

Don't say it! Don't even say the words.

I can't help it. The thought just comes again and again like a … stubborn boomerang. It's like a sick mantra that won't go away. I need a drink I need a drink I need a drink.

Please. Stop.

You know I won't do it. I won't. But I can't help the urge. What's the point in denying it exists? It's always there. Every time I walk past that kitchen cupboard. Every time I open that drawer in the study. My shoe cupboard. The vanity desk. Every single time I crave that glass bottle lip in my mouth.

... I know.

When will it end?

I don't know.

'Good gracious, Miss Douglas, what have you done to yourself?'

Sam blushes as the doctor peels away the cartoon characters.

'I'm usually such a bad sleeper. I can't believe I did so much damage in my sleep.'

'Your inhibitions are lower when you're asleep. You didn't have anyone to tell you not to scratch.'

Sam chokes on air.

'You tried the cortisone?'

'Yes.'

'It didn't help?'

'I thought it was helping. And then I woke up with blood all over my pillow.'

The doctor cleans the wound and applies a fresh dressing. She keeps it in place by winding a bandage all the way around Sam's head, tucking it under her chin.

'I look like a wounded soldier or something. All I need now is a limp and a wooden crutch.'

'At least you can laugh about it,' the doctor says, reeling more and more gauze around Sam's head.

'Is all the bandaging really necessary?'

'It's to stop you from scratching it open again tonight.'

Okay. That makes sense.

'This time we'll give you a full blood work-up. Try to figure out what's causing it. And I'm going to give you oral cortisone. Whether the pills help or not, I'd like you to see a specialist.'

'A dermatologist?' asks Sam. 'That's a good idea.'

Why didn't I think of that?

'A psychiatrist,' says Callie, sitting down at her typewriter. Rolling up her sleeves. 'I'll give you a list of my recommendations in the area.'

'I already have one,' says Sam. 'A psychologist.'

'Oh?' says Callie, mid-clack.

'A counsellor,' says Sam. 'I'm an alcoholic.'

'You didn't tell me that,' says the doctor.

'It was an itch. I didn't think it was relevant,' says Sam.

'In this kind of case, everything is relevant.'

This time Sam is not woken by blood. Her bed linen is wet again, but it's not crimson, like before. It's clear, tinged with pink and green.

You've scratched right through that ridiculous dressing, says the voice.

Oh, God, says Sam. Why didn't you wake me?

I did!

Why did I go to sleep in the first place? I should have just stayed awake. What is this liquid? Is the wound weeping? Is it infected?

This time I really think you should go to the ER. I know it's the middle of the night but —

Okay. I think I will.

The intern on duty clicks his penlight torch and peers at Sam's head. Startles. Shines it into her eyes. He grabs a gurney for her, books an operating room and darts her with an IV.

That escalated quickly, says Sam.

The voice is quiet. Is it still a voice if it is quiet? she wonders.

It looks pretty serious, prods Sam.

There is excited babbling around her.

... They're just being careful. Better safe than sorry, says the voice.

I should probably call the boys.

There's no time.

They rush her under fluorescent lighting that leaves trails in her vision. A long exposure gone wrong till the picture is ruined. Bleached. Blown out. An oxygen mask is strapped to her face. Someone holds her cold hand. Anaesthetic pulls her under; her whole body is dunked by the drugs and the relief.

'Samantha?' says a white lab coat. 'Samantha? Can you hear me?'

Sam groans. Opens her eyes. Her mouth is stuck together. Her head feels like it has exploded. She lifts her hand to touch it but there is only a cocoon of dry bandaging. She tries to swallow the cottonmouth but her swallow-reflex is on strike.

'Waa rara?' asks Sam.

'What happened?' says the lab coat. 'You managed to scratch through —

Scratched through my scalp? says Sam. That's terrible.

'You scratched through your skull.'

That's not even possible. That's not possible, is it?

'It was brain fluid. You actually scratched into your brain.'

Sam can't tell if he is horrified or fascinated. He tells her that while she was out, a neurosurgeon had cleaned and debrided the site, which had become infected. A plastic surgeon had grafted perforated ribbons of her thigh skin over it.

'Thank you,' she says. What else could she say?

'Did you count things as a child?' asks the hospital psychiatrist, pen hovering over chipped clipboard.

Of course I counted things as a child. It was called school.

Sam nods. Her head pounds.

'I mean, count things compulsively,' says the psychiatrist.

'No,' says Sam.

'Did you skip over cracks in the pavement, that kind of

thing?'

'No,' says Sam. 'I'm not obsessive-compulsive.'

'OCD would explain this … situation.'

'I'm not saying it's *not* psychological,' says Sam, 'just that I'm not OCD.'

The psychiatrist purses his lips; not convinced. Sam knows she is inconveniencing him.

The itch remains: furious and all-consuming. A modest flower arrangement arrives: yellow tulips from Pete from Accounting. "Get Well Soon!" the card says.

I don't understand, says Sam.

You don't understand why Pete would send you flowers?

I don't understand why it's still itchy. I mean, it's not even the same skin. It's from my leg.

You're right. It doesn't make any sense.

It's like my actual brain is itchy. I can't stand it. When it's at it's worst, I fantasise …

Yes?

I fantasise about getting a steel brush and just scrubbing away.

Instead, she lies on her side, hands clenched, and

watches the tulips fade.

'Hi,' says a new lab coat. Freshly washed hair, red lipstick, happy clinking gold bangles. Sam envies the doctor's non-itchy scalp. Wonders if she has any of her own hair left under the swathes of gauze. She imagines herself looking like a giant human cotton bud.

'Don't worry,' the red lipstick says. 'I don't think you're crazy.'

'Then you don't know me very well,' says Sam. It hurts to smile.

She seems nice, says the voice.

The neurologist injects local anaesthetic into Sam's scalp. It helps for a few glorious hours, and then the itch comes back. They continue this treatment in waves of itch and relief and itch and relief until the medicine stops working.

Sam wakes up to find that despite the dressings she has rubbed away the skin graft. She is returned to the operating room for a new one. She rubs that one away, too. She is declared a danger to herself and is transferred to a psychiatric institution where they tie her hands to the bedposts at night to stop her from scratching.

We have to get out of here! says the voice.

I don't know. It's not that bad, says Sam.

Not that bad? It's a nut house! You're not mentally ill!

I know.

But?

But it's nice to be taken care of. It's nice to be able to sleep. It's been a long time. I feel better.

One day the man who shares the room with her is gone. He was friendly and always wore quirky socks. Dots and stripes and jolly colours. Liquorice Allsorts. He shared his fruit baskets with her.

There's hope, she tells the voice. See? Mr P has been discharged.

He, too, suffered from a persistent itch and had his hands wrapped up in white. The two were like boxers, the nurses would joke as they performed the evening ritual. Sparring partners. Except that instead of fighting they would sit and have tea together and complain about the early lights-out.

Sam knows that Mr P was not, in fact, cured. She saw the stained sheets, the congealed brown puddle on the floor. The sisters' shiny swollen eyelids. Mr P's itch had been on his neck, over his carotid artery.

A dangerous place to scratch, whispers the voice.

I wonder if the boys will visit, says Sam.

I'm sure they will, says the voice.

Sam is discharged once the staff formulate a way to stop her from hurting herself. She is given a soft helmet to wear at night, and cotton mitts. At its worst the itch is as violent as ever, but Sam protects herself. If she really has to scratch she uses the toddler's toothbrush she hadn't been able to throw away all those years ago. A lifetime ago. She wakes up to the solace of a clean pillow every morning. Her hair grows back in unattractive tufts. She walks with a slight gait: minor cerebrum damage from when she scratched her brain. She plans to return to work. She plans to call the boys and laugh with them on the phone. She plans to go for coffee with Pete from Accounting.

A neighbour's house alarm is howling. It's 4AM. Sam feels surrounded by the night. Her scalp itches.

It's good that you're taking advantage of your situation, says the voice.

My situation? says Sam.

Yes. You're home. You're alive. You're sober. You've got a job. You can walk.

Yes, says Sam, reaching for the toothbrush. She removes the helmet and moves the soft bristles in slow circles over the itch. Sighs at the intense and sweeping relief.

You're lucky, says the voice.

I wouldn't go that far.

You still have a sense of humour.

Do I? asks Sam.

I don't know, says the voice. What do I know?

Sam stretches, swings her legs out of bed. Thinks of Mr. P's candy coloured socks.

Maybe … starts Sam.

Yes? says the voice.

Maybe we can do something today.

❦

3 / THE UNSUSPECTING GOLD DIGGER

When I first slept with Byron I didn't know about the money. I don't think anyone did.

They weren't handing out silver spoons the days we were born. His parents were decidedly middle-class, as were mine, and while we didn't want for much, we were by no stretch of the imagination Trust Fund Kids. We weren't in line to inherit much either, once our folks eventually decided to leap off their respective mortal coils, which looked as if it would be further and further into the future the way they were soldiering on, making themselves raw green juices for breakfast and embracing meditation and tai chi. It's not like I wished them dead — far from it — but I did wonder from time to time how old they would allow themselves to get. It's about being practical: I mean, old age isn't pretty. Letting yourself get any older than 90, I think, isn't respectable. There are plenty of ways you can stop this from happening: it doesn't have to be gruesome. In fact, the whole point is to avoid vulgarity altogether.

Byron and I both went to good government schools in Johannesburg. We had nice clothes but not the best, good sporting equipment but not the most expensive. We grew up middle-of-the-road and although we only met when we were in our mid-30s, we could have easily have known each other for years, because he was exactly like my brothers and the other boys I knew, and I, like his sister. We knew the same jokes and had the same boarding school horror-food stories, which we would still exchange in new company 20 years on. In moments like these it was easy to feel as if we had known each other our whole lives. There was an inherent intimacy in our relationship, something sharp and soft at the same time, embedded deep in our connection with each other. An oyster at the bottom of our ocean.

We met online — not on a dating site, but a travel forum — and our relationship developed quickly. There was no playing hard to get on either side: there was no need. We both saw what we wanted and both got lucky. When you're on your way downhill from 35 and you manage to link arms with a fellow slider who you find reasonably attractive and who makes you laugh you don't think twice about 'moving too fast'. We were comfortable with each other from the beginning; mature enough to be able to just be ourselves. We had similar interests, and a shared love of modern literature, red wine, and any movie starring Will Ferrell. We kind of slid into each other's lives; slid into each other. We ate from each others' plates, split our paperbacks and shared our socks. We kissed before brushing our teeth.

The first warning bell was the size of the diamond he gave me. No, that's not right. The actual warning bell was the diamond itself, and what it represented. The size just magnified the alarm. We had spoken about marriage fleetingly — Byron knew that it wasn't an institution I was particularly fond of — and I had thought that there was no need to mention it again.

I didn't believe in committing to one person for the rest of one's life. At the rate people change, I didn't find it practical.

Our relationship was evermore altered on a humid April morning on Reunion Island. Byron had insisted on waking up early and taking a walk to the beach while it was still empty. I wanted to lie in, doze, and finish the book I was reading. He made bourbon vanilla tea and threw pillows at me, bribing me with how lovely the dawn view would be. I told him to go on his own. He promised a cappuccino and *pain au chocolate* on the walk down, and I acquiesced. Coffee and pastry in hand, gazing at the last of the sunrise, we sat on the still-cool sand while the air around us swirled with something yet unfamiliar to us. There was a peculiar tension, an odd anxiety that I couldn't understand. I brushed it off, thinking I was just out of sorts because of the early rise, but it kept returning, nagging at my mood, like a pebble in a shoe.

"I have something for you," he finally said, breaking the spell of awkwardness.

Thank God, I thought. The unease was just about a small gift that he was hiding, figuring out how to give it to me. Secrecy was the thing making us uncomfortable — we

weren't accustomed to it. I looked at his empty hands, then searched his lit-up eyes for clues.

"I'm not sure you'll like it."

"Well, that's a good start," I joked. He laughed out of nervousness, not at my wit. The pebble was back. Before I could make another attempt at banter he reached into his board-shorts pocket and brought out a small black box hinged with gold. He opened it to reveal an especially large diamond set in a ring. Suddenly the carefully-planned trip to the romantic island made sense: the candlelit dinners; the rose-petal turn-downs. I was usually used to — and happy with — more prosaic accommodation.

"I don't understand," I said.

"Are you going to make me beg?"

"I'd prefer it if you didn't."

"So, then, is that a yes?"

"I'm not sure. It depends what you're asking."

He shrugged, as if he wasn't asking me a question that would change our lives for ever.

"It's yours, the diamond. Whether you want to marry me or not."

I had never been one for jewellery. I didn't like the fuss of accessorising. The same went for marriage. Byron knew all of this, and was asking anyway. I couldn't tell if he was blatantly disregarding my preference or if he had simply decided that his need for me was greater than my

disinclination. That was the moment the trouble started.

It wasn't only the unwelcome proposal that had me worried. Worse still, was that I had accepted. Despite the whirring of my cognitive dissonance, the tap-tap-tapping of better judgement against my skull, I agreed to marry Byron. I knew that if I turned him down it would be the end of our relationship, and I wasn't ready for that. Perhaps not immediately, but eventually it would take its toll. What I didn't guess was that by consenting to his need over mine, it would have the same sad effect. The honeymoon, as they say, was over.

He told me about the money that evening, after a day of stolen glances and tentative affection. I was ribbing him about the size of the diamond, asking if he had had to take a second bond out on his house. Saying the only reason I agreed was the size of the stone: one carat smaller and I would have refused. That's when he told me that he was 'wealthy'. I laughed, saying he could stop trying so hard now, I had already said yes. He was forgetting that I knew him so well, I told him, and that I saw his pilled jerseys and threadbare underwear. Multi-millionaires don't buy toilet paper in bulk, I laughed. But it turned out that they do. I had always known that his company was successful, but had no idea as to the extent. The superfluous funds he kept offshore alone was a hundred times my entire investment portfolio.

The idea of the money came as a warm shock: not unpleasant, but not entirely pleasant either. The revelation, along with the proposal, made my head spin. I understood why he had kept it a secret, but I felt it was duplicitous nonetheless. At a time when you'd expect a couple to feel

most intimate, I found our connection vulnerable, stripped away. An exposed wire. Emotionally, I had taken a decisive step backwards, away from Byron. Unfortunately it turned out to be the first of many.

The rest of our time on the island was spent trying to forget about the awkward engagement. Before, we spent leisurely days on the beach, drank *le Dodo* beer in the sun, ate our body weight in ham and cheese galettes and Nutella crêpes, and had lazy afternoon sex. After, we took a helicopter ride over the volcano and the three cirques, went paragliding, and kept busy conscientiously ticking our way through the travel guide's list of must-dos. The diamond was relentless in its glinting.

When we arrived home and settled back into our regular routine, the money was a constant intruder on my thoughts. Not always unwelcome, but ever-present. I knew from reading articles on lottery winners that such a vast amount of un-earned money could be destructive. I refused to be married in community of property, and insisted that we keep our accounts separate. I was a feminist, after all. Byron wanted me to have it all and more — despite giving a significant amount away, he found he always had 'too much.' Like me, he wasn't a great spender. I didn't need it either, I told him, and he laughed. Asked me what the opposite of a gold-digger was, and when I said I didn't know, he said whatever it was, I was that.

Before we had left for Reunion he had his private banker add me as a beneficiary to his current account, and named me as the sole beneficiary in his will. I now had a credit card that I never had to pay off. It was at first disconcerting — I kept thinking that I would have to pay it

off *somehow* — then surprisingly liberating.

I no longer stood at a shop shelf and compared products versus prices. If I couldn't decide between the Barista Pinotage (R129) or the Chocolate Block (R168) I would just buy them both. I no longer questioned if we really *needed* a wedge of imported camembert: if I thought we would enjoy it, I bought it. When I saw someone in the queue that looked like they could do with a lucky break, I paid for their (usually) humble basket of groceries. There was a certain freedom in it, and I began to enjoy the small day-to-day luxuries that it afforded. I would also get a kick out of the restraint I showed. Looking down at my trolley and seeing the camembert wrapped in its soft foil, and thinking: I have over thirty million rand in the bank today, and I bought a bit of cheese.

The funny thing about the money in the beginning was that although it made no exceptional difference to my everyday life, it felt like it did. I was hardly spending more money than I used to, but I felt rich. I felt a freedom that I had never experienced before, and a security: like a weight I never knew I had was lifted off my shoulders. It was like walking around with a warm secret. Being wealthy, I thought, was more a state of mind than a fat wallet.

Gradually my reluctance waned. A few years on, I couldn't remember why I had resisted the fortune at all.

If anything, I thought I had grown to deserve it by putting up with Byron's moods. Our relationship, as I predicted, had deteriorated. We had a good few years after The Wedding I Never Wanted, but each year hence seemed less satisfying than the one before it. We tried to buoy it by

travelling together, and that worked for a while. It worked for a cycling trip through Brittany, a walk in Cambodia, and a swim in Chengdu. On the good days it felt like we had reconnected for good. It worked less well for Christmas in New York, a beach holiday in Thailand, and a cruise to Iceland, and our holiday in Venice was a disaster. One occasion sums the trip up: after getting lost over and over again, Byron submitted to his sore feet, and to his fury, and sat on a bench, not to speak or be spoken to for over an hour while I had no choice but to hover nearby until his darkness had passed.

I had to learn when I could talk to him and when I couldn't. When he was in a good mood he was his old funny, charming self. He would spoil me with flowers and chocolate and put on music and sling me around the kitchen in a happy dance. We would plan our next holiday, poring over our travel books and Google. We'd drink expensive merlot and he'd kiss me on the lips and surprise me in the shower. These are the times I could relax and be myself. I didn't have to consider every word before I said it out loud. But these moments became more infrequent the longer our relationship progressed. Towards the end, his moods dominated our every interaction. Our house seemed to be carpeted with egg shells. I had to tread accordingly or face his anger, or worse: his contempt.

Our relationship had become complicated. You'd be forgiven for thinking, as an outsider, that the problem was the power in the relationship had shifted to Byron. In fact, the opposite was true. Despite the marriage and the money, all the power was mine for a simple reason: Byron loved me more than I loved him. I realised this when he proposed,

and I didn't have the heart to break his. This started as a small struggle, a gentle push-and-pull, but over time it became a tug of war. I knew it, he felt it, and it was to be our sad and slow undoing.

What do you do with a man who loves you too much? I knew leaving would destroy him. If I even hinted at it he would become desperate. He would have anxiety attacks, skip work, drink too much, as if to show me that he couldn't live without me. One particularly dark night, convinced that I was ending the relationship, he threatened suicide. He had a gun, he said, and pills (he had neither). He couldn't live without me. Wouldn't.

I couldn't live this loitering life: my actions dependent on his state of mind. I refused to live in the ripples of his discontent.

I still loved him but the situation had become untenable. It was getting messy, and I don't like mess. I needed an exit plan. One that was as painless as possible for both of us. I loved him too much to leave him, to break his heart.

I knew that I now depended on his money. Before meeting him I was entirely self-sufficient, but since then I had let my career slide, no longer worrying about cash-flow and only taking the jobs that excited me. I couldn't leave the money behind. Gradually, and without me realising it, my perceived financial freedom had become a gilded cage.

It's not like I sat down one day with a notebook and thought of ways to get rid of him. Killing him didn't cross my mind ... until it did. Once it was in my head it seemed

like the only thing to do. The compassionate thing to do. I would put him out of his suffering; I would do it because I loved him. Even most beloved pets, I reasoned, were put down when the time came.

One morning he snapped at me for asking what we should have for dinner. He was getting ready for a meeting, removing lint from his jacket.

"I can't think about that now!" he barked.

It was clear, I thought, that his time had come.

Even after I had decided what to do, it took me a long time to action it. It was as if killing him was just a fantasy I would retreat to in times of strife. Something I would imagine at great length but never really do. I'd become one of those old ladies with purple-rinsed hair and rheumy eyes, forever fixated on the life they should have lived. Of course I wouldn't actually *kill him*, I told myself. But I knew, deep down, that it was a lie. Still, I did nothing, as if waiting for one day when I would conveniently find him on the edge of a cliff, where I could give him a quick shove while no one was watching.

I couldn't *plan* something, I thought. It would seem heartless, ruthless. An opportunity would have to present itself. This was perhaps a way of putting it off. Maybe, I thought, I didn't have the courage of my convictions.

I found the box of papers one day while spring-cleaning the house. You'd think, with all the money, that I'd pay someone to do the job, but I liked to do it myself. It gave me immense satisfaction to unpack an entire room, and to

clean and de-clutter it. Once a year, I would take a week off work and tick off a room a day. This time, I found the job slightly less satisfying as the rooms were neat and organised to begin with, and, with two days to spare, I decided to attack the space beneath the house.

It's an old house, built over 200 years ago, and while we have made superficial renovations, the core structure has remained the same. At the back of the house there is a small grey wooden door, weathered to the point of crumbling, which is the entry to the small storage space. How a child would love this hobbit-sized door, I thought, as I crept in and began clearing it out. There were to be no children in our future.

It was not all to be thrown away: the dry firewood, laced with spiderwebs, would make excellent fuel for our brazier. Some terracotta pots would do well in our herb garden. There were some lovely old mason jars that we could use in our country-style kitchen. I even kept a sheet of newspaper, finding it quaint, thinking I would have it framed. The most interesting thing I found, however, was a small, ancient-looking clamshell box, dusty black, around the same size as a pack of cigarettes. As I opened it I couldn't help remembering that day on the beach, and the diamond, which still flashed on my finger.

The box held a sheaf of thin off-white papers, that I first took to be cigarette-rolling papers. On closer inspection of the inside of the lid, however, I found a faint stamp: a company logo. A Victorian-era pharmacy. And I knew then how I would kill Byron.

The box seemed to me a gift from fate: the reversal of

the original awkward proposal. I enjoyed the aptness of the solution. Sometimes there is poetry in neatness.

I waited till I was alone in the house, then placed one of the delicate papers on a saucer and poured some water over it. After letting it soak for a few hours, I strained the water into an old perfume bottle of mine and discarded the paper. The box of flypapers found refuge in my underwear drawer.

Poisoning your husband is like falling asleep. It happens really slowly and then all at once. Byron never seemed to notice the drops I added to his tea. I came to understand why arsenic was regarded as a tonic in the old days. His eyes became brighter, his cheeks ruddy. Friends commented on his seemingly good health. He complained of some muscle pain, and his stomach gave him trouble.

I started it almost as an experiment, not sure if I would go through with the whole thing. I wasn't at all convinced that I would be able to do it. I gave him the minutest of doses and closely monitored his reaction.

Worried that someone would find the pharmacy box, I threw it away, out of the window on a highway. I kept the flypapers hidden between pages of my novels. A story within a story.

One night it was particularly bad, and I noted to dial it back a little. I couldn't stand to see him in pain. At my insistence he saw a doctor, was diagnosed with gastro-enteritis, and was told to take some time off work and drink plenty of fluids to stay hydrated. He assured the doctor that I made him endless cups of tea.

Over time, the body builds a resistance to arsenic. I had to stop being coy, stop teasing him with it, and get it over with. There was a delicate balance to be observed: I had to do it slowly enough for it to not look suspicious, but at the same time, there had to be, at a some point, a decisive dose. The whole point, after all, was to avoid suffering.

I procrastinated until the day he brought in The Rat. He had a headache, and seemed confused, so I sent him into the garden to read his newspaper while I was preparing a cold chicken salad for lunch. I looked up from carving the bird and screamed. Just outside the kitchen window Byron was standing, staring at me with his shining eyes, holding a dead rat up by its tail. I gripped the handle of the butcher knife, wondering if I would have to use it. He just wanted to show me, he said. Had I put any rodent poison down? It looks like his stomach exploded, he said. From then on I stopped disposing of the leached flypapers in the compost bin.

A day soon after that, Byron fell ill and had to stay in bed. He could afford the time off. Money kept pouring into our account. I was sitting at his bedside, reading a book.

"Unsuspecting," he said, his face flushed with fever. I asked him to repeat himself. "Unsuspecting," he said again, and my heart accelerated. Did he know?

"The Unsuspecting Gold-digger," he said. "You know, how we described you. As whatever the opposite of a gold-digger was."

"Or … 'unwitting'?" I tried. "Reluctant?"

"No," he shook his head. "Unsuspecting. It's gold, after all."

The next day, Byron was dead. One moment he had light in his eyes, the next, it was gone. He had a heart attack, brought on, guessed his doctor, by stress. The damage to the heart was clear: there was no need for an autopsy. At the funeral people tut-tutted that success does have its price, and when would we learn to not work so hard? At least there weren't any children, others whispered.

I got home that evening as the storm clouds were gathering. I was glad for the thunder: the house was too quiet without him. Unsettling. I emptied the arsenic water down the drain, double-bagged the perfume bottle and smashed the glass with a meat mallet before throwing it in the neighbour's bin.

I stripped off my plain black dress, heels, and stockings. I left my diamond ring on. I soaked in hot bath while the rain pummelled the roof. The lights flickered a few times, as they do in houses as old as ours. The water soothed my aching feet. I wasn't used to wearing heels. Like I said, I've always been a practical person.

I climbed into bed exhausted, as if I had been awake for years and it was finally time to allow my eyes to close. I swapped my pillow with one that was still scented by Byron, and the lights flickered some more. I checked my bank balance on my phone and then reached for my paperback. It was the same every night: bath, silk pyjamas, bed, bank balance, book. It was a ritual that almost always ensured sound sleep. I opened the novel and the delicate bookmark fluttered out: the last flypaper. I picked it up and

dropped it almost immediately, as if it had given me an electric shock. Inscribed on it, in blue ballpoint, was unmistakably Byron's handwriting.

It said "I forgive you."

4 / TRAVELLING SLACKS

Trip Advisor Review:

Coconut Bungalows. 4 out of 5 stars.

I had the great pleasure of staying at Coconut Bungalows at the South Coast, KZN, from the 9th to the 13th of October, 2015. It's a wonderful place. Casual, but still refined in the ways that count. One may walk around freely in short sleeves and short pants without fear of lowering the 'standard' of the place. At the same time, the butter for the scones is served at JUST below room temperature (NOT many places get this right) and the tea cups are delivered warm despite the tropical heat of the climate. It's nothing short of miraculous, really, to find these details attended to while it seems that the rest of the country's hospitality industry is slipping as surely as the polar icebergs are melting.

While I am on the topic of scones, I must note that the pastries were incredible. The cakes were tasty and moist; the croissants were a triumph! Lighter scones do not exist except in my memory of my late Aunt Daphne's homely kitchen, where, as a schoolboy, I would gobble them up by the half dozen, much to her delight. "Now hold on, Jeffrey," she would laugh, hugging me to her jiggling bosom, "Leave some for the rest of us, won't you?" I did love my Aunt Daphne.

I found my room unit small but cosy. I would have preferred accommodation that had a sea-view but I was happy enough with the aspect of the flower garden my room offered me. I especially liked the 'outside shower'. I would have preferred air conditioning to a ceiling fan. The king-sized bed was most comfortable. Slightly firmer than I am used to, but I think it was good for my back. My only criticism of the room was that, despite it being kept 'spick and span' by the cleaning staff, a colony of ants seem to have taken up residence in the cupboard. I brought it to the concierge's attention but the problem was not resolved.

The grounds were kept in immaculate condition, and this includes an emerald green lawn that I found myself being quite envious of. Also worth a mention are the just-refurbished tennis courts and the sparkling pool. What a pity the pool was always frothing over with screaming, horse-playing children! I would have quite enjoyed lounging there, taking in some sun, if it weren't for the gremlins continually wetting my newspaper. Luckily, the Coconut Bungalows caters for adults who prefer the company of other adults, and this is why I spent a great deal of my time in the 'Quiet Lounge', where the little

beasts couldn't wreak havoc. Of course every now and then a child WOULD enter, seeking a parent, and I would indulge them for a moment. But if it looked as if the child wanted to stay I would clear my throat in an authoritative way, and flick my gaze up to the sign that clearly said 'CHILDREN OUT OF BOUNDS'. If the culpable parent didn't get my subtle hinting, I would slam my book closed and glare at them until they all scampered off. A few guests took exception to my tactics, but the 'Quiet Lounge' is the 'Quiet Lounge', after all, a haven for someone like me, who finds children, even on their best behaviour, vaguely (and, let's be honest, sometimes supremely) irritating. In my opinion those guests should take a long, sober look at themselves and ask the question: why do they think the rules don't apply to them? What kind of children will they raise if they flout instructions like they do? Disrespectful offspring, I can tell you right now, and I observed enough proof of that this holiday.

Irresponsible parents aside, I met some wonderful people at Coconut Bungalows. My regular waiter, Bongani, was a lovely chap. A hundred years old in the shade, but he still managed to bring every single meal to the table piping hot. Slightly deaf, he was, but show me a hundred-year-old man that isn't! I was sure to tip him generously at the end of my stay.

The food was certainly above expectations and there wasn't a menu I wasn't happy with, apart from the Thursday lunch, which was a make-your-own-pasta dish. In all honesty I considered it quite cheeky, to expect the guests to cook their own food after paying full board. I have never been a fan of spaghetti.

The coffee was good, but not great. I will take my own blend next time. I did however appreciate the option of warm and cold milk at the beverage station.

The only other complaint I have regarding mealtimes is that there was one particular guest at the table adjacent to mine who INSISTED on (breast!)feeding her baby right at the table! As if common decency had never occurred to her. I found it downright rude and indecent and I told Bongani so, but I don't think he heard. It honestly makes me wonder, sometimes, about the future of the human race. Are we doomed to a vulgar existence where just about anything goes? It was quite upsetting to me, as you can probably tell.

On the subject of inconsiderate neighbours, the dark chap staying in the bungalow next to mine would perform a sort of dance every morning at sunrise, on a rolled out carpet. I wouldn't have minded except that this exercise of his seemed to chase away the birds I was trying to view with my new binoculars. When I asked him to stop he just mumbled something in some oriental language which I'm quite sure he knew I wouldn't understand. Oh, well, perhaps I am in an overly generous mood but I can't fault the owners of Coconut Bungalows for this particular source of vexation. It's not like they can keep 'those' kinds of people out.

The much vaunted 'nature walks' were a slight disappointment. Although the trails are indeed very scenic, the routes are not well signposted and a walk that should have taken 45 minutes took me 3 hours and I was most put out to be told that I had missed my afternoon tea. This, I found unacceptable, and it spoiled the rest of my day.

To end on a positive note, I would like to mention that the private beach attached to the bungalows was most beautiful and pristine. I enjoyed my daily walks along the shore.

What is left to say except that despite some hiccups and minor setbacks, I had a most marvellous stay at Coconut Bungalows, and I give them a well-deserved rating of 4 stars out of 5. I will certainly be returning in the future.

Jeffrey Sacks, AKA @travellingslacks

Dear Travelling Slacks

Thank you for taking the time to write such a long and incredibly detailed review. We are glad that you had a (mostly) wonderful stay and look forward to welcoming you back. I would, however, like to address your various points of discontent.

With regards to your bungalow: On booking your room for your stay you were offered an upgrade to a larger unit with air conditioning and a sea view for a marginal fee, which you declined. Thus, I don't understand why, in your review, you say you would have preferred a larger room. Perhaps next time you will accept the offer of an upgrade.

I have passed on your compliments to our pastry chef. She will be delighted that her scones reminded you of a warm childhood memory. I dare say it won't come as a surprise, however, as she did mention that her baked goods disappeared at quite a rate in the week that you stayed with us.

I apologise again for the ant problem, however, the cleaning staff did report to me that the stash of scones and biscuits you kept in your cupboard was the reason the colony kept returning, despite our house rule that there is no food to be kept in the rooms (for this very reason). The leaking bottle of Baileys that you brought from home exacerbated the problem. Coconut Bungalows offers full board, 3 meals a day, plus morning and afternoon tea, and a full bar. There is also a room service, so you should never have worried about going hungry or thirsty. In fact, most of our guests complain that we feed them too much! Perhaps if you obey our rule, we will be able to avoid the insect problem on your next stay with us.

I'm sorry that you felt the boisterous children spoilt the pool for you. Coconut Bungalows is marketed as a fun, energetic, whole-family resort. I assume you would have gathered that from our website when you made your reservation, as it is full of pictures of 'screaming, horse-playing' children. I am glad that you found relative peace in our Quiet Lounge.

I have passed on your glowing praise of your waiter to him. Bongani thanks you for the R10 tip you left him for the 5 days of 3-meals-a-day service. He tells me that he did offer to make the pasta sauce for you on Thursday's make-your-own-pasta meal, but that you refused. We find that one interactive meal a week is a fun thing to do, and gets our guests chatting amongst themselves and making friends. I'm sorry it did not hold much appeal for you. In future we will warn you of the occasion and you won't have to participate; our chefs will make something special for you in advance.

Bongani also related the story of your disapproval of your fellow guest breastfeeding her baby at the table behind yours. At first I didn't understand the problem. If the woman was behind you, why was she in your line of sight? Even if you did manage to glimpse her, Bongani assured me — despite it being necessary, in my opinion — that the lady covered up and fed her baby most discreetly. He also told me that he offered you another table on the other side of the restaurant, but that you did not want to move. I'm not certain, then, what the actual problem was, but I trust Bongani made certain that you were comfortable. He did tell me that he stopped 'hearing' this particular complaint on the 3rd or 4th occasion. On a side note I must tell you that Bongani is famous for his selective hearing.

I'm sorry you weren't a fan of our coffee. I will let The Roast Beanery — the most highly regarded coffee supplier in the country — know that their particular brand is not your favourite.

Our nature walks are clearly signposted, there are maps at reception, and a hiking guide is always available at a small fee. Perhaps next time you can take advantage of a guide's assistance and make your way back in time for afternoon tea.

Lastly, regarding your neighbour: Professor Abdullah is a loyal and much-respected guest at Coconut Bungalows. He doesn't speak any 'oriental' languages, so I assume what you heard was English. His sunrise 'dance' was, in fact, his morning prayers. The Prof was extremely gracious in that he never once complained about your eccentric habits, such as playing your violin whenever the fancy took you, your loud, drunken conversations with yourself in the middle of

the night, the ants you brought into the area, the immodest Speedo you wore for your daily beach walks, and/or the way you showered in the front of the unit, naked, in full view of the rest of the bungalows. For future reference, the spout you used as an 'outside shower' is really just a tap to assist you in rinsing off beach sand before entering your unit.

Thanking you again for your detailed and exhaustive review.

Kind Regards, Suzy Dos Santos, Owner, Coconut Bungalows

Trip Advisor Review:

REVISED: Coconut Bungalows. 3 out of 5 stars.

Dear 'Suzy'

Thank you for your reply to my honest review of your establishment. I suppose not every owner enjoys it when their guests engage in 'straight talking'! As you can see I have downgraded my rating of Coconut Bungalows from 4 to 3 stars (out of 5), as your response reminded me of other niggles that I thought best forgotten in the original generosity I was feeling when first writing the review. I also feel that the passive aggression in your reply warranted a drop in ratings, as you clearly do not understand nor follow the very important maxim that 'the customer is always right'!

I won't stoop to your level by addressing every separate

point of contention, however I must address one or two issues that I take exception to.

The first is the issue of that rude woman who insisted on breastfeeding her baby right under my nose. Yes, her table was behind mine, but just because I couldn't SEE her actually feeding the child doesn't mean I wasn't aware of it happening behind my back. Yes, she may have covered up her actual breasts while feeding the child, but what use is that, when everyone around her can imagine what is happening under the cover! There are many places that are suitable for a mother to feed an infant: her bungalow, being one! And let me tell you, her feeding was not confined to the dining area either. I saw her doing it on the outside terrace during sundowners and at the pool, too! Bongani was not the only staff member with selective hearing: everyone I complained to just shrugged it off, which I found disrespectful and patronising.

And, yes, I did see the pictures of the raucous children on the website when I booked my accommodation, but I assumed, albeit mistakenly so, that the Coconut Bungalows would strive to accommodate ME and MY particular needs, too.

On another note. Your sarcasm with regards to my taste in coffee did not go unnoticed. The Roast Beanery's coffee is indeed the best in the country. Perhaps you are just not preparing it correctly?

With regards, Jeffrey Sacks, AKA @travellingslacks

Dear Mr Sacks

Perhaps you can send us your notes on how to prepare coffee? We've always been under the impression that you add hot water, brew, and strain, or use the espresso machine. Are we missing something? Is there, in fact, a superior way to make coffee? Please let us know.

It has come to my attention via my cleaning staff that various items from your room are missing. I wonder, did you accidentally pack some of our Coconut Bungalow towels into your luggage? We are also short one cotton bathrobe, a small pillow, a bottle opener, and the large pump-action bottles of shampoo and body wash that we provide for guests to make use of, but not to take home. If you do have these items, please let me know and I will arrange a courier to collect them from you. Alternatively, I can send you the bill to replace the missing things.

Regarding the issue of the guest who was breastfeeding in public: We were so pleased to see that she felt comfortable enough at the Coconut Bungalows to feed her baby wherever and whenever the baby was hungry. Being a new mother is an exhausting job, and we were glad to see her and her little one happy and relaxed. This was more of a compliment to us than any online review.

On the subject, I have taken the liberty of looking up your reviews on various other establishments and am happy I did so. I see your other complaints are in a similar vein. If my memory serves me correctly, one guest relations officer, in particular, offered to gag you and smash your violin over your head to curtail further complaints from his other guests. I thought it was a rather violent thing to say, but I

am beginning to come around to his way of thinking.

I wonder, Mr Sacks, what the real problem is. Are you lonely? Do writing these reviews make you feel more important? At first I thought you were a man of fine taste, noticing the softness of the butter, the lightness of the scones. But now I see that you're just ... well, it appears that you have nothing better to do than to bully the mostly lovely owners of South African travel destinations.

I take back what I said about being happy to welcome you back to Coconut Bungalows. You can keep your R10 tips and your violin and your indecent exposure and your pilfered ant-trailing cookies. You were a disaster of a guest and the truth is that we really don't want you to come back. Ever.

PS. Here's a tip for you: The next time you see a woman breastfeeding a baby and it offends you, STOP LOOKING. Also: STOP WEARING A SPEEDO.

Suzy Dos Santos, Owner, Coconut Bungalows

Trip Advisor Review:

REVISED: Coconut Bungalows. 2 out of 5 stars.

Dear 'Suzy'

I suppose I should have expected this childish response. Not everyone can take constructive criticism. I find that women, in particular, battle with this. I wonder if I should be having this conversation with your husband, instead. I

have told everyone I know about your ghastly communication, and I won't be surprised if, going forward, you see a steep decline in your reservations.

With regards, Jeffrey Sacks, AKA @travellingslacks

Dear Mr Sacks

What my husband knows about the hospitality industry is scary, seeing as he is an investment banker, so I doubt you'd have much luck there. I wonder if I should be having a word with your wife? Perhaps offering my commiseration, at being married to you? I saw a picture of her and thought she looked vaguely Russian. I wondered if you really have a wife — why was she not travelling with you? — or if it was just a photo that you found somewhere on Google images. I looked at your Facebook page and you are welcome to let your small group of friends know not to visit us.

In addition, I have sent your guest profile to all the establishments I know, warning them to not accept a reservation from you. I forwarded the same message to the South African Board of Tourism. If, in future, you can't get a reservation ANYWHERE, you will know why.

I have attached the bill for the items you stole from the room. Please send me the proof of payment at your earliest convenience.

Suzy Dos Santos, Owner, Coconut Bungalows

Trip Advisor Review:

REVISED: Coconut Bungalows. 1 out of 5 stars.

Dear 'Suzy'

As you can see I have downgraded your rating to 1 out of 5 stars. I find your attitude entirely unsatisfactory.

Jeffrey Sacks, AKA @travellingslacks

Dear Jeffrey

You can take your one star and shove it.

Suzy

Trip Advisor Review:

REVISED: Coconut Bungalows. 0 out of 5 stars.

Dear 'Suzy'

The star has been 'shoved'!

Jeff

Dear Jeff

Please stop emailing me. I think this has gone far enough.

Suzy

Dear Suzy

You have no idea how far I can take this.

Jeff

Jeff

Seriously. Step away from your computer. I will no longer be answering your emails.

Suzy

Suzy

I will not be ignored!

Jeff

Suzy? Suzy? I demand an answer!

Dear Suzy

I am going to email you every single day of your life unless you answer me.

Jeff

Jeff

I have called the police and laid an harassment charge against you, as well as one for theft and indecent exposure. They said they will pay you a visit. We have your address on file. It would be in your best interest to stop contacting me.

PS. We have photos of you streaking in your 'outside shower' and we will use them against you if we have to. I hope it doesn't come to that.

Suzy

Dear Suzy

You're right. It's because I'm lonely. Please drop the charges.

Jeff

Jeff

Loneliness is no excuse for being an utter asshole. Didn't your Aunt teach you that?

Suzy

Suzy

You're right, she did. She was a wonderful woman. I used to gobble up all her scones and she'd say: "Hold on, now, Jeffrey, leave some for the rest of us!" How I loved my Aunt Doris.

Jeff

Jeff

Wasn't your aunt's name 'Daphne'?

Suzy

Suzy

You're right. It's Daphne.

Jeff

Jeff, you don't have an aunt Daphne, do you? You made her up.

Jeff? You there?

The host server @travellingslacks is not recognised. This

email address has been deleted. This message will not be re-sent. This is a permanent error message.

5 / SOMETHING BORROWED

I cover my nose and mouth with the ivory silk of the gown and inhale deeply. I want to remember every detail of this day. I run my hand over the beaded bodice: a love letter in Braille. I sit down at the dressing room table and start pinning up my hair. I had it set in generous curls yesterday. The diamanté clips sparkle as I move my head. My make-up is laid out in front of me.

I begin with foundation. Painting my face, I feel like I am performing a rite of passage. This careful, slow transformation, from wide-eyed child-girl to woman. The butterflies start beating their wings: they are in my stomach and in my head. Thoughts alight and flutter away again before I, breathless, can catch them.

It will soon be time to leave for the church. Pop will be coming in the family Bentley to pick us up. He took it out earlier to have it washed and polished. He wanted it to shine like me, he said. He's done so much for Ruth and I; it will be nearly impossible to say goodbye.

At least Pop likes Raymond. That will make leaving home easier. Raymond is like the son Pop never had. They watch cricket and drink beer together. After lunch on Sunday afternoons they sit in the golden light on the verandah, hands behind their heads, in a haze of comfortable silence.

Raymond asked Pop's permission for my hand a week before he proposed to me. How he kept that secret for a whole week I'll never know. Seven breakfasts, seven lunches, seven dinners and Pop didn't do so much as wink at me.

It was a Summer night when Raymond took me to the beach. The sand was still warm. I wore a new skirt. It trembled in the evening breeze. Raymond spoke about the day we met and how much he had grown to love me, and my family. We started to kiss and the world turned on its side. I wondered, then, if that would be the moment I'd give myself to him: that perfect night under the stars. But Raymond had other plans. His hand unfurled like a flower to reveal the diamond he had brought: it had been his grandmother's. It sparkles on my finger now. I was mute but Raymond knew the answer was yes. He is my first and only love. I could marry no one but him.

When I told Ruth she said she was happy for me but I saw the hurt in her eyes. Being older, she imagined she would be the first one to get married. She chafed under Pop's strict house rules. She was always the independent one. On sticky nights she used to tell me her dreams of moving out of the family house, out of the town where everyone's nose was in everyone else's business. Moving to a completely new place, perhaps in Europe somewhere:

Italy, Spain, France. Some place she could be herself. She's my maid of honour today. She has the prettiest green dress.

Ruth introduced me to Raymond. Not in that way: not on purpose. She had taken me along to a picnic with some college friends of hers and there he was, fawning all over her. He watched Ruth with such a determined look in his eyes. I asked her, afterwards, if they were together. She had just laughed and shook her head, her bob swaying.

I bumped into Raymond a few weeks later, at the MonteVista cinema. He remembered me – bought me popcorn and a bag of winegums – as if I was his kid sister. He introduced me to his tall friends and said something to make everyone laugh. My cheeks burned with the memory of how often I had thought of him since the picnic. He pretended not to notice.

I can't remember which film was on that night – my own had been playing in my head. Nothing original: Handsome boy meets plain girl at picnic to the soundtrack of the Beatle's 'Day Tripper'. The universe conspires to bring them together once again at a local haunt. Handsome boy burrows his way into girl's uncompromising father's heart, drops on knee, and story ends in confetti and general wedded bliss.

In the end, our story wasn't quite as twee as that, but it wasn't far off. Raymond was always the perfect gentleman and Pop couldn't help but love him. He was part of the family before he ever asked for my hand.

I was so besotted with Raymond that I offered myself to him. It was the only way I could reconcile the

overwhelming feelings I had. When Pop stopped insisting on a chaperone we would have moments alone: in the corner of a garden at a party; against the rough black bark of a tree during an evening walk. Once in the bedroom of a relative, breathless. I was ready each time but Raymond used to stop himself before my cardigan was unbuttoned.

I want him so much sometimes I want to crawl under his skin. I wish I could get inside his body the way he is inside my mind.

Tonight will be the night. The butterflies have strayed south.

I miss my mom. Of course, this is the time a girl misses her mom. Would she have told me what to expect on my wedding night? Or would she just primly pat me on the shoulder? Either would be fine with me. All I crave is her presence. Pop has tried his best but there are only so many ribbons a father can tie in his daughter's hair. The funeral was the last family function. The wedding planning has brought some sunshine into the house.

I begin curling my eyelashes. Ruth taught me how to do it. Ruth taught me how to do most things. How to blot my lipstick so that it doesn't come off on everything, how to ice my eyebrows before I pluck, how to stop a run in my stockings with a dab of nail polish. And then other things; things that will come in handy tonight. She has always been so generous with her femininity. I apply mascara and separate my lashes. I wonder what's taking Pop so long? I push my face right up to the mirror to examine it. My reflection mists over as I breathe.

With a nervous inhalation I decide it's time to put on my dress. Before I take it down from the hanger I admire it one last time. I stand there in my corset and stockings thinking that it's the most exquisite dress I've ever seen. I step into it carefully and pull it up. I have to wriggle a little to get it over my hips. It's a little tighter than the last time I tried it on. No matter. The zip slides up without hesitation.

I put my shoes on. I battle with the tiny buckle, it's too delicate for my fingers. By the time I look into the mirror the vision is complete. It's everything I've dreamed about.

There's a gentle knock on the door. Only Ruth knocks like that.

"Come in!" I sing, my heart near bursting.

The door opens. It is Ruth, but she's not wearing her pretty green dress. She looks old and tired.

"Is everything okay?" I ask. "You're not dressed for the wedding."

Her face is a mask of despair.

"I'm not kidding, Ruthie," I say playfully. "Pop will be here any minute."

She cannot talk.

"Ruth? What's wrong?"

Her shoulders stoop. She walks to the bed and sits down. Her head disappears in her hands.

"What is it?" I say, starting to worry, wondering what could make her act this way. She looks up at me with so much pain in her eyes that I have to look away. I go to the window and watch the sky. I need some air. I try to open the window but there is a padlock on it.

"Where did you find it?" asks Ruth.

"Find what?"

"That wedding dress. That. Damn. Wedding dress."

Her voice is gruff and I don't know what she means.

"I don't understand," I say.

"Not again, Emily, please, not again."

She's driving me mad! "What on earth are you talking about?"

"What am I talking about?" she says, "What have we been talking about for the past fifty years?"

I'm frustrated now. I feel the beginning of tears but I blink them back. I don't want to ruin my make-up.

"I hid that dress away!" she fumes. "I don't know how you found it. Take it off!"

She claws at me, at the beaded bodice. I push her away.

"I'll get rid of it properly, this time. I will shred it, and burn it, and bury it, and make sure it will never haunt us again!"

"No!" I shriek. "Why would you do that? Why would you say such an awful thing?"

"Because I love you. Because I can't take these episodes of yours any longer."

My mind is racing. Ruth's eyes arrest mine.

"Try to remember, Em."

I start to feel the sharp metal edges of hysteria.

"Remember what?"

"Remember what happened, fifty years ago."

"How can I? I wasn't born yet!"

Ruth shakes her head.

"You were twenty-two years old! It was your wedding day."

"But today is my wedding day."

I look out of the window again. My eyes fall to the locked pane. Ruth's cold fingers turn my head.

"Look at me, Emily! Look at my face. I'm an old lady!"

She does look old. Her hair is grey! I recoil in shock. "What happened to your hair?"

She is gentle now. "Come, look in the mirror."

"No!" I shout. I don't want that white hair, those pale wrinkles.

Ruth grabs a hand mirror off the dressing room table. She forces the image on me. "Look!"

The face I see is ravaged. A cracked doll's face. A cruel caricature.

My heart is beating fast, too fast.

"Where is Raymond?" I ask.

Ruth's anger drains out of her. "He died, Em."

I don't believe her. How can I?

"He was killed in a car accident, on the way to the wedding."

I am sick with shock. I run into to bathroom and heave into the toilet.

Mental images, blurry at first, assault me: Raymond's mother's anguished face at his funeral; the sickly sweet smell of the lily wreath; being assailed by condolence cards, some arriving months after his death. Nightmares of his crushed body. Broken, bloody.

I heave again. Then more harrowing pictures: Another funeral, this time we're the ones throwing soil on the coffin.

"Pop?" I ask.

Ruth is crying now.

"He was in the other car."

Yes. I remember now.

Everyone had said how awful the coincidence had been. What bad luck. Unbelievable, they said. Impossible. But not.

The dress is heavy on me now. My skin itches. I feel like I can't breathe. I struggle with it. Ruth comes over to help. I see the strain on her face. Once I am free of it she holds me and soothes me.

"It's over now," she coos, stroking my hair. "Everything will be okay."

It's an old, battered promise.

With a rush of heat I remember something else. The reason Pop was speeding away in his car. The reason he lost control and drove into the bridge, followed in desperate pursuit by Raymond. Passion allows no time for safety belts or following distance.

Pop had gone over to Raymond's house with a gift. A fatherly premarital gesture, but the intimate words caught in his throat when he saw Raymond's tousled hair, and Ruth's green dress slung carelessly over the settee. Ten minutes later they exploded in a mess of tar and broken glass.

I look up at Ruth. The lines of regret etched into her skin. She looks at me expectantly, waiting, dreading the

next, inevitable, part of the story. But I see she has suffered enough, and she is my sister.

I won't remember that part today.

6 / SHE DID IT

The suspect.

The suspect has one eye swollen shut and blood highlights in her yellow hair. A split lip that sticks so far out that I want to tuck it back into her face for her. What makes dried blood black? What makes eye-skin swell so hard that it buries its own eyeball? Cannibalistic gesture or measure of protection? Too late, eye socket, too late. The suspect stares into space. Saliva shines her chin. She isn't aware of the drool. She's numb. If she's lucky, she's numb. She stares and stares and doesn't see anything.

There is nothing to see here.

She has seen enough.

The suspect was admitted last night. It wasn't the first time.

The suspect? you are thinking. Surely you mean *the victim?*

No, I mean The Suspect. She was found in a puddle of blood. It was mostly her husband's.

What kind of love is this? When the couple's red stuff runs together in tributaries and streams, mixing and morphing into a dark lake of glue. What kind of love is this? Or, more correctly, what kind of love *was* this? For it is no more.

When did it end? When did the crimson petal turn to brown? When did the suspect's skull go from whole to cracked? Now there is a spiderweb, a snowflake etched into the bone. You know the story. But maybe not the whole story. Maybe not the exact story. Every snowflake is unique.

His skull was cracked, too. The husband's. More smashed than 'cracked'. A whole piece of head bone was missing, like a seashell eroded by the sand and tide. I expected to find a sea-brined brain, but it was messier than that. No cool rinsing saline, but instead: hot air and insects. Not too many: there wasn't enough time between the deed and the damning. Just a couple of fat black flies. Their wings vibrating right into our itchy ears.

Blunt force trauma. That old chestnut. We looked around for the instrument (and the puzzle-piece of skull) but it didn't reveal itself. It did not jump up and dance. Isn't it funny that we call it an 'instrument'? As if we could pick it up on a whim and play a tune. A death ditty. A melody of murder. I wonder which song was on when this gory thing was playing out. This blunt game. Every crime has a soundtrack.

She had looked dead, too, until all of a sudden she wasn't. Mottled. Smashed up, but alive. She gasped and chucked up blood, like a possessed puppet in a horror show. Like a victim of an exorcism. But not a victim. Not only a victim, anyway. A suspect, too.

Yes, you can be both. Her husband was both, too. Who else would engrave the snowflake on his wife's skull? Who else would swell her lip? A third party! I hear you shout. An intruder! An evil bastard intent on grievous bodily harm.

It's possible. I have learnt that anything is possible. But evil almost always pitches up at the door with a housecoat on. A comfy old housecoat that smells of home and is invariably scabbed by custard and a snailtrail of last week's roast chicken gravy.

Child molested? You want to blame the ice-cream truck man. (It wasn't him.)

Girl raped? You point a finger at the faceless trenchcoat. (It wasn't him.)

Woman battered to within an inch of her life (and sometimes outside of it) — you see the perpetrator as one of The Others. It wasn't them. Mostly, it wasn't them. Mostly, it was the father, the uncle, the husband. Mostly the evil is deeply seeded inside our circles of love. That's what makes it truly evil.

The suspect lifts a broken finger to the shorn part of her scalp. Runs a dirty fingernail above her ear. What is she thinking about? Is she replaying last night's events? Is the glimmer of light on her stitched-up face the reflection of the

story? How much does she know, and of that, how much will she tell us?

'Mrs Long?' I say, for the third time. Triad, trilogy, troika. Third time lucky, although not for her. She hears me — I can see the faint flicker — but still she keeps staring at the wafer coloured walls. Hospital equipment rattles down the corridor. Metal trollies, and needles scratching paper. Someone's blood pressure cuff exhales.

'Janine?' I say. It tastes wrong, but it does the trick. She cranes her stiff neck in my direction. One eyeball swivels. It's a pretty eyeball. The other is still a prisoner. She opens her lip-balloons to speak but nothing comes out.

DOESN'T ANSWER TO MARRIED NAME, I write in my notebook. It's not the standard police-issue notebook. Those are useless. I like my books tightly bound. When it comes to notebooks, I appreciate strict bondage. When it comes to sex: not so much. I have tied up enough criminals to put me off handcuffs in the bedroom for good.

A ghost of a word escapes her mouth. Then another, then another. Three spook words. A phantom triangle. A triple spectre switchback. Things happen in threes. This is true. I strain my ears. I prime my hammer, anvil and stirrup. I am ready to listen. Not just to hear, but to listen. There is a distinct difference.

I see her teeth are broken, too. That wasn't in the report. Perhaps they were not able to open her mouth when she first came in. Perhaps it had been clamped. Perhaps the horror had wired it shut.

TEETH, I write down.

BROKEN.

I clear my throat.

'Could you ... would you repeat that?' I say in the most gentle voice I possess. It does not come easy. It sounds like a grizzly bear trying to sing a lullaby. It does not come naturally to me. Look at me. Look at me! I am not a tender man.

Of course, it *could* have been an intruder. This is Johannesburg, after all. Sunny South Africa. We are nothing if not a long-festering abscess boiling over with the hot pink pus and frantic squirming oily maggots of crime and violence. And don't you dare act disgusted. It is your doing as much as it is mine. If you take exception to anything it should be your own indifference. At least I am here, in this hospital room. At least I am getting my rough hands dirty.

It could have been a faceless stranger who burst into this couple's bedroom and gave them matching head traumas. He could've handed them identical blows, one for him, one for her. Two for the price of one. Like monogrammed velour bathrobes made in China, His and Hers. Or those old married people who have been together too long and wear matching twinsets with pictures of snowy mountains embroidered on the fronts, replete with a smelly nanny goat, a copper bell at her throat. It could have been *Die Swart Gevaar*, but my gut tells me otherwise. I'd stake my balls on it. And I don't do that lightly. I'd very much like to keep my balls just where they are.

I hand the suspect a plastic beaker with a bendy straw. She won't be eating for a while. She is getting all the hydration and nutrients she needs from her IV but that won't stop her mouth from being as a dry as these wafer walls. She blinks her solitary eye at me in thanks, and slurps. Her injuries do not make for delicate drinking. There is more chin-dribble. In another lifetime, in another story, in a parallel universe I would take a soft cotton cloth and wipe her face for her. I would hold her. Tell her that the worst is over. That she's going to be okay.

But we're not on that particular planet. We're here in this beige private ward and she is the suspect and I am the cop and I need to find out what the hell happened to the purple corpse in the refrigerator drawer that is wearing a wedding ring with her name on it.

I take the beaker back. It's time to talk. I need to hear those three words again to make sure that I didn't imagine them. I angle my body towards her. I steeple my fingers. I wait. I don't tap my feet.

She takes a breath, and then winces at the ribs that curl around her chest like an ivory cage for her heart. Those bones are engraved, too. When I read the medical report I pictured her as a scribbled-on skeleton. Old and new fracture scars running all over her bone and crunchy cartilage like a roadmap to oblivion. How many ribs has she broken? How many arms, legs, cheekbones? How many times can you break a limb before it just won't heal anymore? How many times can you shatter a pelvis before it just gives in and gives up? I pictured her as a tattooed skeleton; so when I came in here I was surprised by her skin and hair. Her modest padding. Her beautiful eyeball.

'I did it,' she says again.

I go back to the top of the page where, hours before I had met her, I had written SHE DID IT.

It wasn't rocket science. I didn't even think it through. Sometimes the deep gut / balls combination just does the work for you. If you can't trust the deep gut / balls combination then you can't trust anything. The penis, on the other hand, the shaft, is another story altogether.

SHE DID IT, I had scrawled in shouty uppercase, sure and arrogant, as if it were a title for a new screenplay, or a song. I tick the words. The ink mark is an inverted shark fin.

Her breathing is shallow from the nerves or the hesitation to re-rupture the ribs. She shouldn't be in this much pain. They should give her some more painkillers. I wanted her *compos mentis* for the questioning, but I'm not a sadist. Besides, I have what I need. I only needed those three words. The rest is backstory. The rest doesn't matter. I ring the bell for the nurse.

The suspect turns towards me, with some effort, and I am confronted by her whole face at once. Or, at least, a face that used to be whole. A face that will never be whole again. It's quite a picture. I will myself to not blink, to not turn away from the mess. To not squirm before the crazy quilt that is her new skin. I need to take responsibility for her condition. It was one of us, after all, that did this to her. A fellow human. A fellow man. Kin, but not kindred.

'I killed him,' she says. 'I killed him.'

She turns her attention back to the beige. I wait for the tears. I wait for her to start rocking and heaving. I wait for her to paint herself with tar. She just stares at the wall. Just when I think that he has finally knocked her into catatonia, she wipes perspiration from her hands and lows in discomfort.

A decade rolls by like ancient grey tumbleweed and a nurse finally arrives.

'Took long enough,' I mumble. He ignores me. What is it about medical people being indifferent to pain? Is it because they see too much of it? Do they become numb by choice or necessity? Can't they see that this woman has been through enough? Look at her! Her skeleton is a scribble! I want to yell at him. Where is the fucking morphine?

His nurse's uniform remains stubbornly starched in slow motion.

You think she's making it up? I want to yell. *You think she's faking it?*

Why am I not indifferent to the pain? I must see more suffering than these people. That is why I smell of the streets and not the dry mist of alcoholic hand sanitiser. I am agitated by their too-clean tunics and their flat empathy. As if they remove their understanding along with the bacteria on their hands. As if they set themselves apart from us, the sad, sorry, roiling society. Quickly! Sanitise! Before you catch it. Before you catch a germ of empathy.

'She's had as much as she's allowed,' he says, looking at the chart at the foot of her bed. 'The next dose will be in two hours.'

The suspect's fists drip with sweat.

Fuck that. Fuck what's *allowed*.

I take a step towards the nurse. I am not a small man.

'Give her more,' I say. 'Now.'

I will be damned if I will allow another man to cause this woman any more unnecessary pain.

I think he's going to stand up to me. I am ready for it, but then he collects a small bag of clear liquid and hooks it up to her IV line. He leaves. I sit and watch it trickle. I urge the plastic bladder to empty faster. It is too slow. Too slow.

But then the groaning stops. Gradually the fists unfurl; blossoming finger flowers. Colour leaks back into her cheeks. We both breathe again.

I offer her more water; she refuses.

'Is there anything else you'd like to say?' I ask.

I need to get away. I didn't mean to spend so long here in this antiseptic purgatory. I have a job to do. I have other blood to sniff.

She swallows. She says, again: 'I killed him.'

'I know,' I say. 'I know.'

I don't want her to feel guilty. What I really want to say is: *I'm glad you killed the sonofabitch.*

I want to say: *I wish you'd done it sooner. Before he broke you in half.*

There is something pulling at her face, at her balloons. I don't want her to cry. I don't want to watch her stretch her stitched-up face. But there is no water in her eyes. The twitching of the lips is not weeping. It is relief. It is triumph. Her eye has stars in it. She has survived.

I start my banged-up Hilux with a twist of key, as if I am turning a dagger in someone's stomach. I can't help the violence of my thoughts. Occupational hazard. My soul has seen too much to be pure. I drive out of the hospital after paying R8 for parking. Bastards, I think, for making the worried and the grieving pay to visit their loved ones. Does no-one in this money-grubbing city have a fucking conscience?

The chevron boom shudders skyward. I accelerate, leaving the beautiful eyeball behind. The sensation of the tyres' traction on the road is good. I feel like I could drive forever on an open road. Instead I'm hemmed in by traffic-tense zippers and clouds of carbon dioxide, and I almost get T-boned by a taxi with gravel for brakes. Red lights are regarded as a suggestion rather than a rule. No point telling Metro. I wave the taxi off with my middle finger. If he takes exception he can take it up with the Glock I have resting in sweat-softened leather against my ankle. I have enough warm bullets for everyone.

'She did it,' says Domino. I can't remember why I call him that. It's not like he is freckled, or especially entertaining. He's not even Italian. He nudges the file into my hand. He wants me to look at it again.

'Of course she did it,' I say. 'I thought you had something new to tell me.'

'Oh, I do,' he says. He is grandstanding, smug, but I don't know why. Had I missed an important detail at the crime scene?

'Did you know that he broke her teeth, too?' I say.

'Did he?' says Domino. It's not a question.

I can feel the minutes ticking by. I have wasted enough time today. I need to get some action. I need to slam a body against my car's bonnet. I wouldn't mind firing my gun, either.

'It's not what it seems,' Dom says. 'You need to look closer.'

'Look closer? She killed her husband in self defence. The details don't matter.'

'The details always matter,' says Dom, as if he is a wise master edifying a recalcitrant student. As if he is goddamned Mr Miyagi. 'You just don't want to see it.'

'Spit it out,' I say, looking at my watch. 'I'm getting old.'

'Maybe if you stopped falling in love with your suspects you'd have a clearer head.'

I take the folder to the restaurant down the road. Their coffee is good but their food is terrible. They know to not bother me with a menu. I start from page one of the file contents and make sure I take in every word. Halfway through my second cup I see the note about broken teeth. So it was in there. I did miss it. What else did I miss? I keep going. My stomach buzzes. I ignore it. I have another cup and I start to get the caffeine-sweats. I hate the caffeine-sweats. My mind begins to wander and then I see it. A psychiatrist's name. A telephone number.

'You saw Janine Long?' I say into the handset. 'She was a patient of yours?'

The doctor won't discuss her on the phone. I grab my keys and leave a pink note on the table.

'A troubled young woman,' he says to me. I am still sweating.

'A walking cliché,' I say. Not that she's walking anywhere at the moment.

We're in his consulting room that smells of vanilla beans and dollar signs.

'You think all young women are troubled?' he asks.

'I think everyone is troubled,' I say. 'It's the human condition.'

The psychiatrist doesn't disagree. I guess we've both witnessed the ugly.

'Let me guess,' I say. 'I'm going to need a court order

before you discuss her particular troubles with me?'

'Not necessarily,' he says, uncrossing his legs. 'What do you need to know?'

'I need to know why she came to in a pool of blood this morning.'

'Her own blood?' asks the doc.

'Some of it was.'

'The rest was ... the husband's?'

'Yes.'

'Ah,' the doctor says. 'She killed him? Let me guess: self defence?'

'Yes,' I say. 'Self defence.'

'Ah.'

'You're not surprised?'

'I'm afraid not.'

'You knew it would happen,' I say, 'and you didn't think to notify the authorities?'

'Of course I notified the authorities,' he says. 'How do you think you got my number?'

'How long did the abuse go on for?' I ask.

'I believe it started when she was 14.'

'14? She knew the victim — her husband-to-be — when she was 14?'

The shrink shakes his head. Begins to say something, then stops.

'Then,' I say, 'there were others?'

It wouldn't be the first time a woman chose one abuser after another. Like being slung out of one revolving door to be sucked straight into the next. The doctor looks confused. He leans forward, resting his elbows on his thighs.

'Who exactly,' he says carefully, 'do you think the abuser is?'

'Was,' I say. 'It *was* her husband.'

His face pops with surprise.

'No,' he says. 'No, not at all!'

It's my turn to look confused. I don't like it.

'Mrs Long suffered from Munchausen Syndrome. That's when — '

'I know what Munchausen is,' I say. 'But it doesn't add up.'

'You're thinking of Munchausen in its narrowest form. It comes in many strains.'

'I don't understand.'

'Mrs Long wouldn't be happy until she was

hospitalised. She learnt to do significant damage so that she wouldn't be turned away from the emergency room. She would tell me how she did it. You wouldn't believe the stories.'

'She would physically abuse herself? Like, cutting?'

'Cutting is different. Don't conflate the two.'

I tap my feet.

'With cutting, pain is the required effect. It's an emotional release. It's secretive. Munchausen is the opposite: Munchausens crave medical attention.'

'I find it difficult to believe that all of her injuries are self-inflicted. You haven't seen the state of her. She was knocked out cold. Her teeth were broken, for Christ's sake.' A rotted picket fence.

'You need convincing. Have you seen her medical history? Decades of injuries.'

'In accordance with an abusive marriage.'

'Yes. Her syndrome does confound the usual scenario.'

'But she was honest with you?'

'I believe she craved attention from me as much as she did from the orthopaedics. And the plastic surgeons.'

'How do you know she was telling the truth? They're notorious deceivers, aren't they?'

'Aren't they, indeed,' he says.

I leave the psychiatrist's office, questions strumming my brain. Ignition, acceleration, autopilot.

'Why kill the husband?' Dom says. 'It doesn't fit with the diagnosis.'

'Shut up, Domino,' I say. 'This is real life. It's messy. Not everything is black and white. Not every psychological profile fits into a neat little box.'

'You're telling me,' he says, 'you're the one with the imaginary friend.'

'Is that what you are?' I say, adjusting the rearview mirror so that I can see him sitting upright on the back seat. He's wearing an especially handsome charcoal suit.

'I don't know what I am,' he says. 'I like to think of myself as a figment of your imagination. Figment. Figment. It's a good word.'

'You're full of shit,' I say, moving the mirror back to its original position. Concentrating on the road.

'You do realise,' he says, 'that you've just insulted yourself.'

The Mini in front of me brakes suddenly and I almost smash into the back of it.

'I've got an idea,' I say. 'Let's drop the witty repertoire and talk about the suspect.'

'I *told* you she was the suspect,' Dom says.

'Is it just me, or is this case not making sense?'

'It's just you,' he says. 'Pretty cut and dried, as far as I can see. You're just hung up. On Her. As usual.' He yawns without bothering to cover his mouth.

'The husband's knuckles,' I say. 'They were bruised.'

'Yes,' says Dom. 'And the bedroom cupboards had holes in them. Maybe he was angry.'

I drum the steering wheel with my fingers. Not convinced.

'Okay, so ... I'm going to give you another clue,' says Domino, as if indulging a particularly slow kid. 'Or, rather, I'm going to emphasise a detail you've already skipped over.'

I stop at a red light. I squint at him in the trembling mirror. 'I'm waiting.'

'What did you miss the first time around?'

'Everything, by the looks of it,' I say.

'Stop with the self-flagellation already.'

'Okay. We couldn't find the puzzle piece. The piece of the husband's skull.'

'RED HERRING!' Dom shouts right into my ear canal. 'What else?'

I think for a while. There was something bothering me. It was her teeth. Why do I keep thinking about her broken teeth?

'BINGO!' he shouts. 'Her chompers. Her pearly whites. Her rotten picket fence.'

'What do her teeth have to do with anything?'

'You want me to spell it out for you?'

God, I can be a bastard.

'Yes, I want you to spell it out for me.'

'I admit, it's left-field.'

'Just get on with it,' I say. I feel like I'm driving in circles.

'Remember that hippie girl you used to date. Brenda.'

Of course I remembered Brenda. Long straight hair. Honey breath. Hazelnut nipples.

'She used to analyse your dreams, right?' says Domino.

'This had better be going somewhere.'

'And you dreamt that weird tooth dream. Where you were keeping all your extra teeth in a tooth mug.'

'I vaguely recollect it.'

'And what did she tell you that was about?'

'Money. It was about money.'

'It was about money,' says Dom. 'What is the supposed root of all evil?'

'Money?'

'Money,' says Dom.

'Not some rare form of Munchausens?'

'Ha,' says Domino.

'But why the long story? Why lead the psychiatrist down the garden path? Why tell half-truths?'

'She had to tell someone something. She's human, after all. We all spin our own stories.'

I sigh.

'Really?' I say, 'Money?'

'Money, money, money,' says Domino. 'Show me the money. Hit me in the moneymaker. Skip to the money shot.'

'I get it.'

'Do you?'

'I do. She did it for the money.'

A couple of calls regarding the husband's bank account confirms the theory. Not that she needed it. She was wealthier than he was.

'I can't believe my deep gut / balls combination let me down,' I say.

'It didn't,' says Dom. 'It said she did it. It just didn't tell you the whole story.'

I picture the housecoat; this time stained with blood.

'Already a multi-millionaire before she met him,' I say. 'She's never had a job in her life. How does that work? Trust fund kid?'

Dom has decided he's helped me enough for the day. He left the back seat while I wasn't looking.

No, I think. No. She's this wealthy because she's done this before. And she got away with it. Over the past 12 years, two large previous payments to her account. Both hefty estates. Who would prosecute a battered wife? She's done this before. She's done it before, and she'll do it again. Third time lucky? Not if I can help it.

I jam my foot down. The accelerator touches the floor. I rush past hooting cars. One vehicle in particular reminds me of the fat black flies from this morning: A Peugeot with tinted windows buzzes around me until I shake it off. When I get to the hospital I drive straight through the parking boom and park in the emergency drop-off zone. I run up the stairs to the private wards and bust down her door. Her bed is empty. Her stuff is gone.

'Where is she?' I yell at the nurse — the one I had given a hard time.

'Gone,' he says. 'Checked herself out against doctors' orders. We haven't even had time to process the paperwork. She took her IV with. Still attached. Strung it up in her hired Peugeot.'

The nurse saunters away, trailing the cold fog of sanitiser.

'Son of a bitch,' I say.

He turns around. 'I knew she was faking something.'

7 / GREY MAGIC

When people ask me what I do, I usually lie. I used to tell the truth, when I was young and had an exoskeleton woven from life-spirit and arrogance, as most young people do. Before that threaded shell was gradually eroded by the hurt in the world: the violence, the bad luck. Now only middle-aged, liver-spotted skin remains, which is no adequate barricr to life's bashing. Now I have to protect myself in other ways; age and wisdom bring another type of armour.

I used to tell the truth, but now the lies slide out of my mouth like spotted eels. Easy and familiar. When I get bored of the untruths, I make up more, to keep things interesting. A year ago, I would have told you, if I had bumped into you at a conference or a cocktail party, that I was a botanist. The trick to believable deception, as I'm sure you know, is to keep it as truthful as possible. I have trained in botany, so it is an obvious one, one that springs quickly to my just-licked lips. But I am also qualified—fib-wise—to be a doctor, an astronomer, a zoologist, an archaeologist, a chemical engineer. Sometimes I surprise myself: my subconscious becomes adventurous, wants to

pursue less lofty careers. I become a marketing consultant, a sous-chef, a yoga instructor.

When I was starting out, I thought I had to tell people what I did—what I really did—in order to get work, but I have since found that when you do the work well, the work will come. The universe, after all, supports action. Now, I only accept referrals from close friends and previous clients (the ones that are still alive, anyway).

The reality is there is never any shortage of demand for the kind of work I do. Telling strangers about my vocation hardly ever translates into real jobs, anyway. I find time-wasters incredibly annoying. I picture them as velcro-legged parasites that cling to my aura until they have unloaded their whole Sorry Story, only to refuse my offer of professional help. It takes all the self-control I can muster to not place some kind of small, irritating hex on them, a monkey on their back, just to cause them the same amount of chagrin that they have caused me. That kind of tit-for-tat may seem childish to you, but it keeps the cosmos nicely balanced. "An eye for an eye" out of the old book was never meant to be vengeful or malicious; it was instead to keep The Balance. If The Balance is off, bad things can happen. Some people call it karma, others say that "the wheel turns." It's all true, no matter how you choose to dress it up, with gory stories of biblical eye-gouging savagery or with glittering, ice-cream-coloured animal gods. The wheel just keeps on turning.

Worse than the time-wasters are the impromptu sermons delivered to me in inopportune places, like on the train, or standing in line for my daily fix. It's awkward. I'm always amazed at how many religious fanatics there are in

our midst, dressed like ordinary people, slacks and crumpled tees, or polka-dotted summer dresses and glass beads, doing things that ordinary people do: eating processed-cheese sandwiches and listening to music on their phones. Using greasy hand cream that smells of roses. They seem so normal from the outside. It's only when they start babbling about necromantic prophets and being "saved" that you realise they have demons in their heads. When you look closely you see black scribbles on their auras. In my opinion, religious fundamentalism is a psychological disorder that has yet to be officially classified.

It's easy for me, in this day and age, to sit in the branches of my oak tree, feeling the light dapple my cheeks, the breeze lifting my hair, as if flying—when all feels right in the world—and ruminate about these people, but my predecessors weren't that lucky. There were no tree-dreams for them. No leisure to sit in a leafy bower and shine acorns, contemplating the spinning cycle of life. Just a couple of hundred years ago I would have been dragged down and lit up. Sometimes I wake up in a fever, as if I am on fire. It spreads from my feet upwards, like I am burning on a stake somewhere in a parallel (or previous) life. The first time it happened, when I was a little girl, I just lay there and blazed. I remember feeling paralysed by the fear of my destiny; perhaps even wished to burn up altogether. Wished to be nothing more than a glint of sad ashes in the creeping morning light. The next day, my legs were covered in blisters. The time after that, I ran an ice bath as soon as I felt it start, which I have been doing ever since. I lie in the arctic water and listen to my heart slow: run ice cubes over my flickering skin, absorbing the cold; the opposite of a sun lizard. Sometimes the fever brings with it auditory

hallucinations: chanting, shouting, the sound of an angry mob. The crackling of a spiteful fire. I don't know if I experience these episodes because my energy has an intense empathy for my foremothers, or if they are echoes of my previous, or future, lives. Whatever the reason, I thank the universe daily for the Age of Enlightenment. Of course, I use the word "enlightenment" loosely. I'm also grateful for my ice machine.

So I lie about what I do because of the fundamentalists and the time-wasters, and also to preserve my psychic energy. I've had enough of the rubbernecking. This fox mantle of dishonesty, this deception, can be lonely, but in my experience—and as parents warn—no good comes from talking to strangers.

At the moment, if anyone asks, I'm a shopkeeper. In a way it's true: I sell all kinds of ideas scratched on paper. I've always liked the idea of owning a bookshop.

It's not only strangers I lie to. I am less than honest with my clients, too. I guess you could say that I place less emphasis on the truth than most people, but only ever for the right reasons. I find honesty for the sake of honesty naïve and often unnecessarily harmful. Sometimes a profoundly dishonest act can have a major positive affect on someone's life. For example, a client of mine—let's call her "Betty"—was having trouble getting pregnant. I could sense, in the first consultation, that she was perfectly fertile (her energy was the colour of a ripe mandarin) but despite this, Betty's womb remained stubbornly barren. I told her I'd have her pregnant within three new moons. All it would take was some skillful spellcrafting, an eggshell sail, and a little resourcefulness on my side. In the Dark Ages we were

called "the cunning folk" for good reason.

It was clear to me that her husband's sperm was the problem, although Betty wouldn't entertain this idea, wouldn't even "insult him" by having him tested, as if he was some kind of caveman with the emotional intelligence of a Sumatran Orangutan. The matter of their infertility was not even discussed in their household, apart from their monthly ritual of him shooting reproachful looks at her tear-stained face, raw and bruised by her steady disappointment.

They had been trying for six years, which was good news for me: 6 is an incredibly fertile number, as you can probably guess from the shape. It also told me that if it hadn't happened by now, it probably wasn't going to happen unless I took some drastic action.

Once I was prepared, Betty was mid-cycle, and the moon was full, it was time to cast the spell. She had invited her sister, Danielle, for moral support, as she was keeping my services a secret from her Orangutan.

"I just want you to know that I don't approve of what you do," were the first words the sister said to me.

"Okay," I said, and continued to unpack my things. I would have preferred "Hello."

"I just don't think it's right," she insisted.

"Oh, Danielle," sighed Betty.

"In fact, I think…" she started. I could tell that she was about to hit her stride if I didn't interrupt her.

"You are more than welcome," I said, "to wait outside."

"Out-side?" she said, as if it was the first time she had ever heard the word. I found myself wishing that she would close her gaping-fish mouth. If we were characters in a comic book I could have waved my wand—abracadabra!—and turned her into a puffer fish, bouncing and flapping on the kitchen floor.

"There is no place for negative energy here tonight," I said, slowly and clearly, to the sister. "If you have a problem, it's best to go, and leave this sacred space." I was hamming it up a bit, for effect. Perhaps I am less mature than I give myself credit for.

"Sacred?" she gasped. "Sacred?" It took remarkable restraint on my behalf to not ask her if English was her first language. If her reaction wasn't interfering with my work I would have found her outrage quite entertaining.

"Look, Dan, this was a mistake."

"Yes! That's what I was trying to tell you!"

"No, I mean, I think you should go," Betty said to her, gently.

"I'm not leaving you with this...this..."

What would she think would happen if she left her sister in my supposedly evil clutches, I wondered? That I would possess her, kill her, steal her soul? I wasn't surprised by Danielle's attitude. You are bound to bump up against some people in my business, people who believe that witchery is wicked. Little do they know that they cast spells

themselves, when they curse other drivers in traffic, touch wood, or blow out birthday candles.

"I need this to work," said Betty.

"Listen to me," whispered her sister, bunching up her fists around the gold crucifix that dangled from her moist and unpleasantly chunky neck. "You don't need to do this. Come to our church! Our cell group has been praying for you..."

"And she has yet to conceive," I said. "You say you don't like spells, what do you think prayer is? You just haven't been saying the right ones."

Blasphemy! her aura shouted.

"And I suppose you know the right ones?" She eyed me: a wolf in wolf's clothing.

"Yes," I said. "It's my job."

I began the ceremony by smudging the room with the sweet smoke of lavender and white sage. With a piece of chalkstone I drew a circle on the pine floorboards around Betty, on which I placed six green candles. I anointed the candles with vanilla oil, lit them, then began my fertility incantation. Betty was instructed to close her eyes and sit as still as possible, as if meditating, and just allow the spell to wash through her. Her hands were placed over her abdomen, sending warmth and acceptance deep into her pelvic chakra. Afterwards, we sailed the eggshell by moonlight while Betty recited a poem she had written, inviting the soul of her baby into her body. I found her vulnerability touching, and couldn't help thinking that she

would make a tender mother. I gave her a silver bracelet with a charm of a carnelian-eyed hare—I had charged the crystal with pentacle-cast spells—as well as a gift of bespoke tea: stinging nettle, red clove and raspberry leaf, which she was to drink every day. She held my hands and thanked me. On my way out, I gave her a syringe I had been keeping warm between my breasts. I told her it was a potion to open and soften her cervix, and that she should keep it at blood temperature and use it before making love to her husband that night.

Six weeks later, Betty was pregnant, as I knew she would be. She has since given birth to a bonny little boy with a full head of hair and an easy smile. Her Orangutan will never know that the child is not biologically his.

The timing of Betty's lunacycle couldn't have been more perfect. I had been consulting that day with another client of mine who was having trouble sustaining his phallus. Feri, or sexual mysticism, is a speciality of mine, and I had been training him in the art of Tantra. This client wasn't dissimilar-looking to the man in the wedding photo that Betty had given me. Without going into too many details, this client had inadvertently given me the means to help Betty. The universe had been particularly supportive that day, as it can be, when you are following a beneficent course of action. Neither client was aware of the transaction, and they were both extremely pleased with the results. Had I been honest with either of them, the outcome would not have been nearly as satisfactory.

The thing about earth magic is that it can go either way. We are all under the influence of so many factors at any one time that it's not an exaggeration to say that

anything can happen. Without even knowing it, our destinies are pushed and pulled by the sparkling cosmos, kneaded and knocked back like baker's dough. You can try your best to stake out your life's path—or others' lives, as I do—but our human influence is limited. There are people— women and men—who become taken with a neopagan lifestyle, study Wicca, indulgently call themselves White Witches. But if they truly knew their craft, they would know that there is no such thing. These dabblers are the moths of the sorcery world, not unpleasant to have around, unless they get confused and start battering themselves against a light-source that is not the moon. Some are elegant and pretty to look at, others leave moth-dust and holes in your winter underwear.

There is no such thing as white magic. Real magic is a wide spectrum encompassing good and evil, and there are very many shades of grey in-between. The reason a spell can never be pure white is because of the cosmic baker's influence. A sorceress may start out with a clear, benevolent purpose, unalloyed ingredients, and a pure heart, and perform the incantation as close to perfect as she can manage, but after that, she has little influence. Once it is out of her mouth, the spell is out of her hands, and cannot be kept un-grubby.

As with magic, is with witches. Just as a person cannot be 100 percent good, a witch, as pure-thinking as she may be, cannot achieve Perfect Snow. Witches are human, after all. She may be milk, ivory, or limestone, or one of the hundreds of shades between them, but never fresh snow. You have this trembling human spectrum overlapping and interweaving with the sure orbit of magic, and it becomes

evident—despite the illusions of the giggling Wiccans—
that a White Witch is nothing but a fairytale.

I am under none of the pagan pretences. I practice grey
magic; more dove-grey than charcoal. Or more accurately:
the colour of a raincloud as it swells and shrinks and
flickers between shades of pearl and slate. I have to be
careful of slipping towards the sooty part of the spectrum.
The darker the magic, the quicker the flame takes, the more
powerful you feel. You have to be on your guard and think
things through: sometimes you set out to do good and the
result is murky, or worse. I once killed someone with a
simple love spell. That may sound like I'm just not a very
proficient witch, but the opposite is true. The spell was one
of my best: refined over and over again to be as simple and
striking as possible. But setting out, I wasn't told the whole
story. A woman had left a man, and the spell was to reunite
them. What I hadn't been told was that the woman had left
the man for someone else. That someone else happened to
meet with an accident the day I triple-cast the reunion
conjuration: an innocent bystander, he was shot in a cash-
in-transit heist. My client, his grief-stricken lover returned,
had been delighted, and paid me double. It had not been my
intention. Apparently they are happily married now. He
still sends me fruit baskets.

Taking lives is not always dark sorcery.
Counterintuitive as it may seem, killing people is sometimes
the kindest, and most important work I do. In a topsy-turvy
society such as ours, where your life is not your own, a
sensible outsider—not bound by popular morality—is
sometimes required. On occasion, a client needs to be
supported in their decision to perform certain actions that

are usually frowned upon by the bleating world at large. This is where my services come in, as a non-judgmental advisor, helper, sponsor, drug dealer, psychologist, relationship counsellor, prostitute, or mercy nurse. Being a witch isn't about spells and trickery—not really—more than anything else, it's about having a completely open mindset, and having the courage of your convictions. In short, to be a consummate witch, you have to have a titanium spine.

I help the client take a psychic step away from their supposed reality, and offer them a perspective that is unconstrained by the values of others. I coax them out of the dogma-box. Although most people seem happy to be trained and controlled by banks, employers and television, it is only when we are unfettered by indoctrination that we can live our free and true lives. I help people with this awakening, but often this bitter-bright truth comes too late, when they are in an acute crisis, or are dying.

The client I am busy working with has stage 4 pancreatic cancer. He joked when he called me, saying: "there is no stage 5". He needed someone who was willing to end his life for him, when the time came, and he found that time rapidly approaching. Just a month ago, he told me, he was driving his Porsche Carrera with the top down, meeting friends for lunch, drinking Scotch, and following the Premier League. But now he finds his appetite vanished, his balance is off. He can't hear properly, doesn't have the energy to drive.

"Could it be true?" he asks me, "That my drive to the café around the corner, for the paper, was my last? That I'll never drive again?"

It wasn't just his beloved car he was grieving for, of course, but his independence. His life as he knew it. He is plagued by a constant "empty" pain in his abdomen that gnaws at his mood. He has no children, his wives are all estranged. His doctor says her hands are tied, there are no more treatments available, that she can only make him "comfortable."

"Comfortable?" he demands. "What the hell is comfortable about dying?"

I wouldn't say he is at peace with his impending death, but he doesn't want to live like this. Not when we know there will be no improvement.

"I should be grateful, I suppose," he says to me, "Going downhill so quickly. It's what every terminal patient hopes for...once you reach the top of the hill, that is."

It's difficult to be grateful when you feel your life is being snatched away. He is not the kind of man who will accept being bedridden, or fed chicken broth with a spoon. He has lost 8 kg in the past two weeks. When he can no longer walk, I take things to cheer him up. He still likes iced coffee but refuses berry pinwheel pastries, his former favourite combination.

On the third day, the heavens open up and blast us with a dramatic thunderstorm. Once the rain slows I follow the sound of mewling outside to discover trees stripped by wind and a skinny-ribbed kitten with opalescent eyes. I rub her dry with a tea towel to reveal tiger stripes and chinchilla-soft fur. I place her on my client's chest, and she soothes him with her loud purring.

I read the newspaper to him as his consciousness swims in and out of shallow sleep. I tell him the soccer score, who has saved a goal, who has been carded. I am with him for five days and five nights. Every hour drains me, although I try not to show it. We do this pretend-dance of patient and nurse until today when he takes my wrist in his cool bony fingers and says he is ready.

The truth is that nothing is being snatched away from him, not permanently. Once his heart stops knocking and his cells power down, his energy will move on to a better place. Not heaven (or hell), not a resting place, but a living place. I have told him that energy cannot be destroyed, only converted, but his imagination cannot stretch that far. It's not a "better place"—not necessarily, just different—like a new day. You don't know exactly what it will hold, but it will surely be kinder to him than this suffering. We are all souls surfing through history. This moving on, this energy conversion, is why I have no problem with ending someone's current life. It is no more sinister than putting a child to sleep.

There is a common misconception that ending a terminal illness requires active euthanasia, but this is most often not the case. The majority of the time, all that is needed is for the patient to sign a living will that refuses any further medical treatment, and for the caregivers to respect his or her wishes. The very last thing a terminally ill patient wants is to be fussed over with antibiotics and feeding tubes in order to prolong his pain, but this is often what families insist on. They panic and press red buttons and jam oxygen masks over their loved ones' faces, despite their clear DNR stickers, because they are the ones afraid of

death.

In most cases I have found that if you cut off all access to medical treatment and are liberal with the painkillers, nature takes its course easily, and the soul is allowed to ascend, un-barbed, to its beckoning place. Sometimes gentle help is needed: extra analgesics, if you can get them, or a steady pillow over a slumbering face.

"I'm ready," he says to me now, clear-eyed. "I'm ready to go."

With a long match, I light the nine black candles in the room, and smudge with sandalwood and willow. I put a smooth Obsidian stone in his palm. I recite the Druidic Death Hex under my breath. The kitten's purring gets louder as the magic electrifies the room. I load up a syringe with morphine, nine times the prescribed dose, and push the needle into one of the beetroot-purple veins that snake over his arms. I can see the effects of the drug cascade over him; his relief is instant. I hold his hand as the spirit leaves his body. I feel a pull, a falling away, and then it's gone. The room exhales. The wheel turns, the cycle spins. There is no need to check his pulse, or put a mirror near his mouth to search for breath. Nothing remains but a sad skeleton in skin. The kitten cries.

I blow out the candles and pack my things, including a fat envelope of cash with my name on it. I wipe the house down to vanish any fingerprints. After a moment's hesitation, I put the moping kitten in my basket, too. I have always resisted having a cat, given my occupation. It seemed a terrible cliché, like sporting a wart on my nose, or flying a broom.

Today, however, I no longer mind the idea. I let myself out of the house, and leave the polished key under the doormat. The wind has picked up, and dead leaves flutter and swirl across my path like ugly butterflies. The moon is waning, and I'm feeling a bit older, colder, bashed-about.

Burnt out. Ashes to glinting ashes.

It will be nice to have a warm creature at home. We can sit in the oak tree together.

❁

8 / PIGEON PAIR

"They're quite pretty things, really," says Juliet.

Edward, intent on smoothing the marmalade on his cold toast in exactly the right way, doesn't hear — or ignores her — and she has to wave at him to break his trance.

"This one isn't quite as good as the thick cut, but it IS easier to spread," he says.

The pair of pigeons coo. It's a gentle, happy sound. Their swivelling necks are iridescent.

"Quite nice to have some birds around," she says.

"The colour is good. You want that golden hue, don't you? You want those strips of blood orange and pink grapefruit. You want that syrupy sheen."

"Edward," says Juliet.

"It's a most underrated condiment, I think. Sweet, with just the right amount of bitterness. And that tang — that citrus tang …"

"Edward! Will you snap out of it?"

Coo! Coo! say the pigeons, beady black eyes watching the couple at the table below.

"What?" he says at last, dragging his eyes off the jar and looking at her. "Did I miss something?"

Sometimes Juliet thinks that she may as well eat breakfast on her own, for all the attention she gets from her husband. Sometimes she would say something — just something small — to make conversation, and he would flat-out ignore her. Not an acknowledging glance, not a mumble of agreement.

"I was just saying that the pigeons are quite pretty. I don't know why they have such a bad reputation."

"Do they?" he asks, taking a bite of his vaunted toast. "Do they have a bad reputation?"

He crunches and grinds the toast in his mouth. Juliet has to talk over the sound or she fixates on it. She hates hearing people chew. Apparently there is a scientific name for it. It's an actual condition. It drives her crazy.

"Yes. People call them vermin," she says.

In the past she had asked him to try to make less noise while eating, and he had flung his head back and laughed. How? He had asked. How does one do that? Even if I wanted to indulge this particular eccentricity of yours. How does one chew quietly?

She had not mentioned it again. He takes another bite

and crunch, crunch, crunch, like a car compactor. Like a bone breaking. Like stepping on crushed glass.

"Vermin?" he says. "That seems extreme."

"Yes," she says, "I agree," and she does.

Misophonia, it's called. She read about it in a magazine. The irrational anger one feels upon hearing others eat. At least she wasn't the only one. His mouth must feel so dry with all that toast and sugar, she thinks. Doesn't he want some water?

"Would you like some water?" she asks, lifting the glass jug. It drips with condensation. He doesn't answer. She pours it anyway.

The pigeons, having had enough of the breakfast show, launch themselves with a clatter of wings off the boundary wall and into the bright sky. The Bentworths watch them fly away.

"Anyway, you know that we need to stop buying that particular underrated condiment," says Juliet.

"This?" he says, showing her his last golden square. "Sacrilege! Why would you say that?"

"It's full of sugar," she says. "You know what your doctor said."

"Oh, please," he says. "I've been eating sugar my whole life and look at me!" He beats his chest, Tarzan-like. "I'm as healthy as an ox!"

"Not according to Doctor Benson, you're not," she

says. "And I don't want you to get diabetes."

Edward grunts and looks away. Rinses his mouth with a sip of cold tea. Juliet picks up the offending jar.

"We shouldn't be buying this anyway," Juliet says. "It's imported from Paris!"

"So?" he says. "That's what makes it good!"

"No," says Juliet. "Its irresponsible."

"It's organic!"

"It's reckless."

"Ha!" he says. "Now I've heard it all."

"It's true," says Juliet. "Think of our trade deficit. We should really be buying local."

"So our pretty birds are vermin, hey?" says Edward. "And now marmalade is reckless. Now I've really heard it all."

"Shall I give them some of these toast crumbs?"

"Don't you dare."

"Why aren't you dressed yet?" asks Edward. He is wearing his tuxedo and is looking especially handsome. Steam is still pouring out of the en-suite. There's probably no hot water left.

"Why am I not dressed yet?" Juliet says, looking down

at her tracksuit pants stained with puréed butternut and crusted with bright blue bubblefruit toddler toothpaste. "Are you serious?"

While Edward had skipped home from work and jumped right into the shower, Juliet had been wrangling the children. Emma had to be fed her baby slop, and topped up with milk. Dean needed fish fingers and peas, which was more of a theoretical exercise in eating than actual eating, seeing as they all landed up on the floor. Juliet had given up and made him two-minute noodles with tomato sauce for what was now the third night in a row. Then they both needed to be bathed and dressed and made ready for bed, which was always an exercise in patience and steel determination, especially with the one-parent to two-kid ratio. The saying about herding cats always came to mind, but a glance at Laila, the family cat, snoozing peacefully on the couch made Juliet feel that herding cats would certainly be easier. A bit of smelly tuna and shaking some kibble in a bowl would probably do the trick. The kids — her kids — her home-made gremlins, required considerably more effort.

"Where's the babysitter?" he says, angling his chin up to the ceiling and looking in the mirror to inspect his freshly shaven throat.

"She'll be here at 7."

He shakes his watch down his arm and looks at the face. Picks up his phone, ready to check the Premier League results.

"You can make their milk and go in and read them a

story," says Juliet, taking off her stained cardigan, "while I make myself presentable."

"It had better be a long story," he says, winking at her.

She throws her top at him. It hits him square in the face and he catches it as it falls.

"Oh," she says. "Before I forget. The pigeons are back."

"Are they?"

"And they brought a few friends with them."

"Is it a problem?"

"I don't think so. They're entertaining, anyway, for the kids. I showed Dean how to shoo them away and it keeps him occupied for ages."

Edward shakes Juliet awake. She opens her eyes but sees nothing.

"What's wrong?" she says, heart-in-throat. *Is something wrong with one of the kids? Has someone broken in? Why didn't the house alarm go off?*

"Can you hear them?" he demands.

Juliet tries to listen but all she can hear is her pulse banging in her ears.

"What?"

"It's the birds. It's those bloody birds."

"A dream?" wonders Juliet out loud.

"You can't hear them? It's like they've nested right next to my head! I can't sleep with them making such a racket."

Juliet hears them. Enthusiastic cooing; wing adjusting; sharp claws grubbing on tin.

"I can hear them," she says. She looks at her phone: 4:30AM. "Looks like we have ourselves a new alarm clock."

"Mama?" says Dean, sleep-walking into the bedroom. She jumps out of bed and swoops to catch him before he tumbles down the two stairs. Brings his warm body into bed with them. Kisses his head.

Coo! Coo! say the birds.

"Ed? You there?" says Juliet into he receiver. "Ed?"

"I'm just walking into a meeting. It's been a hell of a day so far. Can we chat later?"

"It's the pigeons!"

"You're calling me because of the ... pigeons?"

"They've made such a mess. There's just ... there's just feathers and sticks and bird shit everywhere! All over the outside furniture. The settee, the shelves, the flat screen!"

"Can't you just, you know, shoo them away?"

"Shoo them away? There are like, 20 of them."

"Didn't you say that Dean loved chasing them away?"

"He does! He does it all day! It's practically his part-time job. He's not even 2!"

"You said it was cute."

"It used to be cute. He puts his arms up and stomps on the floor — like a gumboot dance — very effective — but even he can't keep up with the way they're flocking in here."

"Let me go in to this meeting. I'll try get back as soon as I can."

"Hmm," says the man in the bright yellow overall. "Hmm."

He sucks his pencil and narrows his eyes and inspects the eaves where the pigeons have been nesting. Dirty patches on white timber trusses where bird feet have been dancing the cha-cha. He makes some notes.

"I can see they've already caused some damage," he says, eyeing the flatscreen TV with a disapproving look.

"I probably should have called you sooner," says Juliet.

"Hmm," the man says.

The timber floor decking underneath the eaves is an abstract painting. Jackson Pollock in guano. The yellow man sniffs. He does not appreciate the artistic merit. The

logo on his overall is the same as the picture on his van: a cheerful looking pigeon holding a suitcase and saluting, as if he is leaving for a quick island holiday. As if these yellow men are really travel agents for burnt-out birds.

"Nine THOUSAND rand?" says Edward, hitting a button on his keyboard over and over again, as if to correct a mistake.

"I know!" says Juliet. "It's ridiculous."

"Are you sure they didn't send us the wrong quote?" he says, hand over brow.

"It's the netting that's expensive. And the spikes. And the labour."

"Netting AND spikes? Is that really necessary? I don't want all this stuff cluttering our space. I spent a fortune on that outside area. I don't want it to look like we're living in bloody Fort Knox!"

It does sometimes feel like a prison, thinks Juliet.

"Is there no other way?"

"I don't know. It does seem excessive."

"Nine thousand rand?"

"He did seem to know what he was talking about."

"Can't we find a way to chase them away, ourselves?"

"I've tried!"

Juliet had dug around in the kids' playroom and found a rubber snake, which she had placed in the birds' favourite spot. They just shat on it.

"They just shit on it," she says, tugging a strand of her hair. "They just shit on everything!"

Edward was used to compliments on his house. They used to please him.

"My God," says his sister, almost losing her grip on her glass of wine before she'd had a sip. "What on earth is going on here?"

"You wouldn't believe it," says Juliet, bouncing baby Emma on her hip. "I've become a guerrilla."

"What the —" she says, trailing off, taking in the odd new decorations. Usually she was proud of the fact that the Bentworths had exceptional taste, but —

"The old CDs hanging like that," says Juliet, "like 80s bunting, is to keep them away. The sun reflects off them and disorients them."

"Disorientates who?" says Sarah.

"You don't know?"

"Know about what?"

"Our problem!" says Juliet.

"We have a feral pigeon problem," says Edward.

"I've put tinfoil on all the surfaces," says Juliet.

"I can see that," says Sarah.

"I chase them with a broom. I throw balls at them. They're so bloody stupid and so stubborn ... sometimes I get so angry I just wish I had a pellet gun!"

"Now THAT'S a good idea," says Edward.

"And I placed fake eggs everywhere. You know, because Google said that they won't nest in another bird's nest. Poor Dean got so excited. He thought we were going to have an Easter egg hunt!"

A pigeon dives in, dodges the CDs and lands on the tinfoil. Emma starts wailing. Juliet get tears in her eyes.

"Juliet? Are you okay?"

"No," says Juliet. "No, I'm not."

Sarah, not good at comforting people, puts her glass down and gives Juliet an awkward hug. Pats the baby.

"You poor thing," she says. "Don't worry. We'll sort these bloody birds out."

A group of men in yellow overalls swarm all over the deck. Ladders are employed; nail guns shoot their columns of steel into the wood with a satisfying bang. Strong black netting is rolled out: the opposite of a red carpet.

"Bird eviction, they call it," says Edward, looking cheerful despite not having slept well in days. "I find that quite funny."

Before their eyes, their minimalist and tastefully decorated outside area becomes a crazy quilt of pigeon prophylactics. Ligatures, gauze, spikes.

"Once the birds have been dispatched," says Edward to the yellow chief (the man who sucks the pencil), "Can we get all this removed?"

Juliet sees the timber trusses being punctured. Penetrated. Perforated. Even if they remove the unwelcome deterrents, the deck will remain scarred.

"Sure you can," says the man. "If you want them to come back."

Edward pays him ten thousand rand.

That evening Edward and Juliet deposit the children in front of the television and drink an aperitif outside, trying to ignore the unsightly eviction gear. They want to see the pigeons swoop in and realise there is nowhere for them to nest. They want to see them get frustrated and fly away. The Bentworths have never considered themselves cruel people but as they sip their scotches in silence all they wish for is to see the pigeons lose hope. They wish for pigeon doom and despair. They swallow their drinks. The birds don't come.

"Do you think it was enough to scare them away?" asks Juliet, as they lie in bed. She wishes he would hold her hand. When was the last time they held hands? "The army

of yellow men, I mean. Do you think the pigeons recognised them and just knew not to come back?"

"Maybe," said Edward, yawning. "He did say that he does a lot of work in the area."

"So we've just chased them to some other unfortunate person's house."

Emma fusses in the cot next to their bed, but settles down without reassurance.

"Maybe, in future, we won't need all that terrible netting," says Juliet. "Maybe we can fill the holes and repaint."

She waits for a reply but Edward is asleep. She leans over him to switch off his bedside light.

Juliet stirs: woken by the scratching. Pins on sheet metal. Before she is even properly awake she knows the pigeons are back. How is that possible? she thinks. How the bloody hell is that possible?

She gets up quietly as to not wake Edward or the baby. Fetches Dean's alligator torchlight, but not before stepping on a piece of Lego and gulping down a string of curses. Uses her remote to switch off the house alarm, but forgets the outside beams. She pads to the back door that leads to the deck, unlocks it, steps down into the cool dark breeze. Sweeps the toy light over the eaves which are free of birds, checks the furniture; the flatscreen. The shadows are still and quiet.

Had she imagined it? Had it been a dream? There was

certainly no evidence of trespassers here. But then there is a flicker in her peripheral vision, which makes her jump. What — she thinks, and then she sees it. A pigeon on her clean white shelf: hiding. Playing dead? Juliet runs towards it to shoo it away, and it gets such a fright it explodes in a clatter of wings and feathers, knocking a flower vase off the shelf, which falls and shatters on the floor. The sound is jarring in the otherwise silent morning. The bird, discombobulated, flies into the wall, then finds his way out. His pitching signals the security beams and sets off the alarm: the siren caterwauls all around her. Emma and Dean are both startled awake and start crying. They both want her but she is sweeping up the shards to protect their tender little feet. Edward tries to hold them back, and then his phone starts ringing, adding to the cacophony. He assures the security company that it was a false alarm. The armed men arrive anyway. The control room had sensed he had been acting under duress.

"Coffee," says Juliet.

"Is that an offer, or a demand?" asks Edward.

"Here." She puts a double shot espresso in his hand. He takes a sip.

"Oh, this is good. What did I do to deserve you?"

"I'm not sure you do deserve me," Juliet says. He knows she is not joking.

"I'm taking the day off," he says, draining his cup. His eyes are red, puffy. He hasn't shaved in a couple of days.

He's looking quite grey.

"Are you that tired?"

Despite his demeanor of exhaustion, there is a sparkle in his eyes.

"It's not that," says Edward. "I'm going to camp out on the deck. I'm going to make sure that those damned pigeons don't come back."

"Really?" says Juliet, warming to him. "Maybe you do deserve me after all."

While Juliet takes the kids to the park, Edward goes shopping to buy supplies for his mission. They rendezvous back at the house. Edward is wearing a new, lightweight camouflage jacket, and beige pants. He looks like a fly fisherman, or an army vet. There are black smudges under his eyes. Had he used her eye-liner? She pulls on her bush outfit: khaki 3-phase zipper pants and a tan blouse. She wipes off her red lipstick and goes with a nude shade instead. Looks in the mirror: feels decidedly German. She joins him out on the deck, puts a thermos flask and Dean's dinosaur-themed tin lunchbox on the table in front of him.

"Sandwiches," she says. "And tea."

Edward nods in approval. Wonders offhandedly what is on the sandwiches.

The provisions she has brought sit in contrast with the weapons on the table: a pneumatic pellet gun, with plenty of pretty copper-coloured BBs. A BirdX Quadblaster QB4, which, according to the box, repelled pigeons with its

ultrasonic waves. A Broadband Ray with Fright Visuals. A Nightmare Sound 4-Speaker. A plastic 'action owl' decoy with a movement sensor. He had already planted the additional spikes he had bought: on the handrail, on the lemon tree, on every inch of open shelf. Her decorative porcelain rabbits and cats now sat behind an aggressive row of metal skewers.

She watches as he loads the air gun. "You're really going to shoot them?" she says.

"Yip," he says, flicking the safety catch off and looking through the rifle's sight. It makes her nervous.

"Be careful of Laila," she says. "Don't shoot her."

"What use is a cat if it doesn't catch the pigeons?" he says. She smacks him on the arm and the gun almost goes off. He forgets to put the safety back on.

"I don't blame Laila," says Juliet. "Would you want a mouthful of vermin?"

"That's a good point," he says. "The cat's a Bentworth, after all. I daresay that a dirty pigeon is quite beneath her station."

Edward installs the various kits he has bought. Juliet assists him: holding ladders, passing screwdrivers, finding extension cables for the electric drill. As she sweeps up after him she can't help noticing how much damage the birds have done. Their acidic droppings have corroded almost every surface she sees. She imagines her precious things covered in diseases and lice. Suddenly she has to drop everything to viciously scratch her head.

"Pigeon lice," she says, scrubbing away. "I'm sure I'm imagining it."

Edward shudders in empathy.

Eventually they are all set up. The deck is unrecognisable, strewn with cables and lights and panels.

"I like the fake owl," Juliet says. "Let's keep him after the pigeons are gone."

"Watch this," says Edward. He runs up to the owl and waves at it. The owl screeches and his head swivels. His eyes are red lasers.

"My God," she says. "That's enough to give anyone nightmares."

Edward chuckles. "Isn't it wonderful?"

He flaps his arms again and the owl responds. It reminds Juliet of the film 'The Exorcist.' Edward keeps laughing.

They send the kids to their Aunt Sarah for the afternoon while they sit in their camping chairs drinking gin & tonics and eating kettle-fried chips. Laila has forgiven Edward, as evidenced by her sleeping on his lap.

"Look at us," says Juliet. If it wasn't the middle of summer they could have matching blankets on their knees. "Sitting here like an old couple."

"We ARE an old couple," says Edward, looking through his binoculars at some birds in the distance.

Juliet thinks he is looking quite handsome, despite his grey stubble.

"We're probably wasting our time," says Juliet. "I mean, there's no way they're coming back now, with all these gadgets."

"Never say never."

Juliet has her iPad and is reading up on feral pigeons. When she finds something interesting she reads it out loud. "Did you know that they don't migrate?"

"Ha," says Edward, pursing his lips. "Just our luck."

"Did you know that they are monogamous?"

"Are they?"

"You only think of lovely, elegant animals being monogamous, don't you? Swans, for instance. Wolves."

"What's that?" says Edward, sitting up straight.

"I was just saying ..."

"Sshhh!" he says, putting a finger to his lips. "What's that sound?"

Juliet listens. There is a murmuring. A distinct pigeon cooing, coming from the roof. They abandon their drinks and scuttle over to the sound.

"There's a pigeon in there," he says. "Inside the bloody roof."

"More than one!" she says. "But how did they get in?"

"I don't care. I'm going to take them out." Edward drags the ladder to the offending area and scrambles up. Juliet hold the ladder still. She hears "Ah - ha!" as he finds their hiding place behind a loose brick.

She wants to call up: Be Careful, but Edward hates it when she says that, so she keeps quiet instead. He forces out the brick and hits the wall next to it to dislodge any feathered vagrants.

Neither of them are prepared for the swarm of birds that erupt from the opening. One hundred, two hundred pigeons, moving together, like an animated, monstrous mass. The fake owl screeches; Laila bolts. The horde flies around and then descend on the deck, on the shelves, on the flatscreen, on the camping chairs, on Juliet and Edward. Everything is covered in twitching grey wings and black-pearl eyes. The Bentworths scream and bat the birds away. Claws scrabble at their skin. Edward's face turns white and he grabs his chest.

Juliet runs towards the pellet gun. The owl screeches again, sending a wave of birds up into the air, and Juliet shoots six birds in a row, without missing. Edward, slightly recovered, picks up Dean's nearby water pistol and starts shooting, too. The BirdX Quadblaster is sending out ultrasonic waves that make the ground vibrate. Juliet kills another five birds, which sends half the flock skittering off. Three more birds with pellets in their hearts fall to the floor, and with the soft, wet smack of the third's body hitting the timber, the rest of the legion wing themselves away. Downy feathers rain like snow down around them.

Juliet and Edward sit together amongst the carcasses and lost plumes. Juliet has ribbons of fresh blood on her cheek where she had been scratched. She doesn't put down the rifle. Edward is still pale, and he has bird shit on the shoulder of his camo jacket. The sun is beginning to set. They look at each other.

"I thought you were having a heart attack," she says.

"Me too," he says. "But it's over now."

"I don't think they're coming back," she says.

"They are definitely NOT coming back," he says. "You made sure of that."

Edward reaches over, and they hold hands.

In the distance, on someone else's property, a pair of pigeons coo and settle in for the night.

9 / THE LITTLE PINK BOOK

Her scream smashes the ceiling. It knocks over a vase of blue chrysanthemums, whips out of the room and into the corridor, bowling over nurses as it goes. It is eardrum-popping, eye-watering, and desolate.

Sister Angelika's disembodied head appears at the doorway. Jesus.

"Is everything alright in here?" she demands, jowls aquiver.

"Yes, Sister." My rubber soles squeak innocence.

"But what is all this noise about? I could hear the bawling from the chapel!"

My smile is glacé. I mop up the spilt water from the fallen flowers.

"Well," I venture, "this is a maternity ward."

Sister Angelika's eyes disappear and reappear in an extravagant show of blinking. I put my hands on my hips.

"A baby's head's circumference is usually around thirty-five centimetres," I add, in case she didn't quite get the point.

An apoplectic jump.

"Well, it's upsetting the geriatrics. They're all in a flurry! They can't hear the television and now they're refusing to take their meds! Could you at least make an effort to keep it down?"

"Oh, of course," I say, "by all means. God bless the geriatrics."

A departing sniff and she is gone.

I take my patient's wrist to measure her pulse against my wristwatch. I wink at her.

"Let's see if you can scream any louder."

Sister Angelika detests midwives. She thinks of us as unnatural. The irony of that, I'm sure, escapes her. I think the whole idea of reproduction escapes her. I can imagine her nose stinging at the thought of it. The steamy interchanging of bodily fluids, the milk-swelling of breasts, the gush of water, the inky blood. Immaculate conception is far more her cup of holy water. If she were residing over a birth the patient would probably be told to lie still, stay quiet and keep her legs crossed. Bless the Catholics.

My patient, Miss June Catrilby, is a lovely woman. (Yes! *Miss!* Sister Angelika would be throwing her frown around if only she knew that an illegitimate baby was causing all this fuss). June and I got along right away. It's

critical that an expectant mother likes and trusts her midwife. When one is in such a vulnerable position one needs to be in the company of only those she trusts. We'll have a doctor on standby, and an attending nurse, but for the most part it will be June and I doing the work.

June told me that the father of the baby ran away, seemingly without a backward glance. June didn't seem too bothered about it; said that they'd be better off without him. He's probably married. Or worse - in politics. I am by no stretch of the imagination a moralist, but I do believe that a child needs a father. At least June knows that I am here for her.

I wanted to be a surgeon but I failed my fifth year of med school. I was the only woman admitted to the medical faculty that year and I skipped eating and sleeping on most days to keep up with the workload until one day I just fell down in a practical exam. My psychologist at the time attributed it to burnout. I had put myself under too much pressure for too long: I was hospitalised for exhaustion. It was a relief. I stuck an IV drip in my arm and spent a few days sleeping. Every insipid meal, every scribble on a clipboard, every blip on the heart machine was a reminder of my failure. I silenced the damning voices in my head with various pills. I thought I would never be able to pay off my many student loans until I eventually found a job that could hoist me out of my debt and beyond. Now I help bring little babies into the world and am sure I'm much better off than someone who has to deal with the gores of surgery. Plus it doesn't hurt to be able to afford new pair of shoes every now and then.

I've delivered over five hundred babies. I keep a record

of each and every one in my little pink book that I carry in my purse. It's for my eyes only. Sometimes, at night, I lie in bed and wonder how all those sweet little babies are doing. Of course all babies are special, but some are more special than others. Some babies you just never forget.

June screams until she can't hold the note anymore. It ends in a blunt groan.

"We're almost there," I assure her, snapping off my glove and being careful to not touch anything with my bare hands. I never touch anything in a birthing room without gloves on.

She has dilated to eight centimetres. It's almost time to push.

She claws my arm. I wince.

"I can't do it," she says, "I can't do it."

Her grey lips plead with me.

"Of course you can," I say, reclaiming my wrist.

She begins to cry. Small, sad sobs.

"You're going to be just fine. It will be like we practised, remember?"

Sob.

I've always been fascinated with babies. The way they grow in their mother's wombs, taking the lion's share of blood

nutrients. How they enter the world, blue and kicking, probably wishing they could go back to their dark, sticky cocoon. Their clenched little fists, their eyes like schoolyard marbles. Even after five hundred and twenty eight babies I still wonder at these sublime little creatures.

I can see that June is exhausted. Her hospital gown is soaked with perspiration. I put a cold compress on her forehead and offer her a sip of water but she won't have it. She is ivory pale. I check her vitals. Her heartbeat is regular but her blood pressure is high. She's not bleeding so there doesn't seem to be anything to worry about.

Tuesdays are always a midwife's busiest day. More babies are born on a Tuesday the world over than any other day of the week. Sundays are, typically, the slowest. Late summer is the busiest time of the year. Boy babies outnumber girl babies, but they also have a lower survival rate. Jacob is the most popular name for boy babies, and Emily for girls.

June seems to have come round and is breathing well. She's getting ready for the next contraction. They are less than a minute apart now. She begins to growl. It looks like we are in business. I beep the nurse that will look after June while I'm busy with the baby. I listen to the baby's heartbeat and it is beautifully even.

Nurse Spencer arrives with a polystyrene cup of tea.

"I thought you could do with it," she froths. "It's Susan, isn't it?"

I look at her blankly. The unruly curls pinned down with her white cap, the straining uniform, the equine teeth.

"Your name?" she prods.

"Oh. Yes. It's Susan."

"It wasn't a trick question."

I half-laugh.

"I'm sorry, it's been a long labour."

I don't want to take the cup but I do.

"It'll be over soon."

I can see that she's not sure of me. She likes people who smile constantly. The tea is cool and weak. She probably doesn't like working with new people.

I'm temping at the moment. Usually I freelance. Homebirths are my speciality. I move around a lot. I like change. I never drive the same car for more than a few months. I'm always colouring, cutting, or extending my hair. I buy new clothes in each new town. It's a kind of tradition, now. I give the 'old' ones away, usually to the Salvation Army. I like to travel light.

June has given up screaming and has settled instead for a primal groan. Nurse Spencer is talking to her in a low, comforting voice. I crunch the polystyrene cup into a ball and slip it into my pocket. I snap on a new pair of latex gloves. My fingers slide into June easily and I can feel that her cervix is now open a full ten centimetres. If all goes well we'll have a baby within the next few minutes.

"Are you ready to push?" I ask her.

I first met June three months ago when she was interviewing midwives. She's the reason I came to Saint Mary's Hospital. I drove the three hundred kilometres to the interview and never went back home. June wanted me and it's a nice town so there was no reason for me to go anywhere else. Sister Angelika looked me up and down and through pursed lips agreed that the hospital would take me on a temporary basis. My new look had worked. Shiny, nut-coloured hair and matching brown contact lenses, all bought from the pharmacy on the way over. A woolly cardigan to go over my collared dress, showing only just enough neck to reveal the third pharmacy purchase: a cheap gold cross necklace.

"Push!" nurse Spencer urges.

June's screwed-up face is flushed now. Her clamped teeth escape her grimace.

"That's good, June. You're doing well."

Pushing, groaning, breathing.

"A few more pushes and we'll have a beautiful little boy."

A frustrated sob. A half-scream.

"We're almost there. I can see his head!"

Nurse Spencer tap dances.

With a bellow from June her baby's head crowns. Before asking her to push again I check that the umbilical cord is not wrapped around his neck.

"The hardest part is over, June," I say, "all you have to do is finish off now."

She half-nods at me. The rest of the baby slips smoothly out.

"He's out," I say, and the nurse dances again.

He's not breathing. His skin is blue. I clap him on the bum and we all hold our breath until his small cry peals out.

Nurse Spencer checks up on June while I attend to the baby. I clamp and sever the umbilical cord in a practised motion. I carry him to the corner of the room, put the suction tube into his mouth and gently wipe his skin. I weigh him. Then I swaddle him tightly in a soft cream cotton receiving blanket.

"You did such a good job," Nurse Spencer is telling June.

"Is he okay?" pants June.

"He's perfect! He'll be with you in a minute. He's just having his toes counted."

June closes her eyes and surrenders to the snowflake-patterned white sheets of her bed. Nurse Spencer fusses around her.

"Nurse," I say calmly, "call the doctor."

Her face jumps.

"Is there something the matter?" she whispers.

The words, now so familiar, need no thought.

"Just call the doctor."

She paces out of the room.

I take the syringe of tranquiliser out of my handbag, attach the needle, and puncture June's IV tube with it. I have learnt to not leave marks. As I empty the syringe, her eyes flutter open and then close again. I pick up the baby, plug his searching mouth with a pacifier, and ease him into the padded tote bag I had hidden behind the metal cabinet. I zip it up. The material is light and breathable but keeps the baby warm. This has almost become too easy. My soles squeak on the polished linoleum floor as I leave the room and turn the corner. I smile sweetly as I pass Sister Angelika in the corridor.

Within two minutes of dispatching the nurse I walk out of the hospital, gently swinging my bag. The sun is bright, the trees are green, and I have a new town to get to.

❀

10 / OFF THE HINGE

The woman at the counter is looking at me very strangely, as if I am a giant, or a midget, or as if I am wearing a shiny salmon for a hat.

'Am I wearing a shiny salmon?' I ask her. Shiny spotty silver singing salmon. Karaoke Sashimi. She blinks her marbles at me. Confusion darkens her face. I don't want to upset her.

'I don't want to upset you,' I say. 'All I need is some milk, for my tea.'

'Milk?' she says, happy that now she knows what I need and can help me.

'Milk for my tea,' I say, and she smiles. I smile back. I am happy. This is good. 'And some bone buttons, and a mouse.'

Her happy teeth disappear again, like shy sea pebbles in the tide.

'Sea pebbles,' I say.

'What?' she says. 'A mouse?'

'A mouse!' I say, laughing in her face. Funny! A mouse.

She moves away from me. Maybe she thinks I am a mouse. Maybe she is afraid of mice. If I am a mouse or not, I mean no harm. I take out my wallet. I need to pay for the milk. I search the empty counter for the white bottle.

'Where is the milk?' I ask.

'We don't sell milk here,' the lady says.

'You don't sell MILK?' I am astonished. Aghast. What kind of shop doesn't sell milk? How will I make my tea?

'I think you might be in the wrong place,' she says, windmilling her arms at her wares. 'You see, this is an antique shop.'

I look around. I see ceramic soup tureens and copper candlesticks and crystal snifters. I want to smash the crystal, although I can't think why. I'm not angry. Maybe I just want to see what will happen. I want to see the rainbow shards and splinters. I want to feel powerful. I want to destroy these pretty things and stomp them into the floor and lift my arms and bellow like King Kong.

'Is there someone I can call for you?' asks the crystal snifter lady. She is worried. I know this because her voice is a tall, pink, wobbling jelly. Raspberry?

'Hmm?'

'Your husband?' she says, then, looking at my naked ring finger: wrinkled. 'Or a ... friend?'

I don't know why she has to mention Larry. What does Larry have to do with antiques? I spin the imaginary wedding band. It's something I used to do.

'I can call someone for you, and make you a cup of tea, while you wait.'

'I *would* like a cup of tea,' I say. The truth is I feel like I could kill a cup of tea. No, that's not right. How does the saying go?

'Let me pay you for it,' I say, paging through my wallet. How much does a cup of tea cost? I have no idea.

50 cents? 50 rand? Maybe it costs 50 cents but they will charge me 50 rand and then they would have 49 rand 50 of mine that they don't deserve. That they've fleeced me of. It appears that antique dealers are not to be trusted.

'No, no,' she says, hiding her marbles with eyelid-skin at seeing my open wallet. 'It's not necessary. Really. Please, take a seat.'

She motions towards an over-waxed mahogany piece carved with balls and claws. It has a balding maroon velvet seat. There is dust in the air. I can't see it but it is tickling the end of my nose.

I don't want to sit on the antique chair. It looks untrustworthy. Also, it might bite me. I put my hands behind my back to protect my buttocks. Ball and claws. Buttock. Buttock. Buttock.

'Buttock,' I say, but the lady has vanished. She has time-travelled to the next century where she is looking for a kettle to boil. I am glad. Now I don't have to sit on the buttock-biting chair. I think she will probably be a long time, so I will leave this old copper candlestick shop and go to get the milk.

On the way out I pick up a plate. The heirloom is seashell-thin: begging to be broken. Someone has drawn a French pastoral scene on it, in powder blue. It begins to burn in my hands. I am torn between taking it with me, and throwing it against the floor as hard as I can. I want to take it in my bag. I want it to shatter. I want to hold it against my chest like a newborn baby. I want it in smithereens. The word 'smithereens' makes me think of polystyrene.

'Polystyrene,' I say. I slip the plate into my bag and step out of the shop.

There are lots of people on this road. Lots of cars. I need to walk upright so that the shiny salmon doesn't fall off my head. In school they would award certificates for deportment. Walk like you have a rodding iron for a backbone and get a gilt-edged certificate. A golden backbone. A Mary Poppins song pops into my head. The one about flying kites. There it is, the song, barbed in my brain, and the words come over and over. LET'S go FLY A KITE, UP to the HIGHEST HEIGHT. The lyrics boomerang between my temples. I hum along. I try not to stomp in rhythm with the song. I don't want people to stare. Like that man over there in the silly chef's pants, with his arms crossed in front of his chest, white smoke trailing out of his nose like a magic dragon. As if he has swallowed fire.

He is looking at me. How rude. I will just walk right past and ignore him. He keeps looking. His eyebrows are steep, and too dark. Much too dark. I don't like them one bit.

'Buttock,' I say, and keep walking.

The sun is a big hot ball travelling the sky in slow-motion. I'm really thirsty now. I find a shop that looks like it might sell milk. I go straight up to the counter. Spit-Spot. No dawdling.

'Do you sell milk?' I ask, perhaps a trifle loudly. A trifle loudly. A loud trifle. Goodness. That sounds delicious. I would like to eat a Loud Trifle. It sounds like something out of an Enid Blyton fantasy novel.

The young man in the shop is too skinny. He could do with eating a Loud Trifle. I want to tell him so, but what good will come of that? I bite my tongue.

'Milk? Like, a glass of milk?' he says, as if he doesn't understand. As if milk is a philosophical concept that is difficult to grasp. His hair is pointing in all different directions as if he has just woken up from a particularly frightening dream. His skin has writing on it. He could do with a good wash.

'A bottle of milk, for my tea,' I say.

'So you want *tea*?'

Perhaps he needs more than a good wash. A lesson in English comprehension, for one.

'Yes,' I say slowly. 'Milk. For. Tea.'

He is embarrassed now (I would be too!) and rubs his head pelt possum pear.

'So,' he says, cleaning the sleep from his eye, 'do you want tea, or do you want milk?'

Am I not speaking clearly? Is the idea of buying milk just too complicated for mere mortals like this dirty skeleton to comprehend? I feel instantly exhausted by the dire hopelessness of the human race. I feel drained. Doomed. I need to sit down. Luckily there are lots of tables and chairs in this shop. Perhaps it is a furniture shop. The chairs here are not dusty and they are not buttock-biters. It feels good to rest my golden spine. The grubby skeleton brings me a glass of milk and a cup of tea. This does not help my cause whatsoever. I need to leave, to find a bottle of milk to take home with me. Poor Larry, he has probably keeled over from his lack of tea this morning. Keel peel kipper. Shiny Salmon. I can't drink the tea on the table in front of me, as much as I want to. It wouldn't be fair to Larry. How would he feel, if he saw me here, knocking back a good, hot cuppa while he is in the very process of keeling over from the thirst? No. I can't take a sip. Not one. I need to leave. I make it out the door and 3 shops down before the unwashed calls me.

'Your milk!' he shouts. 'Your tea!'

I scrabble over the cobblestones. I can smell the sea in the air. I'm afraid the skelly will follow me but he just stands there, wiping his hands on his floury apron of defeat. I don't know what I was doing, looking to buy milk at a

furniture shop. My head needs checking. I try to swallow the dryness in my throat.

I want to walk faster now, but am feeling lightheaded. When last did I eat? I keep going. There must be some kind of corner shop, some kind of convenience store. Damn it, what kind of street is this, anyway? I shiver; my golden backbone is chilled from head to tail. Perhaps my pelvis is turning into metal, too. What kind of award would present you with a golden pelvis? I'm not sure I'd like to know. I should have had that tea at that furniture shop. It looked like a good cup of tea. It's not easy to find a good cup of tea. Larry wouldn't have been happy, but then, is Larry ever happy?

The light is evaporating. The sun has had enough of shining. I feel a bluebottle of adrenaline shoot through my veins. How can it be so late? Larry will be worried! He'll be furious. I'm quite sure that I left the house this morning, not more than an hour ago! What has happened to the day? I wrap my cardigan around me. I can't go home without milk, though. Then it'll become A Story. No, no, no. I will not go home empty-handed. I will not be butt of yet another bitter joke. I'll try one more shop. I could assassinate a cup of tea. No. I could … execute a cup of tea?

The wind is picking up and I feel the grey shadows creeping along the pavements and up my legs. I count the signs shouting 'CLOSED' until I run out of fingers but then there is one store with a front door flung open with golden light and laughter. I dispense with formalities and just yell 'Milk!' to the people inside. They are wearing cocktail dresses and sipping rubies from glasses. When they notice me they stop and peer over. There are too many steep

eyebrows on this street. I don't like it one bit.

'Milk!' I yell again. I lift my wallet at them, as if to signal that I will pay for it. I don't care how much it costs. I will pay 50 rand for a bottle of milk if that's what they want. I hear dead leaves gusting along the street. They flutter up against the glass façade. There are tears in my eyes, but I'm not sure why. I blink them away and see art on the walls. I want to tell them about the antique lady who is now in another time-dimension searching for teabags and sugar, and the barely-skinned skeleton with writing on him. I want to tell them about Larry who will most definitely have something to say about me going out for a bottle of milk for tea and disappearing for 10 hours.

I'll never hear the end of it.

My mouth is dry; glued together. I try to use spit to un-stick my tongue.

I'm about to tell them that I have an extremely fragile plate in my bag when I see the distaste in their painted faces. They don't want me here. They don't want to hear about my bottle of milk. There may be luxurious light all around them but there is no light in their eyes. They are all wearing masks. They are aliens. Not the kind that abduct you.

I turn around too quickly and stumble; hurting my bad ankle. I feel the twinge all the way up the left side of my body. I grit dry teeth in lieu of a gasp. I limp.

'Wait!' I hear from behind me, but I don't stop, because I don't want to talk to the aliens, even if they don't want to

abduct me.

'Wait!' I hear again, closer, almost in my ear. There is a young woman at my elbow. I recoil at her extra-terrestrial touch. She is breathing hard, as aliens are known to do. It's the atmosphere here on earth; the thin air. It's not good for them.

'I must get on,' I say. The sooner I leave this alien art gallery the better.

'Where do you stay?' she asks. 'Let me call you a taxi. My treat.'

That's what aliens say just before they abduct you.

'No, no, no,' I say, trying to get away. She laser-beams my face with hers until she no longer looks like an alien wearing a mask but a real person with tiny red veins in her eyes and pores on her nose. Lunar craters. I stare at her nasal moonscape. I don't know how she did that. It's a good trick.

'That's a good trick,' I say to her.

'Please,' she says. 'It's cold outside and you're hardly wearing anything.'

This takes me by surprise. I look down and see that I am still in my nightgown. A pair of dog-gummed slippers and a moth-eaten cardigan complete the look souk sunny. Funny.

Bone buttons.

'I can't go home without the milk,' I say.

'I don't have any,' she says, looking around at the rubies and champagne. 'If I did, I would give it to you.'

I don't want her alien milk, anyway. It would probably taste like mice. Larry wouldn't approve. I reclaim my elbow and leave.

The street is dark. The shops are closed. I don't know how I'm going to find milk now. The people have all packed up and gone home. They don't see me skipping over cracks in the pavement in my white cotton dress. They don't see an ancient white fairy gliding down their lonely black road.

I am so thirsty, I feel like I could drink the moonlight. It would taste like home-made ginger-beer. It would prickle and pop in the back of my throat.

'Stop,' says the tall man with the massive dog's head on his shoulders. I have never seen such a big dog's head. I have never seen a man with a dog's head. He is a Husky. He has those keen blue Husky eyes and black triangles for ears which would disappear against the night if he wasn't in the habit of shaking them at me. There is something in his voice that makes me obey. No, that's not right. It's not something *in* his voice but his *actual* voice that makes me stop. A Husky's voice will do that.

The wind is a wet sheet on my back, but I don't move. Perhaps he is the antique watchdog, sent from an outer-century.

'You've come for the plate?' I ask. 'I didn't mean to take it.'

'No,' says the dogman, with the ginger-beer reflection

in his eyes.

'The plate is of no use where we are going,' he says. He adjusts his handsome black cloak. It looks warm.

'We?' I say, shivering.

'We,' he says.

'How can a plate be of no use? A plate is always of use,' I say. I don't mean to argue with the Husky but, ultimately, common sense must prevail.

'That is true,' he pants, 'but broken plates are less useful.'

I stick my hand into my bag and feel the daggers of the broken plate. Smithereens. Polystyrene. I am sorry. When the crystal-snifter lady gets back from her time-travelling I will apologise, and pay for the plate. I look down at my wallet, wondering if I have enough money.

'What are you doing?' asks the Husky.

'I'm counting my money,' I say. 'This is my wallet.'

'That's a funny-looking wallet,' he says. I want to say that he is a funny looking man, or a funny looking dog, but I don't. I don't want to be rude. I look down at my wallet again and see what he means. It's not a wallet at all, but a book. No wonder no-one would sell me a bottle of milk. I was trying to pay them with a secondhand paperback.

'What is the story about?' says the dog. He speaks right into my face, like dogs do, but he does not have dog-biscuit breath. Perhaps he doesn't eat dog biscuits. His whiskers

are fishing lines that cast around for things. I don't know what things yet.

I look down again, turn the book over in my hands. It is familiar to the touch. I have held this book for a long time. The cover art is blurry. I can't read the title. I try to concentrate, to force it into focus. Finally, the words appear. OFF THE HINGE, it says. It rings a bell.

The dogman tries again: 'Do you know what it's about?'

'What are all stories about?' I say.

'Love,' pants the canine. 'Loneliness. Redemption.'

'Yes,' I say. I watch his pink tongue vibrate. 'Where are we going?'

He starts to howl. You'd think that it would make me feel uncomfortable, standing there on the street, watching a wolfman howl, but I'm not. It feels right. I won't join in, even though I am tempted to. It's a beautiful sound. When he stops howling it's like a sound-vacuum. Like the world will never be complete again until the howling recommences. I'm amazed at how I have spent my whole life without it.

'Is it time to go?' I ask.

'Yes,' says the dog. 'Are you ready?'

'I don't know.'

All of a sudden it's like being in a stress-dream where I am woefully unprepared: sitting naked in class during an exam, or realising the morning of my wedding day that I

had forgotten to buy a white dress. My underarms start to perspire, although I can't see how. I thought there was no moisture left in my body.

'What about my husband?' I say. 'He'll keel over without me.'

'Larry?' says the dog.

'Of course, Larry,' I say. 'Do I have any other husbands?'

'Larry left a long time ago,' says the wolfman. 'You do not need to worry about him.'

There's a lightning bolt of recognition in my brain. The keeling over of Larry is not a thought, but a memory.

'He left?'

'Metaphysically speaking,' barks the dog.

'He died?' I say, and as the words leave my mouth I know that it is true.

'There is no such thing as 'death',' says the giant dog head.

I am relieved. Mostly because I am no longer in trouble with Larry.

'What do I need to take with me?' I say. 'I suppose a shiny salmon will not come in handy?'

'I have eaten the salmon,' says the dogman. 'It has served its purpose.'

I feel for my hat and it is true: there is nothing on top of my head.

'To be prepared,' says the Husky, 'you will need a book, a baby, and a bag.'

Oh dear, I think. Where will I find a baby at this late hour?

'Look inside your bag,' pants the dog. I peer inside, expecting to see the French shards, but instead there is a tiny mewling baby with writing on her skin. It is the powder-blue pastoral scene. I lift the baby out and hold her to my chest. I shush her and tell her that everything will be alright. I pat her back until she's quiet.

'Will there be milk, where we are going?' I ask, not without hope. He fixes his ginger-beer cataracts on me.

'There will be milk.'

I'm not convinced. He makes it sound so easy to find milk, and I know that it's not. My mouth is a cotton ball.

Buttock.

'Will there be enough?' I ask. The tattooed baby sleeps peacefully in my arms.

'Where we are going,' he barks, 'there is enough of everything. Come gently, now. It is time.'

'But, specifically, milk?'

'There will be rivers of milk,' he fibs. A dairy-white lie. 'Cream waterfalls. Gushing dams of liquid lactose. A deluge

of moo-juice. Enough to bath in. To swim in. To canoe in. To sink an ocean-liner in.'

The Husky takes my face in his hands. They are velvet. He opens his mouth and leans towards me with his non-biscuity breath. I think he's going to kiss me but then his shiny salmon tongue is combing my hair. He tames my grey bird's nest. He grooms me as if I am a stray kitten. Perhaps that is what I am.

My eyes are watering again. I think it must be the relief. He swishes his coat until it covers all three of us and we begin to walk together. His whiskers trawl the night air. We walk off the edge of the Earth, where the universes are hinged together. The night explodes with stars.

The metallic tasting meteor-light cuts through my every need.

It's a different kind of milk, thinks the Husky, and I can hear his thoughts.

Of course, I think back at him. I get it. When you have this, you don't need milk. It's the same as having enough milk to canoe in. It's actually better.

Yes, pants the Husky. You get it. It's better.

✵

11 / STICKY FINGERS

I learnt how to keep a secret when I was three years old.

It started on an ordinary day — a sunny Jo'burg afternoon. I was in my mom's arms while she was buying cigarettes from the sweet counter at Checkers. She used to smoke the Dunhill 30s that came in a wide red and gold box, (with gold foil inside!), and a white underside that was perfect for scribbling shopping lists and working out math problems. When making this smoker's stop after doing the grocery shopping, she'd always let us choose a few little chocolates for the sweetie bowl at home. Maybe it made her feel less guilty about spending money on cigarettes, or smoking around us. Maybe it was just her being kind; even on a teacher's salary she was always generous.

She'd give us each a silver bowl and my older brother and I would be allowed to choose a few different treats. We always went for the chocolates – the other stuff was a waste of time. My favourites were the chocolate-peanut clusters, followed closely by the chocolate-coconut clusters. The bowls were then weighed and paid for: a sweet ritual.

That day, while everyone else's eyes were on the scale, including mine, a little three-year-old hand reached out towards the sweets and, before I knew it, there was a chocolate toffee finger melting in my pocket.

I don't know what made me steal it. Mom had already bought me the chocolates I had wanted (I'm not even sure I liked chocolate toffee fingers). Perhaps I was just born an opportunist. Maybe my kleptomania was inherent to my make-up, along with my bad temper, green eyes and big feet.

Sometimes I wonder if I would still be a thief if that first incident hadn't happened … if I hadn't experienced that hot thrill of having something that didn't belong to me.

If, for some reason, I had resisted that first childish impulse to grab, perhaps my restless heart wouldn't be forever waiting for The Next Nice Thing To Steal.

Was I too young to understand right from wrong? Perhaps. I did show off my loot the moment we got into the car, which makes me think that I didn't know what I had done was wrong. Wasn't it quite clever of me to get something for nothing? I don't remember if I was expecting praise or punishment. I did learn then that I shouldn't show anyone what I had stolen, no matter how urgent the desire becomes. That's when I learnt how to keep a secret.

When I was five I kidnapped two dolls from nursery school. I sneaked them out in my scruffy cardboard suitcase. It wasn't so much 'stealing' in my mind, then, it was more the fact that I loved the dolls so much that I thought they

should be living at home with me. Their names were Nadia and Devon. Once the stowaways were discovered, my mother marched me to the teacher to return them, and apologise. The teacher was so very kind about it – not only did she not scold me, but she agreed that, as I was such a good 'mother' to the dolls, I should be allowed to keep them. She was sure that they would be happier with me. Looking back now, I wonder if this confused my developing moral compass.

Whatever caused it, bad genes or bad luck, I am, and (most likely always will be), a thief. It took me a while to admit it, but that doesn't make it any less true. There is no arguing with the two hundred and sixty four lipsticks I have stashed under my bathroom sink, or the army of restaurant salt and pepper cellars that take up an entire double-cupboard in the kitchen. In my 20s I referred to myself as a 'collector'. I was making a stand against soulless industrialisation and crass materialism: 'Look,' I thought, 'I can take this without anyone even *noticing*.'

Row upon row of similar trinkets: my cupboards looked like Andy Warhol installations. I thought I was smart, ironic. I wasn't fooling anyone.

Sometimes I take things for specific reasons. I was at a cocktail party a few months ago and the hostess was this awful person. She had a horsey face and kept guffawing all over the place. She kept forgetting my name and calling me 'love', and I know it was because I'm a housewife and she thinks I don't matter. I turned my back on her soggy canapés but it wasn't enough: I knew I'd have to take something of hers, and I did. She didn't deserve to have the sweet ceramic rabbit miniature I found in her display

cabinet, and I was certain he was much happier when he left in my clutch later that night.

It could also be due to nominative determinism. You know, like when your name is Bolt and you become the fastest sprinter in the world. Or Candy, and you become a stripper. Maybe that last example isn't such a good one; that's more like just changing your name to suit your talent. My name is Nicolette, and people call me Nicky or Nick. It's quite funny, I think, and I catch myself wanting to tell people, but of course, I can't.

It's lonely, being a klepto. So much of your existence revolves around your conquests and close calls, but you can never share that part of your life with other people. Last week I took the most beautiful orange and cream silk scarf from Poetry (scarves are one of the easiest things to steal, apart from panties and lipstick) — but I can't tell anyone about it. It has the most charming elephant print on it. I can't even wear it, because if Derek, my husband, sees it, he'll demand to see the receipt.

Sometimes I fantasize about an online dating site that caters to people like me. Of course I wouldn't actually date anyone — I'm happily married! — but it would be wonderful to just meet some like-minded people and share our stories.

Derek keeps giving me more cash. He sneaks it into my wallet and I pretend that I don't notice. I already have two credit cards that he pays off every month. He has always had so much money ... it frustrates him to not be able to pay to make this problem go away. But it's not about money. He doesn't understand.

My best friend, Sylvia, is the only one I can really talk to, but I can't tell her everything either. She is one of the least judgmental people I know, but even she has her limits. I have to be careful to select only the stories I am bursting to tell, and hide everything else, like the fake pearls I took from my sister-in-law's jewellery box on Saturday, and the sandalwood-scented candle I got from the esoteric shop at Rosebank Mall. Esoteric shops are so easy to lift from: they are all too often dimly lit, have poor security measures, and the shop assistants simply don't expect their customers to steal. Bad karma, and all of that.

When I hold back from telling Sylvia for a few weeks she gets this bright look in her eyes. 'You're getting better!' she'll say. Or, 'You've turned a corner!'

She can be so naïve.

She's never really had any money, not much anyway, but I'm sure she hasn't stolen a thing in her life. A few years ago she made me start writing down, item for item, the things I was taking. She thought I was in denial about the extent of my 'problem' (I'm not). But I enjoyed the exercise of recording my acquisitions, and I still do it. I have 12 (stolen) notebooks full of excited entries. They read like accountant's ledgers. The pages are well thumbed ... one of my favourite things to do is to go through the lists and remember the moments they brought with them. It makes me feel like a 'collector' again. It makes it more real, in a way. More ... honest. The books are stacked underneath our bed. Only Sylvia knows about them.

I met Sylvia years ago at one of Derek's company's functions. They worked in the same building but had never

met. I actually introduced them, and now we're all great friends. We've got a lot in common. Over the years she's become part of the family. The kids love her. Did I mention we have kids? A four- and a six-year-old – a boy and a girl (I resisted the urge to name them Nadia and Devon). I'm sure that we look like the picture-perfect family to some. To those who don't know about my habit. Sylvia is like the kids' fairy godmother, always wooing them with gifts and food.

She's like my fairy godmother too, I guess. A couple of years ago I was caught shoplifting a pair of Dolce & Gabana sunglasses from Sandton City. Depending on your technique, sunglasses can be an easy lift, because you end up trying so many pairs on, there are bound to be some floating around the shop, unattended to. You have to do it when the shop is relatively busy — sales are always a good time — and you should arrive with a similar pair to the ones you want to nick, preferably perched on your head. Once you choose a pair, you replace the old ones with the new, *et voila*, out you flounce with a new pair of shades.

This has worked for me over and over, but on that unlucky day the security guard was paying attention. Perhaps my lipstick was too red: it was Revlon New Cherry. Bold make-up on a shoplifting spree is never a good idea; people don't trust women whose lipstick is too bright. But one gets complacent and neglects the rules. I hadn't been caught for so long that I stopped believing it could happen. Started thinking I had some kind of magical power. Ignored the bad karma of stolen lipstick.

So I made the switch quite near to the exit, and then turned to walk out, and next thing there was a strong hand

grabbing me, like a headmaster would yank the arm of a troublesome child. It was shocking, but expected, at the same time. I tried to act confused, concerned, then indignant, but I could see the guard wasn't buying it. He was quiet and kept glancing up at the red LED light of the security camera, as if waiting for someone to come down and give him the go-ahead to slap some cuffs on me. After a perfunctory exchange on his walkie-talkie, he escorted me through the mall and sat me down in a dingy office near the food court. There was another stern-looking man there. All I could smell was Cinnabon.

They weren't sure if they were going to press charges, and wanted to speak to my husband before 'taking any steps'. I gave them Sylvia's number instead. An hour later she had charmed and cajoled the two men into giving me a warning (well, a warning and a life-time ban from entering the store). She made up this story about how my husband was having an affair and I was having a minor nervous breakdown. I was impressed at what a convincing liar she was — I had never guessed it. From then on she called me 'Sticky Fingers'. She'd poke me in the ribs and say 'Take that, Sticky Fingers.'

The smell of cinnamon still unsettles me.

The next time I was caught I wasn't that lucky. Sometimes I wonder if I actually *wanted* to get caught. Either way, I guess that it would have happened sooner or later. I mean, I wasn't going to stop stealing, so it was inevitable. My lucky streak, my magical power, wasn't going to last forever. I had had so many close calls over the years, over a lifetime: my Sticky Finger Magic was due to run out.

Derek and I were staying in a luxury hotel in Camps Bay, with a room that overlooked the sea. The kids were with his mother for the weekend, and we decided at the last minute to hop on a plane to Cape Town. We were pretending to be spontaneous: it's something rich married people do to try to keep the relationship exciting. It's weird, because it's like you're pretending to be someone else for the weekend: someone young, childless, passionate, romantic. And you try to reconnect with your significant other, but he is also pretending to be that other, lighter, person, but really neither of you are yourselves. So you drink more than usual and have kinkier sex than usual, but when Monday rolls around and he is pulling out his hair looking for his favourite tie for a meeting and you are wiping toothpaste off your toddler's cheeks and this is your real life and did the weekend in Cape Town actually even happen?

But there we were, in the hotel spa, after a full body Swedish massage and a quickie in the Rasul chamber. We went to our respective change-rooms to shower and before I left I did what I always do — I checked all the lockers. It's like checking a casino slot machine or a basement parking ticket machine for abandoned coins, except that some women are lulled into such a secure stupor by their privileged lifestyles that they don't even bother to lock away their things. I got three quarters of the way through when I hit the jackpot: a shiny new snakeskin Louis Vuitton handbag, with matching wallet and belt. The bag was too big to steal, and I had no need for the belt, so I took the wallet. It was a thing of beauty, not more than a few days old. The fact that it was a wallet meant that they would probably assume that a member of staff took it, for the cash,

although I left behind her jewellery. It was gaudy: diamonds and Tanzanite. I held the necklace against my collarbone to see how it would look, just as a matter of interest. It confirmed what I already knew: blue stones are not my style.

A lady in a white spa bathrobe came in just as I was sliding the wallet into my own handbag. I played it cool, pretended that I was doing nothing unusual. I was just a woman putting her wallet into her bag. But, unfortunately for me, the robed lady happened to be the owner of the Louis Vuitton. It took a while for her to register what I was doing. I think she must have first thought: Oh, look, that lady has the same wallet as me. But then her eyes travelled to her locker, saw the door was open, saw that it had been plundered. Her face, previously scrubbed and blissful-looking, jumped into ferocious mode, and she proceeded to throw the biggest hissy fit I have seen. She was like a toddler on a double espresso. The words she was shouting at me didn't even make sense. I tried to calm her down, explain that it was a misunderstanding. I thought that it was my bag but then I realised I had brought my *other* bag, so I was putting it back. It's when I saw the jewellery that I had realised that it wasn't my locker. Tanzanite, I said, I never wear Tanzanite. That's what made me realise.

It was an unlikely story, but weaker ones had worked before. People are desperate to believe the best in other people.

... But not this manic madwoman. She seemed half outraged, half delighted to have a bit of drama in her day. Despite my constant assurances that she had misinterpreted the situation, she turned and fled the room to call security. I

used my towel, still damp from the shower, to quickly wipe down her locker and the things of hers I had touched. Now it was her word against mine.

I glided out and headed in the opposite direction to the noise she was creating at the spa reception. I left through the back door and scuttled my way up to our hotel room. Derek was asleep, naked, on the bed, and I sat on our patio, looking at the sea, waiting for the knock at the door.

It took the hotel manager 20 minutes to figure out my name and room number. It had been staring out at him from the spa appointment book. He knocked softly at first — it was easy to ignore — then louder, and he started calling my name. Derek stumbled out of bed, confused but overly alert, the way you are when your nap is (rudely) interrupted. I threw a gown at him before I opened the door.

The man doing the knocking looked apologetic the moment he saw us.

'Terribly sorry!' he kept saying. 'Terribly sorry to inconvenience you, but could you come down to the hotel reception?'

'What is this about?' Derek demanded.

'Terribly sorry! There seems to be some kind of ... I'm sure it's a misunderstanding.'

'Is there a problem?' my husband asked, still pale from sleep.

'There may not be?' said the manager. They looked at

each other for a good time, perplexed.

'I know what this is about,' I said. 'Some crazy woman at the spa was accusing me of going through her locker. She was screaming at me ... she kicked up such a fuss!'

'Yes,' said the man, clearly relieved that he wouldn't have to make an allegation. Derek sighed.

'I should have complained,' I said to both of them. 'Being accosted like that.'

'Yes ...' said the man. 'A misunderstanding. That's what I told her. Will you come down so that we can clear it up?'

I paused. An innocent woman would have flown downstairs to clear her name. I sensed that if I went down there I would get into a vast amount of trouble. Both men sensed my hesitation. The manager's eyes pleaded with me to co-operate, to not make his day any more difficult than it already was. Derek jumped in.

'Well, was anything actually taken?' he asked.

'Taken?' said the man.

'Stolen! Was anything stolen from the woman?'

He paused. 'She's not making much sense — the lady — she's very upset. It's hard to know.'

'So can you please then explain to me why you don't just tell this lady to stop fabricating defamatory stories about my wife?'

I loved Derek so much in that moment. I felt so loved, so protected. He would get me out of this. He started to close the door, but the manager stopped him. Both men were gentle; there was no tussle. The man looked intensely uncomfortable. Eventually he blurted out: 'It's the ring!'

'What ring?' asked Derek.

'That ring,' he said, motioning to my left hand. I looked down and saw a diamond and Tanzanite ring on my index finger. I didn't even remember putting it on.

Things moved both quickly and agonisingly slowly from then. The police were called and I was arrested almost immediately, and charged, but the waiting in between was torture. Hours of staring at the grimy jail cell walls. Hours sitting on cheap cracked chairs waiting for some kind of admin to be done: paperwork to be processed, questions asked, answered and repeated *ad nauseum*. When they told me that my lawyer was getting on a plane to Cape Town I wanted to tell them — tell everyone — not to bother. I wanted to say, just give me the orange overalls and tin mug and bus me to wherever the hell I'm going to end up. At the time it seemed preferable to waiting for a lawyer to make his way to me all the way from Jo'burg.

Derek had, of course, hired the best lawyer money could buy, and when Mazarakis did finally walk into the beige room they were keeping me in I was very happy to see him. You would never have said that it was a Sunday, or that he had just been on a plane, with his sharp suit and alarmingly clear blue eyes. I, on the other hand, felt that I had aged 20 years in the last few hours. I looked different, felt different: I was a completely disparate person to the

woman who had a loving husband and two beautiful children, or the woman who had had a massage overlooking the ocean that morning. My skin was whiter, thinner; my pores larger; my body vulnerable. The enchantment had been broken. I had been exposed for who I truly was.

Mazarakis was calm and measured, and explained what I was to expect in the next few hours, and days. I'd have to stay in custody overnight as they could only apply for bail on Monday morning. He was apologetic at that, as if it was his fault I had stolen the ring. He never asked me if I did actually steal anything — I think Derek must have told him about my 'problem'.

After bail was set, I was allowed to fly home with Derek. He was angry with me, cold, but still sat next to me on the plane despite lots of free seats in the first class cabin. It's a terrible feeling, knowing you have let someone down so badly. The exigent guilt settles into your body, your organs become heavy with dread.

We refused the complimentary Graham Beck brut, and the cheddar straws. They had no place in this new, upside-down world of ours. Derek had a Business Day open on his lap but I could tell he wasn't reading it. I could almost hear the thoughts crowding his head: 'What was she thinking?'; 'Why would she risk so much?'; 'What if she has to go to prison?'; 'She doesn't even *like* Tanzanite!' and, of course, 'What about the children? Who will be their mother?'

Of course, the same questions had been haunting me for years, and I could never answer them. I am dishonest by nature, but this is true: if I could have fed my addiction in a less destructive way, I would have.

During the trial, Sylvia stayed at the house with the kids. She fed them, bathed them, took them to school. She kept photos of them in her wallet and on her phone to show me when we caught up, in snatched spells during proceedings. She brought paintings that they had done for me, showing us as the perfect little family, standing outside our perfect little house. I couldn't help noticing that the mother in the picture was starting to look more like Sylvia than me.

I was so grateful that she was there to support Derek; he was taking it very badly. She would sit next to him in court, with a brave face, positively glowing in comparison to him. Every time I caught his eye he gave me this pained expression, as if he already knew it was all over.

Sylvia brought me things from home — small comforts: pajamas, toiletries, books. Even homemade chocolate peanut butter cookies, that she had baked using my recipe, in my oven.

We would have won the case, Mazarakis said so. He said there was absolutely no evidence against me, apart from that damn ring, which he creatively — and successfully — explained away as a 'misunderstanding'.

There was no convincing evidence against me, until on the day of sentencing the prosecutor received a delivery from an anonymous source. It was a large brown box full of notebooks — my lifted ledgers — full of years of detailed entries of all the things I had stolen. Of course, they were in my handwriting, and covered with my fingerprints.

When I recognised the covers and realised what they

were, it felt like I had been stabbed in the chest. A quick, nimble blade, between my ribs. In-and-out. And then a slow cold bleeding.

It turned out that I hadn't learnt how to keep a secret at all.

Only one person had known about those notebooks, and where they had been hidden. As the prosecutor introduced them to the court, and they were admitted as evidence, I looked at Sylvia, but she wouldn't return my gaze. It was then that I saw her hand on Derek's lap, and his hand on hers.

And I could hear her voice in my head, saying: 'Take that, Sticky Fingers'.

12 / ESCAPE

'He's suicidal,' says The Father. The People laugh.

'Seriously,' he says, turning back to the braai and the hot spitting sausages.

The Mother clicks her tongue. Shakes her head. Tips warm Shiraz into her mouth.

'Don't be such a drama queen.'

I make my monkey noises and she hoists me, inelegantly, onto her lap. I warm my evening-chilled cheeks on her chest. The woman who sits in The Mother's usual chair shrieks with laughter.

'You're too much,' she warbles to The Father. 'You're just too much.' She wears her perfume in a cloud. The Mother shifts irritably on the couch. Perhaps it's not as comfortable as her usual chair.

'I'm being serious, Peg,' The Father says.

Peg? I think. That's a funny name for a big lady.

'Why do you say that?' the woman asks, once her belly has stopped jiggling. 'That the baby's suicidal?'

'He has absolutely no concept of danger,' says The Father.

'That's completely normal,' says The Mother. 'How is he supposed to know not to ... not to crawl into a fire, for instance?'

'Surely they have some sense of self-preservation?' asks the man with the funny eyes who is eating all the potato chips.

'Ha!' shouts The Father, snapping his tongs. 'If only.'

I can smell red coals. Smoke and meat. Lamb chops.

'You can't expect him to know *not* to crawl into a fire,' says the Mother. 'He's a little baby. Look at the size of his head!'

'Hey?' says The Father.

'His brain is still tiny. His pre-frontal cortex hasn't been developed yet.'

'Pre-frontal cortexes have nothing to do with self-preservation. Besides, he has a bigger brain than Mojo and Mojo knows not to crawl into a fire.'

Mojo's ears shoot up at his name being mentioned. Do the humans need him? Is it time for a walk? A game? A snack? He gets up to investigate but then feels the nip in

the air; decides to go back to sleep instead. He turns around and around on his bed before he feels he is in exactly the right position and then whimpers down.

'He's a dear little thing, isn't he?' says the Peg. She means Mojo, not me.

'Yes,' smiles The Mother. 'He's a darling pup. Lovely nature. Although he did chew up Dave's slippers the other day.'

'Ah, they were old,' says The Father. 'Good riddance.'

'And he ate one of Kade's toys. Naughty puppy,' says The Mother. She says 'naughty' but she's using her vanilla voice which means that she's not really cross.

'Kade didn't seem to mind.'

'As long as it wasn't his cuddle-bunny,' says The Mother.

I am holding Cuddle Bunny by his ear. That's my favourite way to hold him.

'Nice, for a lad to have a dog,' says the man with the funny eyes. 'I expect that they'll be good friends.'

'They are, already,' says The Father. 'Mojo is very good with him.'

With everyone's attention on the dog I leap off The Mother's lap and hurtle towards the verandah floor. I hit my head hard (but not hard enough). The People gasp. There is a shocked silence, and then I wail with all my might.

'My God,' says The Father, flinging the tongs down and rushing towards me. He grabs me under the arms, lifts me up towards the light, inspects my forehead for injury. 'Did you just *drop* him?'

'No!' shouts The Mother, in pale skin. 'He just ... he leapt off!'

My forehead throbs. It grows an egg. I wail and wail like an ambulance.

'You see?' he demands of the Peg and the man with funny eyes. 'You see what I mean?'

Peg clutches her pearls.

'I think you should stop drinking,' says The Father, eyeing out The Mother's wineglass.

'Don't blame me!' shouts The Mother. 'He jumped!'

I'm getting tired now. I tone my cries down to a sad blubbering. The Father hugs me and Bunny to his woolly chest.

'Is there any ... damage?'

The man takes off his funny eyes, shines them on his flannel shirt, and puts them back on. He peers over at me as if I am a curiosity.

'Probably,' says The Father, roughly mussing my hair and kissing the top of my head.

'Mama,' I cry. 'Mama.'

'Poor little brain,' says The Mother, taki
and swaying me to the ballad in the backgrou

'Is there anything I can do?' asks the Peg.
packs more chips into his mouth.

'Yes,' says The Mother. 'You can knit him some kind
of cotton wool helmet. Some kind of … thud-guard. Or
better yet, a full-body suit. A bubble-wrap onesie.'

'A what, dear?'

'She's joking,' says the chip man, dusting his greasy
fingers.

'Kade would probably find a way to suffocate himself
with the bubble-wrap,' sighs The Father.

I don't know why they call me 'Kade' when my name is
Aaron. I wish I could tell them but the only words I have
are 'Mama,' 'Up,' and 'Bye.' It's difficult to describe my
existential angst to them with such a limited vocabulary.
How do I tell them that there's been a mistake? That I'm
not supposed to be here, with them? That I don't belong in
this body?

'It's very stressful,' says The Mother, pushing the
coleslaw around on her plate.

'Of course it is!' says the Peg. 'Having small children is
…'

'It's relentless,' says The Father. His hair has a new
glint of grey.

'Exactly,' says The Mother. She holds a hand to her

emple, as if she is the one with the egg.

I am patting Mojo. He is pretending to sleep. We are both good at that.

'I just never realised,' says The Mother, 'how … dangerous the world was, before I had Kade.'

'We spent a fortune baby-proofing this place before he was even born —'

'The pool net alone cost thousands —'

'But it's like he has a built-in danger-seeking radar.'

'If there is a sharp fork and a plug point he *will* find them both and force it in there,' says The Mother.

'If there's a ladder to climb —'

'— Or *anything* to climb —'

' — He'll climb as high as he can, and then fall.'

Or jump, I think.

'Or jump!' says The Father.

'He's like a little monkey, but without the balance,' says The Mother.

'A monkey with a death wish,' says The Father. He looks straight at me. There is affection in his frown.

The man with the funny eyes chuckles. He doesn't finish his boerewors roll. His stomach is full. He has eaten too many chips.

Chips! I think. I want some. I drop my bottle of milk and toddle over to the coffee table. I press my palm into the chip bowl. A chip sticks to my hand and I graze it off. So salty. I put all my fingers into my mouth. Yum.

'He's allowed chips?' asks the pearl-clutcher.

'Not really,' says The Father.

'Not at all,' says The Mother.

'I say,' says the man with the leftover roll on his plate, 'I say: let them shred twenty-rand notes if it keeps them quiet!'

The People laugh. I look up from my chip bowl and laugh, too. There are some spit-soggy chips in my open mouth. They look at me and laugh some more. The Mother moves towards me to take away the salty bowl. I protest.

'Shame, love,' says The Father. 'Just let him have them. It makes him happy.'

'They're not good for him,' says The Mother.

'You can't be afraid of everything, dear,' tuts the cloud of perfume.

'Easy for you to say,' mumbles The Mother under her breath.

'Here,' The Mother says to me, 'have some apple.'

She feels bad about taking the chips away. I grab the peeled slice from her hand and jam it into my mouth. The cold fruit feels good on my gums. The sweet juice leaks. I

grab another piece. I like holding food in both hands at once.

'Slowly!' she cautions. I inhale a big chunk. It's stuck. I can't breathe. The white flesh is like a cork in my throat.

Mojo is up like a shot, and barking madly.

'He's choking!' shouts The Father.

My eyes feel like they are going to pop.

Without hesitating, The Mother swoops, bending me over her haunches, so that I am upside-down with her knee buried in my stomach, and whacks me on the back so hard that I vomit all over the terracotta tiles. The apple cork is dislodged. There is a collective gasp. Air stings my lungs.

The Mother's cheeks are burning. Her eyes shine. Is she angry with me? She pins me to her breasts, not caring about the sour vomit gluing our chests together. Not angry. She starts shaking.

'Holy shit,' says The Father. 'Did that just happen?'

'I got such a fright,' cries The Mother into my scalp. 'I got such a fright.' Her limbs form a vice around me; I struggle, but she won't let me go. I relax. I burrow into her. I'm a grey mouse.

The apple-choke wasn't on purpose. It was just a happy accident. Sometimes that happens. Other times I have to get creative.

'Do you know,' says The Mother, once I am feigning sleep in the travel cot nearby and The People are discussing

my imminent demise over Pavlova, 'that he climbed into the oven once?'

'No!' says the Peg, helping herself to more dessert, licking a crumb off her thumb. 'He didn't!'

'He did!' says The Mother, topping up her wineglass. 'Don't look at me like that, David,' she snaps. 'I'm off duty now.'

The Mother calls The Father 'David' when she's upset.

'I wasn't looking at you!' says The Father. 'God knows after that we all need a stiff drink.'

The Mother blubs.

'Will you be alright, dear?' asks the Peg. 'You must have gotten such a shock.'

'He climbed into the OVEN,' she says. She wants to say more, but instead she zips her mouth closed and pushes her plate away.

'It happens. You said so, yourself. Babies don't know what is good for them,' says the man with cream on his moustache. He has found space for pudding even though he didn't finish his roll.

The Mother blubs some more. The Peg hands her a paper serviette off the table. She blows her nose. It's louder than I expected. Usually she only blows her nose loudly when we are alone.

'I'm not crying about the choking,' says The Mother. 'I'm crying because ...'

'Because you're exhausted!' says The Father. 'We don't blame you!'

'No,' says The Mother, dabbing at her nose and then making the serviette disappear in her fist. 'It's because he won't give up.'

'What do you mean?'

'If he's not flinging himself onto the floor or choking on an apple or climbing into the oven he'll do something else! It's like he won't stop until he ... until he kills himself!'

'Karen!' they all say.

'That's not true.'

'You're just upset!'

'It's just been a bad day.'

'You said so yourself,' she yells at The Father. 'He's suicidal!'

The Father laughs. 'I was joking!' he says. 'Kind of.'

This is not good for anyone. I need to escape soon. I am fond of The Mother. I don't like to see her cry.

'Why don't we take him off your hands for a couple of hours, sometime?' suggests the man with the flannel shirt. 'How about next weekend? Saturday?'

The Peg looks at him strangely.

'What?' he says. 'We managed to keep our kids alive,

didn't we?'

The Peg is clutching at her pearls again.

'You know, just so that you two can have a break. See a movie or something.'

The Mother guffaws. I think the wine is making her feel better.

'That's kind,' says The Father, 'Thank you.'

'I wouldn't be able to relax,' says The Mother. 'I feel like I am the only one who understands what a Kamikaze Kade is.'

It's *Aaron*, I think. I don't know what a Kamikaze is.

'I'm sure that within minutes he'd find a way to do some grievous bodily harm to himself.'

'Now who's being a drama queen?' asks The Father, touching her arm in a kind way.

'You know what happened at your mother's house,' she says, moving her arm away from his, knocking over her empty glass. It doesn't break. The man catches it before it rolls off the table, puts it out of the way.

'The one time I asked someone to look after him,' she says to The People, 'we almost lost him.'

'Lost him?' says the man.

'Literally and figuratively,' says The Father.

'What on earth ...?' asks the Peg.

The Father clears his throat. 'He loves buttons, you see.'

'Buttons?'

'Pressing buttons,' says The Mother. 'All babies love pressing buttons.'

'So, my mom —' starts The Father, but The Mother jumps in.

'So Dave's mother leaves her house keys — with the garage door remote on them — lying around.'

'I'm sure she didn't just leave them *lying around,*' says The Father. 'I'm sure —'

'She did, David. Okay? She did. Because she wasn't bloody well thinking.'

'It's difficult to be cross with her, because she was doing us a favour by babysitting,' says The Father.

'Speak for yourself!' says The Mother.

'And the baby —?' says the Peg.

'Kade!' says the Mother.

'K— Kade opened the garage door?' asks saucer-eyed Peg.

The Father rubs his face with his hands; warms the back of his neck. Looks out into the dark leaves of the

garden. The full moon floating in the pool.

'Not only did he open the door,' says The Mother, animated by the drink or her fury or both, 'but he CRAWLED OUT OF THE PROPERTY AND INTO THE STREET!'

'No!' says the Peg. 'No!'

'Into the busy street!' says The Mother, happy at Peg's alarm.

'We all make mistakes,' shrugs The Father. The Mother gives him a look that would sear steak.

'You know what the worst part is?' she says.

'You mean that wasn't the worst part?' gapes the Peg.

'The worst part is that she didn't even *realise he was missing*. He was NINE MONTHS OLD and crawling in the road. Do you know how small a 9-month-old is? There is no way a car would have seen him in time.'

'Heavens,' says the Peg.

The Mother barks a laugh. It's not a nice sound. Mojo twitches in his sleep.

'So what happened?'

'The security patrol car found him. Saw the open garage. Put two and two together. Rang the doorbell.'

'Oh my God,' says the man. 'You were so lucky!'

'Lucky?' splutters The Mother.

'We were,' says The Father. 'Incredibly lucky.'

'What is lucky,' demands The Mother, hot-cheeked again, 'about almost losing my child?'

She stands up with a clatter and begins clearing away the cream-smeared plates. There is no more talking. I watch her through crescent eyelids. Soiled serviettes roll like tumbleweed into the bin. She sweeps meringue rocks in after them. Tears stream down her face and out of her nose. She swipes at them with her sleeves.

The People get up from the table. They begin rinsing glasses and loading the dishwasher. The Father takes The Mother aside and takes the cutlery out of her hands. Hugs her. He can tell that she is on the verge of some kind of explosion, or deflation. She resists at first, then melts into him. He pats her hair, not unlike the way I pat Mojo. That's what friends do.

I can see that my time has run out. This can't continue. I have to escape tonight. I have no choice. Tonight is the night.

'Thanks for helping,' sniffs The Mother once the kitchen is clean and the tea towels have been hung to dry. She eases the door of the dishwasher closed and turns it on. The water splashes through the machine. The arm whirrs. The soap pocket springs open. She leans against it, as if to keep the door closed. As if, without her weight, it would leap open without warning and douse everyone with foam. Her eyes are black. I don't know why The Father doesn't

tell her to wash her panda-eyes off.

'Why don't you sit down, dear,' says the Peg, her pearls hanging freely now. 'We'll make you a nice hot drink. A cup of tea?'

The Mother sags under the sympathy. She sags all the way down onto the couch.

This is good. If they stay in the lounge they won't be able to see me climb out of my cot. I wait until the kettle is boiled and the teaspoons stop tinkling in the mugs and the milk is put away. When I am sure they are all settled in the lounge I use Cuddle Bunny as a step (I have been practising this while The Parents sleep) and climb to the top of the cot and from there I crawl onto the counter. Success! I love being this high up. Getting down, on the other hand, proves to be tricky. Usually I would just jump but I need to be very quiet now.

The People are talking in muted tones. I can no longer make out what they are saying. I hear ceramic mugs being set down on the glass coffee table. I guess that I have five minutes, at the most, before my absence is detected. I'll have longer if The People want to leave and The Parents go outside to wave. I climb down from the counter onto the floor without making a noise but then my fluffy one-piece pyjama-suit makes me clumsy and I trip over the rippled edge of the oriental carpet and fall spread-eagled onto the floor. Mojo barks.

'Sssh!' I say to Mojo.

The People stop talking. They strain their ears.

'Was that Kade?' asks The Mother, of no one in particular.

'I'm sure he's still fast asleep,' says The Father. 'If he starts crying I'll go to him.'

'Has he always slept in that travel cot? In the dining room?' asks the Peg.

'Yes,' says The Mother. 'I need to have him close-by.'

Ever since I tried to suffocate myself with my baby duvet The Mother monitors my slumber compulsively.

'Do you want to check on him now? Will it make you feel better?' asks the man.

'No,' sighs The Mother. 'No, I'm sure he's fine.'

I wait a few seconds and then start making my way to the back door. There is a small step which I almost always forget, but not this time. I hop down into the cold night air. There is still warmth coming from what is left of the fire. The last of the embers glow in the breeze. I scamper across the wide verandah and onto the cold black grass. The ground is uneven and I fall again, but this time it's a soft landing. I crawl the last metre to the pool.

I love the pool. During the day when the sky is in it, it looks like such a happy place. A blue invitation. Now it has swallowed all the night around it. It's an oily abyss.

I crawl to where Mojo has chewed an opening in the pool net. There is no time for goodbyes. I turn around and lever myself in backwards, as if I am scuttling down stairs.

In a way, I am. I slip in silently.

People think drowning is a noisy affair. They imagine shouting and splashing. But when it's a toddler doing the drowning it's as quiet as falling asleep. Once the baby slides underwater you can't hear their flailing. Those are the babies that don't want to escape.

There is no flailing for me. I do not struggle as I sink. Taking the first slug of water is difficult but after that I relax. The water is a lead blanket of calm and my heart begins to drift away. The water tips my chin upwards and lifts my arms, as if inviting me to dance. My body slowly turns and I can feel the darkness is stealing me away: black smoke wrapping itself around my mind, taking me apart.

Fulfilling my destiny is everything I imagined: a soul-searing joy; a terrible bliss. Death is a welcome vacuum. As the last of my thoughts roll away, I think: Finally, I am where I should be.

The darkness is splintered by a cacophony. Urgent barking that goes on and on until there are hurried footsteps and I am hauled rudely out of the water and into the light. Screaming. Shouting. Shaking.

'He's not breathing!' a woman yells. 'I can't find his pulse!'

People are talking urgently. There are strange warm lips on mine. My sleeping lungs balloon. My ribs crack. My bliss evaporates as I cough and choke. I spew water from my mouth. Air assaults my insides. What is happening? Where am I? Who are these People hunched over me with

their anxious bulging faces? Why is that creature making such a noise? Is this what it is like to be born? I was happy in the water but this is so cold. So very cold.

The woman who has been pumping my chest cries out when she sees that I am awake. Breathing. She strips the wet fabric from my marble body and puts me under her shirt, directly onto her hot silk of skin. She smells right. She crushes me. She cries. I realise: this must be The Mother. This feels right. There is a man standing: dripping. He stops yelling into his phone and envelops us in his arms. He is The Father. A blanket is thrown around us.

'Kade!' sobs The Mother. 'Kade!' She doesn't have any other words. The Father sobs too.

Kade, I think. That must be my name. That feels right.

I am very tired. I snuggle in, to stop the shivering. I breathe in the milk-silk scent of The Mother. I feel like I am home.

The dog finally stops barking.

✿

CONTENTS

JAM

This book is dedicated to Julia-Ann Malone,
my Patron Saint of Short Stories.

2016 Paperback edition

ISBN-13: 978-0-620-71672-7

Published in South Africa by Pulp Books.

The following stories have been previously published: "Grey Magic" in *Wax & Wane,* "Bridge Gate" in *Common Thread.* In addition, "Bridge Gate"; "The Itch"; "The Unsuspecting Gold Digger"; "Travelling Slacks"; "Something Borrowed"; "She Did It"; "Pigeon Pair"; "The Little Pink Book"; "Off The Hinge"; "Sticky Fingers" and "Escape" were commissioned, produced and broadcast by SAFM.

https://pulpbooks.wordpress.com

Book design by JT Lawrence • Cover photograph courtesy of Canva.com

STICKY FINGERS

A Collection of Short Stories

JT LAWRENCE

ALSO BY JT LAWRENCE

The Memory of Water (2011)

Why You Were Taken (2015)

The Underachieving Ovary (2016)

Grey Magic (2016)

How We Found You (2017)

A NO-FRILLS APPROACH TO PUNCTUATION

For most of us, what we know about punctuation is derived from early education and from subconsciously absorbing how punctuation is used in the material we read. This has provided us with the knowledge to get by in most situations. To progress from that point to a reasonable mastery of punctuation is a fairly simple task using the following framework.

The basic element of the English language is the sentence. Sentences may be of any length, from one word, to hundreds. No matter how long or short, sentences always contain three basic elements: (1) subject (who or what), (2) verb (what the subject did), and (3) object (who or what the subject did it to).

> John drove the car.

In the sentence above, John (who) is the subject, drove (what John did) is the verb, and the car (what John drove) is the object. The sentence is terminated with a period, which indicates to the reader that it is a simple statement of fact. If the sentence were to end in a question mark:

> John drove the car?

the reader would read the sentence as a question, and mentally add a rise in tone to match the way it would sound if spoken. If the sentence were to end in an exclamation point:

> John drove the car!

the reader could read the sentence as if it was said in anger, as if the speaker were surprised, or if the speaker were elated. The true intention of the sentence would depend on how it was used in context.

The period, the question mark, and the exclamation point are terminating punctuation marks. Commas, colons, dashes, and ellipses may also be used as terminating marks.

Commas, colons, and dashes are frequently used to terminate introductory elements added to a sentence:

> There was no denying it, John drove the car.
>
> The sheriff was sure of it: John drove the car.
>
> They all agreed on one point—John drove the car.

Dashes and ellipses are used to terminate incomplete statements in dialogue:

"John drove the car; I'm convinced of—" George stopped as John entered the room.

"They all say John drove the car, but what if . . ." The inspector's voice trailed off as he contemplated a new line of thought.

Punctuation marks are also used to separate parts of sentences. Termination of introductory elements, illustrated above, is one example of how punctuation separates one part of a sentence from another. Commas, semicolons, and dashes are all employed as separating devices. Commas are also used to separate main clauses in a sentence:

Dave supplied the gas, but John drove the car.

[Main clauses are complete sentences, able to stand alone if separated.]

Semicolons separate independent statements when they are joined in a compound sentence because of their close relationship:

John drove the car; Joyce and Debbie only went along for the ride.

Dashes are used to separate parts of a sentence the writer wishes to emphasize:

One fact stands out above all else—John drove the car!

A third function of punctuation is to enclose parts of sentences or independent statements to improve clarity. Used in pairs, commas, dashes, parentheses, quotation marks, both double and single, and brackets are employed for this purpose.

A large portion of the enclosing function is to set apart parenthetical elements in sentences. These are words, phrases, or clauses that amplify or explain something in the main sentence, or offer a digressive statement related to it.

Incidental parenthetical elements in a sentence are enclosed by commas.

John, in fact, drove the car.

[A transitional parenthetical expression.]

John, the boy who dated Julia last summer, drove the car.

[A parenthetical appositive. An appositive restates, amplifies, explains, or further identifies the noun or pronoun that precedes or follows it.]

Dashes are employed when the writer wishes to emphasize a parenthetical element:

John—boy would I like to get my hands on that kid!—drove the car.

Parentheses are used when the information enclosed is more of an aside to the reader than closely related to the main sentence:

John (I wish I could remember his last name) drove the car.

Double quotation marks enclose words quoted from a speaker, or a text:

"John," he said, "drove the car."

On page five, he wrote: "John drove the car."

Single quotation marks enclose quoted material within quoted material:

"I watched as he wrote, 'John drove the car,' in his report," he told the inspector.

Brackets are used to enclose remarks by the writer that are not a part of the main text:

John drove the car. [Once this was known, the mystery was solved, and the inspector closed the case.]

The examples above illustrate three basic uses of punctuation: *terminating*, *separating*, and *enclosing, to set off*. These three functions represent the majority of applications for punctuation in the English language, and offer a framework for mastering its use.

Notice that in each case, the basic sentence, "John drove the car," remained the same. Introductory elements and parenthetical information were added to increase the amount of information presented, and to clarify the meaning. Each time something was added to the original sentence, it was set off by punctuation marks. Each example illustrates the original premise that punctuation shows the reader what words to read together, where to pause for emphasis or importance, when to separate closely-related thoughts, and where one statement ends and another begins. Understanding these simple basics is the key to understanding punctuation. Learn to apply the principles of *terminating*, *separating*, and *enclosing*, and you have learned how to punctuate.

We want to make it clear at this point, that there is a difference between punctuation and grammar. Grammar is the study of the classification of words, their inflections, and their functions and relationships in sentences. Punctuation is the practice of inserting standardized marks in sentences to clarify meaning and separate structural units. Knowing how to punctuate will not by itself make you a better writer, but it will make what you write more understandable.

Because punctuation and grammar go hand-in-hand, a mastery of punctuation will increase your awareness of grammatical sentence structure. In time, your writing will improve to the extent that your subconscious mind has absorbed the principles of grammar from your early education and from your reading. You can accelerate this process by studying additional texts.

Punctuation marks are listed in alphabetical order in this handbook to allow quick reference. We encourage you to browse through the text to pick up general information, as well as use it as a reference manual. By applying the basic framework concept described in this chapter, you can rapidly assimilate the most common principles of punctuation use. A solid mastery of punctuation should follow soon after.

Please note as you read through the text, that the main purpose of this handbook is to present as complete and clear a presentation of the principles of punctuation to as wide an audience as possible. With this in mind, the authors have made a conscious effort to use as few technical words or expressions associated with the study of grammar as possible. Technical words or expressions that are used, are defined in a glossary following the main text. Lesser-known terms are defined both in the text immediately following their use, and in the glossary. To help clarify some rules of punctuation, portions of example sentences are underlined to highlight the area under discussion.

APOSTROPHE '

The apostrophe is used to show possession, to form plurals, and to indicate the omission of letters or numbers.

I. USE AN APOSTROPHE TO INDICATE POSSESSION

A. Add an apostrophe and an "s" to singular nouns and proper nouns not ending in "s" to form the possessive:

Sam's chair	President Reagan's strategy
the cat's collar	his mother's husband
a ship's captain	the car's windshield

B. Singular nouns and proper names ending in "s," "ss," or an "s" sound form the possessive by adding an apostrophe and an "s":

Dickens's *Great Expectations*	the waitress's pen
the boss's office	Mars's beard
the gas's odor	Yeats's poetry
Porfirio Diaz's regime	the bus's door

(1.) The names "Jesus" and "Moses" are traditional exceptions. The possessive case is formed by adding only an apostrophe.

Jesus' parables	Moses' law

(2.) Greek or hellenized names of more than one syllable ending in "s" or with an "s" or "eez" sound take only and apostrophe to form the possessive.

Archimedes' inventions	Parmenides' philosophy
Dionysius' torture	Theocritus' poems
Orestes' life	Xerxes' reign

(3.) Traditionally, certain nouns that end with "s" or "ce" and are followed by a word beginning with "s" take only an apostrophe to form the possessive.

for goodness' sake   for appearance' sake

for conscience' sake   for rightousness' sake

C. Add an apostrophe and an "s" to plural nouns not ending in "s" to form the possessive:

the deer's favorite drinking spot   the men's club

the children's toys   the alumni's dinner

D. Plural nouns and plural proper names ending in "s" use only an apostrophe to form the possessive:

the puppies' food   the Smiths' apple trees

the Joneses' party   the four dentists' chairs

a teachers' meeting   the two churches' rummage sale

E. Compound nouns use an apostrophe and an "s" on the last word of the compound to form the possessive:

my mother-in-law's books   the man-of-war's guns

his brother-in-law's business   the president-elect's files

the mothers-in-law's books   *[plural compound]*

F. To show joint ownership, the last noun is possessive and takes an apostrophe:

his grandmother and grandfather's trip to China

Mr. Kefauver and Ms. Townsend's bar

Muriel and Dan's dog

the Katzes and the Rosses' beach house

G. To show separate ownership, each noun is possessive and takes an apostrophe:

Eva's and Scott's exam

the hamsters' and rabbits' food

Wilson's or Harding's or Hoover's presidency

the professors' and the students' and the administration's grievances

H. Indefinite pronouns use an apostrophe and an "s" to form the possessive:

one's car	someone else's cup	each other's
everybody's responsibility		no one's mistake

I. Certain general expressions of possession use an apostrophe:

cow's milk	traveler's check
writer's cramp	confectioner's sugar

(1.) An apostrophe is used with some expressions even when actual ownership is not indicated.

a stone's throw	two weeks' worth
wit's end	a day's work

J. A double possessive uses both "of" and an apostrophe and an "s":

that hobby of Guy's	an appointment of my mother's
a daughter of Jim's	these books of the Wheelers'
	[Plural: the books belong to all of the Wheeler family.]

K. A gerund (verb ending in "ing" and used as a noun) is generally preceded by a noun or pronoun in the possessive:

Albert's coming to New York surprised his lawyer.

They were all worried about Judy's drinking.

Someone's whispering upset the seance.

We objected to the tower's swaying.

L. When writing geographic names, the titles of books, the names of business firms, organizations, and institutions, use of the apostrophe to indicate possession should follow the original form designated by custom or usage:

Boys' Clubs of America   Harpers Ferry

Authors League of America   Kings Canyon, California

Lion's Gate Bridge   *Jane Fonda's Workout Book*

Weight Watchers Fast and Fabulous Cookbook

II. USE AN APOSTROPHE AND AN "S" TO FORM PLURALS

A. Of small letters:

There are four "i's" in Mississippi.

Remember to cross your "t's."

All "p's" over by the window; "q's" line up here by the door.

B. Of abbreviations with periods, and capital letters that would be confusing with only an "s":

There are nine M.D.'s in this building.

How many Ph.D.'s?

Look under the "I's," the "M's," and the "U's."
[Without apostrophes, the sentence would read: Look under the "Is," the "Ms," and the "Us."]

C. The plural of words used as words is usually formed by adding an "s" or "es." Both an apostrophe and an "s" are used if the "s" ending alone would cause confusion:

You have too many "ands" in that sentence.

You have too many "as's" in that sentence.
[Without the apostrophe, this sentence would read: "too many 'ass'."]

How may "I do's" do we have?
[Without the apostrophe, this sentence would read: "how many 'I dos'."]

III. USE AN APOSTROPHE TO INDICATE OMISSIONS

A. An apostrophe is used to form a contraction by marking where one or more letters have been omitted:

shouldn't	(should not)	I'll	(I will)
could've	(could have)	she'd	(she would)
isn't	(is not)	they're	(they are)
there's	(there is)	you're	(you are)

B. Use an apostrophe to show where numbers have been omitted:

the crash of '29   (1929)

the class of '85   (1985)

Richard Nixon was reelected in '72.   (1972)

She was born in '21.   (1921)

IV. DO NOT USE APOSTROPHES

A. To form the possessive of personal pronouns:

I — my, mine	we — our, ours
you — your, yours	they — their, theirs
she — her, hers	it — its
he — his	who — whose

B. To form the possessive in expressions where one noun modifies another:

The state capitol in Salem.   *[wrong: The state's capitol in Salem.]*

They put him in the Oregon State Penitentiary *[wrong: They put him in Oregon State's Penitentiary.]*

He pulled a quarterback sneak.   *[wrong: He pulled a quarterback's sneak.]*

C. To form the plural of numbers:

1930s   (not 1930's)   8-½s   (not 8-½'s)

747s   (not 747's)   sixes, tens, fourteens

The veterans were in their fifties and sixties.

D. To form the plural of most terms containing all capital letters, or single capital letters, used as words:

Two CPAs share a suite.

We saw six UFOs last year.

This school still teaches the three Rs.

ASTERISK   *

The asterisk is a reference symbol used after a word, figure, or sentence that directs the reader's attention to additional information in a note at the bottom of the page. When used in a table, the asterisk note is placed at the bottom of the table instead of the bottom of the page.

I. USE AN ASTERISK

A. To mark a place in the text that directs the reader to related information that may be incidental, or may disrupt the narrative if included in the body of the text. The asterisk alerts the reader to go to the bottom of the page where a note containing the related information is usually placed. The note is marked by a matching asterisk.

B. As a reference symbol when noting specific parts of tables, particularly if the table consists of figures, equations, or formulas. Use of the asterisk (and other symbols) avoids mistaking the notes for parts of the equations or formulas.

(1.) Symbols used as reference marks are placed in a superior position from (one-half space above) the line of text, or information in a table.

(2.) Do not use more than three asterisks for notes (***) on a single page or table. Use additional symbols or letters as needed, but do not use a combination of asterisks and other symbols, numbers, or letters (*ab).

BRACE   { }

A brace is a mark used to show that a relationship exists between one group of lines, equations, or statistics and another. The point of the brace is directed toward the logical flow of information, or toward the fewer number of lines, whichever is most appropriate.

I. USE A BRACE

    A. To show the connection between one group of lines and another:

Kent
New Castle }   Counties of Delaware
Sussex

Henry Knox
Timothy Pickering }   Secretaries of War under George
James McHenry   Washington

1 kilometer {   0.621 mile
                3.2815 feet

BRACKETS   [ ]

Brackets are used in pairs to enclose the author's comments about the text.

I. USE BRACKETS TO ENCLOSE

A. Author's interpolations, comments, or translations:

One comment about the Masterson papers [most authorities agree on this] is that they contain unusual insights to life in a seventeenth century manorhouse.

He announced that he had just heard from the stationmaster and more beer was on the way [cheers and thumping of mugs on the table].

For his tombstone, they ordered the Latin inscription requiescat in pace [may he rest in peace].

B. Notes indicating omissions, corrections, or descriptive information:

They [the South American countries] will have to get their financial houses in order before the world banking community will feel comfortable dealing with them again.

With a shaking hand, the old man wrote, "I grew up in Ronok [Roanoke] Virginny [Virginia]."

According to Jamison, they arrived on July 10, 1936 [1938] and moved into the big house.

C. Notes indicating the reproduction of errors found in source material:

"The tenth of May we arrived at the Canaries, and the tenth of June in this present yeere [sic], we were fallen with the Islands of the West Indies. . . .

— Arthur Barlow in a
report to Sir Walter Raleigh

II. **WHEN BRACKETED MATTER TAKES UP MORE THAN ONE PARAGRAPH, START EACH PARAGRAPH WITH A BRACKET; PLACE THE CLOSING BRACKET AT THE END OF THE LAST PARAGRAPH ONLY**

COLON   :

The colon is used as a break in a sentence to emphasize what follows. Its effect is more formal than that of a semicolon. Rather than indicating a pause, the colon signals the reader to go ahead with focused attention on what comes immediately after.

I.   USE A COLON TO SEPARATE

A. When introducing an independent statement, a formal extract from a text, or a speech in a dialogue:

The question to be debated was: Should the student body benefit from profits made by the University book store?

In his well-known book, *Critical Path*, Buckminster Fuller had this to say about copper: "Copper is the most plentiful of the most efficient electric-power-production and conduction metals."

Tammy: I'm too scared to go in there.
Roger: Come on, there's nothing in there that can harm you.

B. When setting off separate clauses in compound sentences when the second clause amplifies, explains, or illustrates the first:

John didn't like the cafeteria food: he felt it was too salty.

Monday was terrible: I overslept, was late to class, and got my feet wet because I forgot my galoshes.

It was a beautiful painting: a sailboat silhouetted on an orange, red, and silver sea in front of a huge setting sun.

C. When introducing a list or a series:

The Commission's study focused on three areas: the downtown core area; the Burnside renewal area; and the waterfront.

The mayor announced three objectives:
1. Lower the city budget.
2. Improve residential area police patrols.
3. Clean up the waterfront.

(1.) Periods are used after entries in a vertical list only when at least one of the entries is a complete sentence. When a list completes an introductory sentence, no final period is used unless the listed items are separated by semicolons or commas.

(2.) Use a colon with "as follows" or "the following" when items in the list or series follow immediately after.

The areas focused on were as follows:
1. The downtown core area
2. The Burnside renewal area
3. The waterfront

(3.) But do not use a colon with "as follows" or "the following" when the introductory statement is complete, and is followed by one or more sentences:

The Commission focused on unused land, business, and residential property, with emphasis on the following.

1. Underused commercial property in the downtown core area was identified.

2. Historically important buildings in the Burnside renewal area were tagged for special attention.

3. City-owned land along the waterfront was evaluated for park development.

(4.) Use a colon with "namely," "for instance," "for example," or "that is" only when the series consists of one or more complete sentences.

The Commission's study covered three downtown areas, namely, the downtown core, Burnside, and the waterfront.   *[no colon]*

The Commission's study covered three areas, namely:
The area between Burnside and Jefferson Avenue and
from Second to Ninth Street was designated as area
one. From Burnside Avenue north to Lovejoy Avenue was
designated as area two. From the waterfront to Second
Street was designated as area three.   *[colon used]*

(5.) Do not use a colon when the list or series introduced
is a complement or object of the introductory statement.

The Commission's focus areas are (1) the downtown
core, (2) the Burnside renewal area, and (3) the
waterfront.

*[Items (1), (2), and (3) are complements of
"focus areas."]*

The Commission is planning to investigate
   1. the downtown core;
   2. the Burnside renewal area;
   3. the waterfront.

*[Items 1., 2., and 3. are direct objects of the
introductory clause.]*

D. Formal salutations from a body of text:

My Dear Sir:

Ladies and Gentlemen:

To Whom It May Concern:

E. The parts of Biblical and other citations:

Mark 1:39

II Corinthians 9:5

The Historian 46:4

F. When dividing titles from subtitles:

*Editing Your Newsletter: A Guide to Writing, Design,
and Production*

The Peter Principle: How to Make Things Go Right

G. When indicating proportions:

Mix water and vinegar 30:1

His chances of success are 10:1 against.

H. When dividing hours and minutes in clock time:

10:21 p.m.   6:15 a.m.

II. USE OF COLONS WITH OTHER PUNCTUATION MARKS

A. Always place colons outside quotation marks or parentheses.

B. When a quotation taken from a text ends with a colon, drop the colon and add an ellipsis.

COMMA   ,

For the English language, the comma is like salt on food; it brings out the flavor. It is used in more places than any other punctuation mark, and is therefore considered to be complex. This is not true. The comma follows the simple principles of separating and enclosing parts of a sentence to clarify its meaning.

Commas separate amplifying, explanatory, or digressive information from the beginning and end of sentences. They are used before and after the same type of information when it is in the middle to set it off or highlight it from the rest of the sentence. Commas are also used to separate items in a list, so it can be identified as a list.

It's as simple as that. Keep these three uses in mind and you will rapidly master the use of commas.

I. USE COMMAS TO SEPARATE

A. Elements in a series. Place a comma between all words, phrases, clauses, letters, or figures in a series of three or more, including before a conjunction preceding the last item:

Marty kept books on physics, history, poetry, and computers on his shelf at home.

She returned home, fed the cat, did the laundry, then cooked dinner.

Did you choose a, b, c, or d?

His locker combination was 20, 8, 17.

Note: Some authorities advocate omitting the comma before the conjunction preceding the last item in a series. The authors disagree with this practice, since the writer must make a judgement each time the rule is applied as to whether or not the resulting sentence can be misunderstood. Nothing is gained by omitting the final comma in a list, while clarity can be lost in some cases through misreading.

(1.) When a conjunction is used between the last two elements in a series, place a comma before the conjunction. A conjunction is a linking word that ties together clauses, phrases, or words.

The boys asked for a baseball, a bat, <u>and</u> four gloves.

(2.) Do not use commas when the elements in a series are all joined by conjunctions.

The orchestra played compositions by Mozart <u>and</u> Brahms <u>and</u> Chopin.

(3.) Do not use a comma between the last item in a series and an item being described.

He wore his old, faded, <u>stained   jeans</u> to work on his car.

(4.) Do not use a comma between items in a series that are employed as closely related pairs or sets.

The establishment offered comfort, solitude, a well-stocked library, and <u>bed and breakfast</u>.

The menu listed <u>eggs and bacon</u>, <u>eggs and ham</u>, and <u>eggs and hash</u>.

(5.) When one or more of the elements in a series contain commas, use semicolons instead of commas to separate the elements.

They travelled through <u>Denver, Colorado</u>; <u>Ogden, Utah</u>; and <u>Pasadena, California</u>.

Some of the members picked <u>fruit, cotton, and vegetables</u>; <u>others worked in banks, bookstores, and restaurants</u>; <u>still others were employed as doctors, lawyers, and stockbrokers</u>.

B. Chapter and page references:

Jason's quote is in <u>Chapter 12</u>, <u>page 237</u>.

C. Parts of an address when the address is joined in a line:

The book was sent to 4891 Elm St., Portland, Oregon 97865.   *[Do not use a comma before the Zip Code.]*

D. Parts of a date:

I left for Europe on Wednesday, June 15, 1990.

The meeting was scheduled for November 1, 1986, but was actually held two days later.

(1.) No comma is used between the month and year when the day of the month is absent.

The book was published in March 1967.

(2.) No commas are used when the day of the month is written first (a style commonly used by the military and in Europe).

8 April 1924   27 June 1764

(3.) No commas are used between dates and holidays, seasons, or the abbreviations A.D. and B.C.

The last time they came was Christmas 1936.

The class was scheduled for spring 1987.

The 774th year of the Roman Empire is equivalent to 29 A.D. on our calendar.

E. Numbers of more than three figures signifying quantity:

6,045 $78,900.00   4,580,991

F. Inverted proper names:

White, Stanley   Clark, Alvin T.

G. Names of places:

<u>San Diego</u>, <u>California</u>   <u>Dublin</u>, <u>Ireland</u>

They wrote to him through the express office,
<u>Trafalgar Square</u>, <u>London</u>, <u>England</u>.

H. An informal salutation from the body of a letter:

Dear Joan,   Dear Mom,   Dear Aunt Gail,

I. The complimentary close of a letter from the signature:

Sincerely yours,   Truly yours,

Affectionately,   Always,

J. Words or figures that otherwise might cause the reader confusion (try reading the following examples without the commas):

Instead of a few, thousands came.

Instead of 40, 70 were sent.

During 1956, 460 athletes competed for the award.

Toward Marsha, Martin was very cool.

The way it was, was okay with them.

II. USE COMMAS WITHIN A SENTENCE TO SET OFF OR EMPHASIZE

The use of commas to set off, emphasize, or enclose phrases or clauses is frequently controlled by whether the phrase or clause is nonrestrictive or restrictive.

(1.) If the phrase is not essential to the meaning of the sentence, it is nonrestrictive, and set off by commas.

Bill Dixon, <u>who spoke to the group</u>, represented the
State Energy Commission.

The Senate, <u>by a narrow margin</u>, passed the bill.

(2.) If the phrase is necessary to, or restricts the meaning of the sentence, it is restrictive, and not set off by commas.

The man who spoke to the group   represented the
State Energy Commission.

The Senate passed the bill by a narrow margin.

A. Clauses joined by a coordinating conjunction in a compound sentence. The most common coordinating conjunctions are *and*, *but*, *for*, *nor*, *or*, *so*, *still*, and *yet*:

Sara wanted a new dress for the dance, but she
didn't have enough money.

The desert is beautiful, yet it is dangerous to
the unwary.

(1.) Some authorities allow elimination of the comma when the connected clauses are short (three to five words).

Edna washed the dishes and John dried.

George held the horse's head and Sue mounted.

She went in but he hesitated.

B. An introductory modifying phrase, or adverbial clause from an independent clause that follows it:

By setting aside money earned during the summer,
Laura was able to pay her tuition.

Moving quickly and quietly, Henry wrestled the
boxes onto the truck.

C. An ending modifying phrase or adverbial clause from an independent clause that precedes it:

Roger sailed the boat upstream, careful of the
channel buoys.

Sally first drove the car around the block, slowly
and cautiously.

D. Direct quotations from the rest of the sentence (always place commas inside quotation marks):

When associates complained to Lincoln that General Grant was a heavy drinker, he said, "<u>Can you tell me what kind of whiskey? I should like to send a barrel to some of my other generals.</u>"

— Ida M. Tarbell,
The Life of Abraham Lincoln

"<u>I should like,</u>" said Lincoln, "<u>to send a barrel to some of my other generals.</u>"

(1.) Omit the separating comma if you use only part of a quotation, or if you introduce it with "that."

When told General Grant was a heavy whiskey drinker, Lincoln asked for the brand, so [that] he could "<u>send a barrel to some of my other generals.</u>"

Lincoln asked the brand of General Grant's whiskey, that he might "<u>send a barrel to some of my other generals.</u>"

(2.) Do not use commas to separate indirect quotations.

Lincoln said he <u>would send a barrel of General Grant's whiskey to his other generals if he could find out what brand he drank.</u>

E. Adages, maxims or other special expressions from the rest of the sentence (always place commas inside quotation marks):

"Who first coined that old saying, 'Blood is thicker than water?' " asked Jim.

Only one aphorism, <u>You cannot help loving who loves you</u>, has remained in my mind.

F. Tag questions from preceding independent clauses:

You've just returned from the store, <u>haven't you</u>?

She put the book on the shelf, <u>didn't she</u>?

You are sure, <u>aren't you</u>?

G. Contrasted elements or expressions in a sentence:

He lives in apartment <u>A</u>, <u>not B</u>.

Pat turned <u>35</u> last year, <u>not 29</u>.

He plays <u>golf</u>, <u>never tennis</u>.

She parks <u>in the garage</u>, <u>seldom out on the street</u>.

H. Two or more adjectives modifying the same noun:

Polly wore an <u>old</u>, <u>threadbare</u>, <u>brown</u> sweater.

(1.) When consecutive adjectives modify equally, no comma is used. This is especially true for adjectives that refer to age (young, old, new), size, color, or location. Two simple tests are to mentally place "and" between the adjectives, or to switch the sequence of adjectives. In either case, if the resulting sentence seems awkward, the commas may be left out. If the resulting sentence appears to read correctly, use commas.

They accepted his <u>revised</u> <u>draft</u> <u>manuscript</u>.

The <u>small</u> <u>white</u> <u>knob</u> on the stove.

It was one of those <u>old</u> <u>one-street</u> <u>frontier</u> <u>mining</u> towns.

I. The person speaking, or spoken to, in dialogue (always place commas inside quotation marks):

"I don't think," <u>said Peter</u>, "I'll ever understand statistics."

"Go to the kitchen, <u>Nancy</u>, and help Tom with the vegetables."

(1.) Note that in dialogue, where appropriate, a question or an exclamation mark may replace the comma.

"Are you back again<u>?</u>" asked George.

"The potatoes are boiling over<u>!</u>" shouted Theron.

J. Initials or personal titles after proper names:

Eva Kubinsky, <u>D.D.S.</u>, is on the board of directors.

Professor Alfred Miller, <u>Ph.D.</u>, made the introductions.

Jerry Anderson, <u>Sr.</u>, started the business in 1904.

Dennis Noble, <u>chairman</u>, criticised the new incumbent.

III. USE COMMAS (BEFORE AND AFTER) WITHIN A SENTENCE TO SET OFF

A. Parenthetical words, phrases, or clauses that amplify, explain, or offer a digressive statement without changing the meaning of the sentence (nonrestrictive phrases):

The senator, <u>however</u>, refused to comply.

Rodney, <u>his heart beating rapidly</u>, donned his parachute.

The Portland Building, <u>which was controversial when it was first built</u>, is now a valued addition to the city.

B. Absolute phrases: a phrase within a sentence with an informal relationship, but no clear grammatical relationship, to the rest of the sentence.

He saluted, <u>a nostalgic lump forming in his throat</u>, as the flag passed by.

C. Words in apposition (adjacent nouns, pronouns, or groups of words where one of the expressions restates, amplifies, explains, or further identifies the other):

<u>My wife</u>, <u>Josephine</u>, bought a goat last week.

<u>We</u>, <u>the undersigned</u>, agree to support Roosevelt for President.

<u>His company</u>, <u>the shoe factory in Brockton</u>, showed increased profits this year.

(1.) When an appositive is restrictive, it is not set off by commas.

The <u>sailor</u> <u>who was the first to volunteer</u> was designated the leader.

Steinbeck's book <u>"The Grapes of Wrath"</u> described Midwest dustbowl conditions in the 1930's.

The <u>quotation</u> <u>"The only thing we have to fear is fear itself"</u> is from Franklin D. Roosevelt's first inaugural address.

D. Vocatives (nouns, pronouns, and other terms used in direct address). Vocatives may also appear at the beginning or the end of sentences, and are set off by commas:

Let me assure you, <u>Bob</u>, your job is secure.

I promise you, <u>fellow Democrats</u>, I will represent you to the best of my ability.

Take your seats, <u>ladies and gentlemen</u>, the play is about to begin.

E. "Of" phrases:

John Maxwell, <u>of the firm Taylor and Young</u>, represents our firm in London.

Captain Kangaroo, <u>of television fame</u>, spoke to our communications class.

(1.) When a place name is generally accepted as a part of a person's name, it is not separated by commas.

<u>Montgomery of El Alamein</u>   <u>Jesus of Nazareth</u>

IV. USE COMMAS TO INDICATE OMISSION

A. Of a word or words, understood through the context of the sentence:

Helen was elected president; Cheryl, <u>[was elected]</u> vice president; and Valerie, <u>[was elected]</u> treasurer.

Last semester, the assignment was ten pages; this
semester, [the assignment was]fifteen pages!

V. DO NOT USE COMMAS:

A. Before the first item in a series.

B. After the last item in a series.

C. To separate a subject from its verb in a compound predicate.

Bill went to the meeting and met with the nominating committee.

F. Between two independent clauses where a stronger mark (semicolon or period) is required.

G. With restrictive words, phrases, or clauses.

H. Together with a dash or parentheses.

I. Before an ampersand (&).

J. Between the name or number of an organized unit.

Teamsters Local 233   American Legion Post 24

DASH   --

The dash is used to indicate a sudden interruption or sharp break in thought, or to add an air of surprise or emotional tone. It can always be replaced by some other punctuation mark, and should be used only where strong emphasis or stylistic effect is desired.

In typed manuscripts, a dash is formed with two hyphens with no space separating it from the words before and after. In typeset copy, it is optional whether or not to place spaces before and after the dash, and is frequently dependent on the typesetting system being used.

I.   USE DASHES TO SEPARATE OR SET OFF

A. Nonrestrictive modifying phrases or clauses:

No one in the fraternity—not even David—dared to oppose the Dean's ruling.

The Muses—nine sister goddesses in Hellenic mythology—were a source of inspiration to the ancient Greeks.

B. Nonrestrictive appositives (adjacent nouns, pronouns, or groups of words where one of the two expressions restates, amplifies, explains, or further identifies the other). Appositives may also occur in the middle of a sentence:

She could forgive him everything but this—the theft of her grandmother's pearls.

Steven was motivated by three things—wealth, power, and prestige—in his race up the corporate ladder.

C. The summary of a thought, a series of thoughts, or a list of items from that which it summarizes:

Food, clothing, shelter—these are considered basic to survival.

She studied English, German, French, Italian, and Spanish— languages she would need to conduct tours in Europe.

II. USE DASHES TO ENCLOSE

A. Parenthetical elements that cause a sharp break or interrupt thought:

I've sent Eddie and Guy—those boys can certainly eat—to the store for chips, dip, and soda.

(1.) When a modifying phrase or clause set off by dashes calls for a question mark or exclamation point, the appropriate punctuation is placed in front of the second dash.

Jeff and I—do you know Jeff?—are going to the opera on Saturday.

B. Parenthetical elements you wish to emphasize:

The blankets—soft, warm, and colorful—were made of wool.

C. Parenthetical elements used for stylistic effect:

He was irritated beyond belief—irritated by the incessant hum of the transformer.   *[reiteration]*

He was relieved—oh was he relieved!—when his financial aid check arrived.   *[dramatization]*

III. USE DASHES TO TERMINATE

A. An expression, the meaning of which is completed by two or more parallel elements (items of equal importance expressed in the same grammatical form) that follow:

The committee recommended that material for recycling—
  1. be placed at curbside;
  2. be collected once a week;
  3. be transported to the county recycling center.

The girls said their good health was the result of—
    frequent exercise;
    a high fibre diet;
    adequate sleep.

(1.) Do not use a dash when enumerated elements are used in a continuous sentence structure.

a. In a compound sentence with more than two elements:

The committee recommended that material for recycling: (1) be placed at curbside, (2) be collected once a week, (3) be transported to the county recycling center.

b. In a compound sentence with only two elements:

The committee recommended that material for recycling (1) be placed at curbside and (2) be collected once a week.

c. In a sentence containing a list:

The girls gave three reasons for their good health: (1) frequent exercise, (2) a high fibre diet, and (3) adequate sleep.

B. An unfinished word or sentence:

"I don't mean to be—"

"The word 'emphasize'—"

"The word 'emp'—"

(1.) Use a comma following a dash to separate unfinshed quotations from the speaker.

"I don't care—," began Henry, as the noise from the passing train cut him off.

C. In-line subheadings:

Key Outline— The desired area is . . . .

START EARLY— Begin thinking about . . . .

D. Run-in questions and answers in testimony:

Q. <u>Was he with you?</u> — A. <u>No</u>.

E. Dates when indicating an indefinite span of time:

George Potter (1951—)

The American industrial age (1880—) shaped the country's cultural perspectives.

IV. USE DASHES TO INDICATE OMISSION

A. Of letters or words in a sentence:

<u>Marie D—</u> was the key witness in the drug dealing case.

"That's a <u>h—</u> of a way for you to act!"

[See hyphens for a similar use in text.]

V. MISCELLANEOUS USES OF DASHES

A. To indicate halting or interrupted speech:

"It was—well—you know—it was bad. There was blood everywhere, and—my God—I couldn't see where the door was, and Barb was—she was screaming, and—God, it was terrible."

B. In place of a colon, where preceded by a question mark or an exclamation mark:

<u>What do you think of this?—</u> "House for sale, $200,000."

C. To precede a credit line or a run-in credit or signature:

How do I love thee? Let me count the ways.

—Elizabeth Barrett Browning
"Sonnets From the Portuguese XLII"

Give and it shall be given unto you. . . .

—Luke 6:38

D. In place of commas or parentheses, if clarification is improved (where emphasis is not otherwise desired):

The school's top decision makers—the chancellor, the president, and the vice president for finance—represented the university during the negotiations.

Three of the four sisters—Mary, Nancy, and Joan—took jobs with the gas company.

VI. DO NOT USE DASHES

A. Immediately after a comma, colon, semicolon, or period.

ELLIPSIS   . . .

The ellipsis (plural ellipses) is used almost exclusively to indicate the omission of text from quoted material. Ellipses are formed by typing three periods, with letterspaces between them. The ellipsis is always separated by a letterspace from words or other punctuation marks preceding or following it. When ellipses represent words omitted from a direct quotation, they are placed within the quotation marks.

Quoted material employing ellipses to indicate deleted material should always retain the basic meaning intended by the original author. It should also retain a sense of grammatical correctness and express a complete thought.

I.   USE ELLIPSES TO INDICATE THE OMISSION OF TEXT FROM QUOTED MATERIAL

Original sample text

When the depression struck, businessmen took the view that the various phases of the business cycle were inevitable and that, in time, prosperity would return. Some said the economy was sound, and that the only thing wrong was the people's lack of confidence.

No one could truly ignore the depression. It penetrated every aspect of life in the United States. A year after the crash, 6 million men walked the streets looking for jobs that did not exist. In 1931, unemployment in the nation rose to 9 million, and in 1932 climbed to about 15 million. Thousands of banks failed, prices dropped, foreign trade shrank, and business failures increased.

By the summer of 1932, steel plants were operating at twelve per cent of capacity. Many factories had shut down completely. People lost their savings; they could not make mortgage payments, so they lost their homes; charity soup kitchens opened in the cities, and long bread lines formed; the jobless slept where they could—on park benches or in the doorways of public buildings; many suffered from cold, starvation and malnutrition.

—Current, DeConde, and Dante
United States History

Shortened sample text, using ellipses

When the depression struck, businessmen took the view that . . . in time, prosperity would return. . . .

No one could truly ignore the depression. . . . A year after the crash, 6 million men walked the streets looking for jobs . . . . In 1931, unemployment in the nation rose to 9 million, and in 1932 climbed to about 15 million. Thousands of banks failed, . . . and business failures increased.

. . . Many factories had shut down completely. People lost their savings; . . . charity soup kitchens opened in the cities; . . . many suffered from cold, starvation and malnutrition.

A. When text is omitted from the middle of a sentence, insert the ellipsis only:

When the depression struck, businessmen took the view that . . . in time, prosperity would return.

B. When text is omitted from the end of a sentence, insert an ellipsis in the position of the missing words, and follow it with the original punctuation of the sentence:

A year after the crash, 6 million men walked the streets looking for jobs . . . .
[The last dot is the period.]

NOTE: Some authorities advocate placing the punctuation before the ellipsis when text is deleted from the end of a sentence. The writers of this handbook feel such placement would confuse readers. This potential for confusion is eliminated, it is felt, when the ellipsis is consistently placed in the position of the omitted text, and punctuation precedes or follows it as in the original sentence.

C. When text is omitted following the end of a sentence, or between sentences (including between paragraphs), follow the original punctuation mark with an ellipsis:

No one could truly ignore the depression. . . . A
year after the crash, 6 million men walked the
streets looking for jobs . . . .

[In the first sentence, the first dot is the period ending the sentence. In the second sentence, text has been omitted from the end of the sentence, so the last dot is the period.]

D. When an incomplete sentence follows a punctuation mark preceded or followed by an ellipsis, and is the beginning of a complete thought, capitalizing the first letter is optional:

No one could truly ignore the depression. . . . men
walked the streets looking for jobs . . . .

or—

No one could truly ignore the depression. . . . Men
walked the streets looking for jobs . . . .

or—

No one could truly ignore the depression. . . .
[M]en walked the streets looking for jobs . . . .

E. When text is omitted from the end of a paragraph, end the last sentence with the original punctuation, then add an ellipsis:

When the depression struck, businessmen took the view
that . . . in time, prosperity would return. . . .

[The first dot is the period ending the sentence, and is not separated by a space.]

F. When text is omitted from the first part of a paragraph, whether whole sentences or the beginning of an opening sentence, retain the original indentation and insert an ellipsis in place of the deleted text:

   . . . Many factories had shut down completely.
People lost their savings; . . . many suffered from
cold, starvation and malnutrition.

G. When one or more paragraphs are omitted when using widely spaced portions of a quotation, insert a single ellipsis in place of the deleted material:

When the depression struck, . . . 6 million men
walked the street looking for johs. . . .

H. When appropriate, retain original punctuation before or following the ellipsis representing deleted text:

People lost their savings; . . . charity soup
kitchens opened in the cities; . . . many suffered
from cold, starvation and malnutrition.

In the early days . . . , property was readily
available.

The list was clear, but ridiculous . . . : raisins,
snails, copper flasks, and bed curtains.

"Money and politics, . . . !" she shouted.

I. When a direct quote is grammatically incomplete, use an ellipsis only, with no punctuation unless an exclamation point or question mark is called for:

"I wonder if . . ." Susan began.

"I resent the implication that . . . !" the old lady
screamed, as he shut the door on her.

"Do you need a . . . ?" Tom started to ask.

[Used in this manner, the ellipses infers that the speaker intended to continue, as opposed to the sharp interruption indicated by a dash used for the same purpose.]

J. When one or more lines of verse are omitted, indicate the deletion with a row of spaced periods approximately the same length as the last line quoted.

Original sample text

All day the waves assailed the rock,
I heard no church-bell chime,
The sea-beat scorns the minister clock
And breaks the glass of Time.

                    —Emerson, "Nahant"

Shortened example text, using ellipses

All day the waves assailed the rock,
. . . .
The sea-beat scorns the minister clock
And breaks the glass of Time.

II. ELLIPSES MAY BE USED (INFREQUENTLY AND WITH DISCRETION) IN NARRATIVE PROSE

A. To indicate an implied expansion of thought:

She wants me to go, but . . .

B. To indicate the passage of time:

The night grew cold . . . the moon rose . . . stars appeared . . . still we waited.

III. DO NOT USE ELLIPSES

A. Before or after a partial quotation used in a complete sentence:

They wrote "6 million men walked the streets looking for jobs," and government statistics support their statement.

B. Before a quotation set apart from the main text, and beginning with an incomplete sentence that completes the last sentence in the main text:

After the stock market crash the depression struck, and

businessmen took the view that the various phases were inevitable and that, in time, prosperity would return.

C. Following a quotation set apart from the main text that ends with a complete sentence, unless it is considered necessary for clarity. See III B (immediately above) for the example.

D. To indicate missing words or letters in the original copy (see hyphens).

EXCLAMATION POINT   **!**

The exclamation point is a mark of terminal punctuation that indicates or expresses strong emotion or emphasis. Use exclamation points sparingly, and do not use more than one at a time, or its emphatic force will be weakened.

I. USE AN EXCLAMATION POINT WITH A WORD OR SENTENCE

A. To show strong feeling or emphasis (may occur in a declarative sentence):

Help!

Turn off the light!

She loves me!

How right you are!

(1.) The exclamation point should be placed inside quotation marks when it is part of the quotation.

[Note the omission of the comma in the following sentences.]

"You fool!" shouted the artist. "You've ruined the painting!"

"Ouch!" cried Tommy. "That hurts!"

B. To indicate a forceful command or request:

Stop! Come back with my car!

Go to your room now!

Get that dog away from the table!

"Please give me something to eat!" the starving man cried out.

(1.) The exclamation point may occur in an interrogative sentence.

[Note the omission of a question mark in the following sentences.]

"Where are you going!" shouted Glen.

Who is yelling, "give me liberty or give me death!"

HYPHEN   -

Hyphens are primarily employed to improve reading comprehension by connecting parts of compound words or phrases. Common usage also supports a wide range of other applications.

I. USE HYPHENS TO JOIN THE PARTS OF COMPOUND WORDS OR PHRASES

Compound words may consist of: (1) two or more distinct words written as one (footnote, bookstore); (2) two separate words, which, when joined by a hyphen, express a thought more than, or different from, the words used individually (penny-wise, break-in); (3) or a root word joined to a stressed prefix (ex-boyfriend, pro-government).

Compound phrases may consist of: (1) commonly employed prepositional phrase compounds containing three or more words (mother-in-law, man-of-war, government-in-exile); (2) improvised descriptive compounds (lighter-than-air, first-come-first-served).

The use of hyphenated compounds constantly changes in English language usage. Many combinations that began as two-word descriptions have evolved into single-word compounds through an interim step as a hyphenated compound. Base ball (a ball game played with bases that the player must run to and touch), for example, evolved first to base-ball, and is now written as baseball. Book store, which evolved into the single word, bookstore, is another example.

The only dependable way to determine if current practice calls for hyphenated or solid spelling of a compound word or phrase is to consult an unabridged (or at least a collegiate) dictionary. Most, but probably not all, of the noun forms and many of the adjective forms will be listed there. Note that all the dictionary entries are divided into syllables. Your dictionary's explanatory notes will tell you how to distinguish between the marks used to separate syllables and hyphens joining parts of a compound word.

A. Hyphenated noun-compounds consist of two proper nouns so closely associated that they constitute a single concept when used together, but are spelled individually and joined by a hyphen:

cure-all	place-name
blood-alcohol	scholar-poet
dog-ear	author-publisher
father-confessor	crop-year

B. Hyphenated adjective-compounds consist of two or more words that express a single thought, which in turn, precedes and modifies the meaning of a proper noun, or of a closely related single word and the noun it modifies:

cat-like	old-fashioned	great-uncle
orange-red	trade-mark	fellow-member
light-haired	high-ranking	off-the-record
law-abiding	half-baked	all-encompassing

(1.) When a compound adjective follows the noun it modifies, the hyphen is usually dropped:

His manner was old fashioned.

His contracts were always awarded to fellow members.

Their testimony was to be off the record.

Their plan was only half baked.

C. Hyphenated prefix-compounds connect a prefix to the noun it modifies:

ex-president	pre-Columbian
anti-Communist	co-author
de-water	trans-Pacific
pro-Ally	un-American
self-employed	mid-ocean

D. Hyphenated phrase compounds are three-or-more-word combinations expressing complex descriptive titles or thoughts:

stick-in-the-mud	one-man-one-vote
brother-in-law	18-year-old
hard-and-fast	know-it-all
grant-in-aid	what-you-see-is-what-you-get

II. MISCELLANEOUS USES OF HYPHENS

A. To divide words carried over from one of line text to the next:

The advantage of this process is the achievement of multiple color effects.

(1.) Words carried over from one line of text to the next are always divided at a syllable break.

(2.) Never divide a word between two lines of text in a manner that leaves a single letter by itself on either of the lines.

(3.) Divide hyphenated words only at the hyphen:

self- employed	**not** self-em- ployed
ex- manager	**not** ex-mana- ger

B. To join single letter modifiers to nouns:

A-bomb	I-beam
U-turn	S-curve
V-neck	T-square

C. To join capitalized names when indicating relationship or distance:

The Washington-Moscow talks

The New York-Paris flight

D. To distinguish between the word used, and another, similar word:

co-respondent	(correspondent)
re-solve	(resolve)
co-op	(coop)
re-creation	(recreation)

E. To avoid doubling vowels or tripling consonants:

pre-eminent	shell-like
pre-empt	co-opted

F. To terminate the first part of a hyphenated compound when used with another related hyphenated compound:

a two- or three-wheeled bicycle

a first- or second-level decision

three-, four-, and five-year-old cheese

G. When writing compound numbers between twenty-one and ninety-nine.

H. Between numerator and denominator when writing fractions:

a three-fourths majority

one-tenth liter

but

twenty-two twenty-fifths

sixty-seven one-hundreths

(1.) Some authorities advocate elimination of the hyphen when the first two words in a numerical expression serve as a modifier for the second.

three fourths of a majority *[modifies majority]*

one tenth of a liter *[modifies liter]*

I. Between a numeral and a unit of measure:

5-inch	16-day
40-hour	12-foot
six-mile	three hundred-yard

J. As an equivalent of "up to and including" when used between numbers or dates:

Sept. 21-29	from 10-16 miles
6-8 cups	about 3-5 days
pages 212-218	pages 212-18

K. Between letters of a word to show spelling or construction:

She spells her last name T-o-m-p-k-i-n-s.

C-a-u-g-h-t and c-o-t are homonyms.

L. To represent deleted letters or illegible words in copy:

I'll be d---ed!" she exclaimed.

The mi---ng letters had faded from the page.

M. To suggest stuttering:

I d-don't know y-y-you v-very well.

III. DO NOT USE HYPHENS

A. With adverbs ending in "ly."

highly	tightly	slowly

B. In civil or military titles denoting a single office:

ambassador at large	notary public
major general	secretary general
sergeant at arms	under secretary

(1.) Use a hyphen for double titles.

secretary-treasurer   treasurer-manager

general manager-secretary

PARENTHESES   ( )

Parentheses are used in the same manner as commas and dashes to set off amplifying, explanatory, or digressive information contained in, or immediately following, a sentence. The choice of which of these three punctuation marks to use depends on the relationship of the information to the rest of the sentence. If the parenthetical material is closely intertwined with the rest of the sentence, use commas. If it is desired to forcefully emphasize the information, use dashes. When the parenthetical material is used as if it is a whispered aside to the reader, employ parentheses. Parentheses are most effective when used sparingly. Used too often, they can become tiresome and distracting.

I.   USE PARENTHESES

A. To enclose supplementary, parenthetic, or explanatory material which requires more highlighting than indicated by commas, and when the material does not change the meaning, or has only a slight bearing on the rest of the sentence:

It is difficult to imagine why any unexpected person would (or how any unexpected person could) have come around the calmly seated Elwell (whose chair, with its back to the wall, faced the fireplace), stood squarely in front of him and shot him between the eyes.*

Had he been old enough to serve in what, in those days, we all naively referred to as the Great War? (Oh, yes.)*

By the quaint but familiar device of moving that the salary of the First Lord of the Admiralty (Mr. Reginald McKenna) be reduced by one hundred pounds, the honorable member for Kingston (Mr. Cave) started the ball rolling.*

B. To enclose a quotation source or other matter when noted in text:

For Humphrey . . . is recognized among geneticists as a first-rate original scientist, whose work has been published by Johns Hopkins (*Working Dogs: An Attempt to Produce a Strain of German Shepherds Which combines Working Ability and Beauty of Conformation,* by Elliott Humphrey and Lucien Warner, with a foreword by Raymond Pearl, Baltimore, the Johns Hopkins Press, 1934), and a few years ago . . . .*

* All examples marked with an asterisk are from: Alexander Woollcott, *Long, Long Ago* (New York: Viking Press, 1943).

C. To enclose numbers or letters used to enumerate a series when the series is run into text:

It is not easy to think of any other American play with so good a chance of being acted a hundred years from now. Perhaps (1) *Our Town*, (2) *The Green Pastures*, (3) *The Wisdom Tooth*, or (4) *Heartbreak House*.*   *[Paraphrased from the original.]*

D. To enclose numbers confirming a number spelled out in the text:

This memorandum will serve to confirm our order of thirty-seven (37) dozen conference notebooks with our school seal engraved on the front.

Your expenses for the trip should not exceed five hundred dollars ($500.00).

E. To enclose question marks or exclamation points when you wish to emphasize doubt, irony, or amazement:

The doctor told Emily she would only (!) have to reduce her food intake to 1200 calories per day to lose two pounds a month.

They visited us September 16 (?), 1943.

F. To enclose reference directions:

The amortization table (see p. 70) clearly shows that the investment is sound.

The company based their defense on a section of the environmental laws (Article III) that allowed local storage of radioactive material pending final disposition.

II. FOR FORMAL PAPERS, USE BRACKETS AS SUBSTITUTE PARENTHESES WHEN THEY ARE USED INSIDE EXISTING PARENTHESES. FOR INFORMAL PAPERS, A SECOND SET (OR MORE) OF PARENTHESES MAY BE USED WITHIN PARENTHESES TO ENCLOSE MATERIAL

Formal

The vending machine sells a variety of foods (sandwiches, soft drinks, milk, fruit, [and sometimes canned soups]).

Informal

The cafeteria has hot food (hamburgers, hot dogs, soup (and once in a while, casserole dishes)).

III. PUNCTUATION USAGE WITH PARENTHESES

A. Material enclosed in parentheses within a sentence may contain commas, semicolons, and other appropriate internal punctuation marks as required, but it is not begun with a capital letter except in the case of formal names, titles, or personal pronouns requiring a capital, and is not ended with a period including when the material consists of a complete sentence:

[Oscar] Levant (who, by the way, makes a fleeting appearance in one of Dashiell Hammett's books, under the guise of Levi Oscant) could be heard muttering under his breath, "An evening with Gershwin is a Gershwin evening."*

I have since forgotten every experience except that we used to roar a song called "Lightly Row" at the top of our lungs, and that Miss Snooks (I am reasonably sure that was her name) once caught me in the ungallant act of thumbing my nose at a little girl . . . .*

B. Material enclosed in parentheses but not contained in a sentence begins with a capital letter and ends with a period, question mark, or exclamation point placed inside the parentheses:

To acknowledge these he stood, pen in hand, at the high schoolmaster's desk in his home on I Street. (He always held that the seated position encouraged verbosity.)*

C. When the material enclosed in parentheses is a question or an exclamation, the appropriate punctuation mark is used within the parentheses:

Although the honorable member for Leicester, Mr. Ramsay MacDonald, was so far out of key as to call the motion an attempt to blackmail the Treasury (cries of "Shame! Shame!"), the resulting debate went to the heart of the matter . . . .*

D. Punctuation marks belonging to the sentence containing the material enclosed in parentheses are placed outside the closing parentheses:

The new home was a penthouse in East Seventy-Second Street, New York City, a bachelor apartment of fourteen rooms (counting the trunk-room).*

E. No punctuation should be used in front of a beginning parenthesis unless it is being used to enclose a number or letter enumerating an item in a series that has been run into the text. Internal punctuation required for the sentence containing material enclosed by parentheses is usually placed after the closing parenthesis:

I could not completely respect any man unless, like Robert Louis Stevenson (or, for that matter, Jane Austen herself), he was just a little bit in love with Elizabeth Bennet of *Pride and Prejudice*.*

F. When material enclosed in parentheses requires more than one paragraph, start each paragraph with a parenthesis and place the closing parenthesis at the end of the last paragraph.

PERIOD   .

The period is used primarily as a mark of terminal punctuation, indicating a complete stop at the end of a sentence. It is also employed in a wide range of secondary applications.

I. USE A PERIOD TO TERMINATE

A. Declarative sentences:

The certificate is hanging on the wall.

Helga's towel is still wet because she left it wadded up on the beach after she went swimming.

(1.) Periods should always be placed within the closing quotation mark (including double sets of quotation marks).

Suzanne replied, "I believe educating students and controlling them are almost always mutually exclusive."

B. Indirect questions:

Lisa asked when we were coming home.

He wondered if they wanted automobile insurance, or a life insurance policy.

C. Commands or polite requests:

Come quickly.
[Imperative sentence fragment.]

Will you please turn off the lights.
[A polite request, not a question.]

I expect to hear from you soon.

D. Sentence fragments:

When will you graduate? Next month.

How much money did you make last year? Not enough.

"What's new?"
"Plenty. Lost my job."
"Laid off?"
"Fired."
"What for?"
"Hitting the boss."

(1.) A sentence fragment is not a complete sentence with a subject and a predicate, but when a fragment expresses a complete thought, it should be punctuated as a complete sentence.

II. MISCELLANEOUS USES OF PERIODS

A. Use a period with some abbreviations and initials:

Mr. Albertson	M.D.
S. W. Wheeler Ave.	R. J. Wagner
Warren G. Harding	Yeates Co.
Tetco, Inc.	J. E. B. Stuart

[Personal initials are separated by a space.]

(1.) When a person becomes known, or is referred to, by his initials, no periods are used.

FDR   (Franklin Delano Roosevelt)

LBJ   (Lyndon Baines Johnson)

JFK   (John Fitzgerald Kennedy)

(2.) Some abbreviations, because they are recognized and used frequently, are written without periods.

PTA   (Parent-Teacher Association)

FBI   (Federal Bureau of Investigation)

UFO   (Unidentified Flying Object)

AFL-CIO   (American Federation of Labor-Congress of Industrial Organizations)

UPI   (United Press International)

(3.) Acronyms are pronounceable words formed by combining initial letters of other words, or the letters of the major parts of compound terms. Acronyms are almost always written without periods.

OPEC	(Organization of Petroleum Exporting Countries)
BASIC	(Beginners All-purpose Symbolic Instruction Code)
NATO	(North Atlantic Treaty Organization)
FORTRAN	(formula translation)
sonar	(sound navigation ranging)

(4.) An abbreviation at the end of a declarative sentence uses the final period of the abbreviation to end the sentence.

Myron is taking the train to Washington, D.C.

(5.) An abbreviation ending an exclamatory or interrogative sentence keeps the abbreviation period and adds a question mark or an exclamation point.

Will Myron take the train to Washington, D.C.?

It's 4:00 A.M.!

(6.) An abbreviation inside a sentence retains the abbreviation period, and is followed by any necessary punctuation.

He will leave tomorrow at 8:00 A.M.; I will leave tonight.

This is the meaning of D.V.M.: Doctor of Veterinary Medicine.

B. Use a period after numbers or letters in a vertical list or outline:

1. Orange	A. Cotton
2. Blue	B. Wool
3. Mauve	C. Linen

I. Holidays
  A. Christmas
    1. Church
    2. Trees
      a. Ornaments
II. Vacation Days
  B. Trips
    1. Beach
      a. Shells

(1.) If one or more of the items in a list are complete sentences, periods should follow each of the listed items.

A. Your prose should be clear.
B. Your prose should be succinct.
C. Your prose should be without affectation.

(2.) If the list is introduced by a sentence, a final period is used if the listed items are separated by commas or semicolons.

I was certain
  1. that Thomas did not own a gun;
  2. that Thomas had no motive for killing Fay;
  3. that Thomas had left the city before the murder.

(3.) Enumerating a list with letters or numbers is optional. The period is eliminated from the end of the list unless the items are separated by colons or commas.

The following kinds of tea are served regularly:

lapsang souchong
jasmine
mint
chamomile   *[No period at the end of the list.]*

C. Use the period as a decimal point:

$8.95	4.78 percent
6.8 meters	$.10
22.25 sq. ft.	7.2753

D. Use a period to separate parts of literary works:

Hamlet II.iii.5   *[act, scene, line]*

Moby Dick XV.78   *[chapter, page]*

F. Use a period after a run-in sidehead:

Getting started. Read through the directions carefully, and then locate the tools you will need.

3. Vegetable-fruit group. Four or more servings of fruit and/or vegetables should be eaten daily.

III. DO NOT USE A PERIOD

A. After title lines denoting major parts of a text, or after column titles in a table.

B. After numbers used to indicate order or position:

1st, 2nd, 3rd, 4th, 60th

the 2nd Ohio Volunteer Infantry

C. After Roman numerals used to indicate order or position:

King Henry VIII   Pope John XXIII

D. After chemical symbols, though they are abbreviations:

Al (aluminum)   C (carbon)   NaCN (sodium cyanide)

QUESTION MARK   ?

The question mark is used to end a sentence that asks a direct question, indicate a series of questions within a sentence, and may be used as an editorial mark to express uncertainty.

I. USE A QUESTION MARK

A. At the end of a sentence that asks a direct question:

Can you come here for dinner Thursday evening?

What is he doing in there?

Who will volunteer?

(1.) When a quoted sentence asks a question, the question mark goes inside the quotation marks. If the question does not apply to the quoted material, the question mark goes outside the quotation marks.

Emily asked, "Is he working now?"

When did she say, "I've come to sing, not to talk"?

(2.) When both the quoted sentence and the sentence it is contained in are questions, the question mark is placed inside the quotation marks.

Why was he shouting, "Who is at the door?"

(3.) The question mark is placed inside parentheses only if it is part of the parenthetical matter, and another mark of punctuation must be used to end the sentence (first example). If the question mark is not part of the parenthetical material, it goes outside the parentheses (second example).

Helmut toured the Robert Mondavi winery (or did he?).

What is your favorite kind of pie (I mean fruit pie, not cream pie)?

(4.) When both the sentence and the parenthetical material are questions, one question mark is used, and is placed outside the parentheses.

How will we ever explain the pigeons in the kitchen (and who would believe us)?

B. To indicate a question or a series of questions within a sentence:

What does she want from me? Mark wondered.

When will the war end? is the question of the day.

How do you like your steak? rare? medium? burned?

Who is your favorite? Nancy? Kathy? Liz?

Did you lose your violin? or was it stolen? or did you leave it in the car?

(1.) The first letter of questions within a sentence may be capitalized or not, at the writer's discretion, unless the questions begin with proper names, or other words that require capital letters.

(2.) When a parenthetical question falls in the middle of a sentence, the question mark goes inside the parentheses, or before the second dash.

I was at the library yesterday—have you been there lately?—and was amazed at the changes that have been made.

It was fortunate that Franklin drove by (wasn't he supposed to be with you?) and picked me up.

C. To indicate editorial doubt or uncertainty:

John Alden (1599?-1687) sailed on the "Mayflower" in 1620, and settled at the Plymouth colony.

The professor believed that both ginger(?) and cloves were used.

(1.) The question mark is usually enclosed in parentheses when used to express the writer's doubt. Authorities are mixed as to whether a space should be used between the parenthesis and the word or number that precedes it. We recommend no space.

II. DO NOT USE A QUESTION MARK

A. With indirect questions:

Bob wondered whether to buy a new mini van.

B. With polite requests disguised as questions:

May I have a copy of that bill.

[Does not require a response.]

QUOTATION MARKS   " "

Quotation marks are primarily used to enclose direct quotations—the exact words of a speaker or writer—in the text. Certain kinds of titles are enclosed in quotation marks. And quotation marks are used to call attention to words or terms that may be unfamiliar to the reader.

I.   USE QUOTATION MARKS

A. To enclose direct quotations in the text:

"How long will you be in Germany?" Peter asked.

Gary volunteered to answer questions about his "philosophy of the hungry"; no one in the audience responded.

Who shouted, "Everyone down on the floor"?

B. To call attention to words, letters, or numbers that the writer is defining, explaining, or using as special terms that may be unfamiliar to the reader. An underline may be used instead of quotation marks for this purpose. When typesetting, attention is usually attracted by setting the words, letters, or numbers in an italic typeface. The same style (quotation marks, underlining, or italic type) should be used consistently throughout the document:

"Cold type" is a term covering a number of nonmetallic typesetting methods.

A "prompt" is a message or a symbol that the system displays when it is ready for the next command.

These "slugs" of lead, each containing a line of text, are then assembled in a holding frame.

He is the only dog I ever knew who could pronounce the consonant "F."

C. To enclose certain titles:

You must read Stephen Crane's short story "The Blue Hotel."

"Annabel Lee" by Edgar Allan Poe.

They studied Chapter Two, "The German Revolution."

Television's "Hill Street Blues" has become a success.

Cyndi Lauper sings "Girls Just Want To Have Fun."

The article in <u>Inc.</u> magazine was called "The Spirit of Independence."

(1.) Titles of articles, chapters, short stories, essays, short poems, TV and radio programs, songs, unpublished dissertations and theses, and manuscripts in collections are among those enclosed in quotation marks rather than underlined (see underlining).

II. PUNCTUATION USAGE WITH QUOTATION MARKS

A. An expression that introduces or explains a quotation is followed by a comma. An expression that interrupts a quotation is set off by commas before and after it, unless a stronger mark of punctuation is needed.

<u>Clifton exclaimed</u>, "I'll never leave!"

"We've just arrived in Germany," <u>remarked Clifton</u>, "and I feel very much at home here."

B. Commas and periods always go inside quotation marks, including double sets of quotation marks (see "D." below). Question marks and exclamation points are placed inside the quotation mark when they apply only to the quoted material, otherwise outside.

C. Longer quotations that are not part of a conversation, and are not set off from the text, are usually introduced by a colon:

Financial advisor Howard Ruff writes lucidly about gold contracts: "Gold contracts have value under certain, carefully structured conditions. They will not come into general use, as government is not about to hedge in the futures market against its obligations, nor is it about to tie its fortunes to a fluctuating commodity."

—Howard Ruff, *Howard Ruff From A to Z*

D. A quotation within a quotation is enclosed in single quotation marks (' '):

Michael answered, "It was Thoreau who said, 'Nations are possessed with an insane ambition to perpetuate the memory of themselves by the amount of hammered stone they leave.' "

(1.) A question mark or an exclamation point goes inside the single quotation marks if it applies to the material inside the single quotation marks, but outside the single quotation marks if it applies to the entire question:

Tony said, "I went over to Buddy's dorm, and he asked, 'Where's the pizza?' "

Tony asked, "Why do they call it 'pizza for a lifetime'?"

E. If a quotation is more than one paragraph, quotation marks are put at the beginning of each paragraph, but at the end of only the last paragraph:

"Again the whippoorwill called. And on this second invitation another whippoorwill answered courteously. For nearly half an hour they carried on their spirited duet.

"My small raccoon sat listening intently, well aware of the exact direction from which each call was coming. Having had his afternoon nap, he was now ready to make a night of it."

—Sterling North, *Rascal*

F. When quoting poems or excerpts of poems that are set off from the text, no quotation marks are used:

The fog comes
on little cat feet.
It sits looking
over harbor and city
on silent haunches
and then moves on.

—Carl Sandburg, "Fog"

G. When quoting poetry in the text, quotation marks are put at the beginning and end of the quote, and lines of the poem are separated by virgules:

"The fog comes / on little cat feet. / It sits looking / over harbor and city / on silent haunches / and then moves on."

H. Dialogue is always enclosed in quotation marks, and generally a separate paragraph is used for each change of speaker:

"And they carry the women to the island," said Joe; "they don't kill the women."

"No," assented Tom, "they don't kill the women—they're too noble. And the women's always beautiful, too."

"And don't they wear the bulliest clothes! Oh, no! All gold and silver and di'monds," said Joe with enthusiasm.

"Who?" said Huck.

—Mark Twain, *The Adventures of Tom Sawyer*

III. DO NOT USE QUOTATION MARKS

A. With quotations set off from the text:

Charley likes to get up early, and he likes me to get up early too. And why shouldn't he? Right after his breakfast he goes back to sleep. Over the years he has developed a number of innocent-appearing ways to get me up. He can shake himself and his collar loud enough to wake the dead. If that doesn't work he gets a sneezing fit. But perhaps his most irritating method is to sit quietly beside the bed and stare into my face with a sweet and forgiving look on his face; I come out of a deep sleep with the feeling of being looked at. But I have learned to keep my eyes tight shut. If I even blink he sneezes and stretches, and that night's sleep is over for me.

—John Steinbeck, *Travels with Charley*

(1.) Usually any quotation longer than four lines is set off from the rest of the text as a block quotation. The entire passage is indented and single spaced. Setting the passage off from the rest of the text indicates to the reader that it is a quotation.

(2.) A quotation within a block quotation is enclosed in double quotation marks:

> It would be pleasant to be able to say of my travels with Charley, "I went out to find the truth about my country and I found it." And then it would be such a simple matter to set down my findings and lean back comfortably with a fine sense of having discovered truths and taught them to my readers.
>
> —John Steinbeck, *Travels with Charley*

B. With indirect quotations:

Kate Daniels, the senior editor, said that <u>she expects to buy more material next year</u>.

Craig <u>answered no to all the questions except the last</u>; he had received one traffic ticket.

(1.) Yes and no should not be enclosed in quotation marks except in dialogue and direct quotations.

C. With indirect questions:

Why is everyone crying, Morton wondered.

Then he asked if I would shut the door and take a seat with the other candidates.

SEMICOLON ;

The semicolon would be more accurately named if it were called a "semiperiod." It is used almost exclusively to join independent clauses or statements sharing a close relationship that would, except for that relationship, otherwise be written as separate sentences. The semicolon is also used as a substitute for commas to improve clarity in some complex sentence structures. The semicolon indicates a sharp break in continuity stronger than a comma, but just short of the full stop called for by a period.

I. USE A SEMICOLON BETWEEN TWO PARTS OF A COMPOUND SENTENCE NOT SEPARATED BY A CONJUNCTION

A. Between independent or coordinate clauses:

The population of West Linn is 12,386; in the past year the city has grown by 800.

She felt reluctant to go on the plane; he was excited by the trip.

B. Between separate statements too closely related in context to be written as separate sentences:

Yes; you were right.

No; they shipped only half.

Wait; I'll go with you.

C. Before conjunctive adverbs or other transitional expressions. Some common conjunctive adverbs are: *then, however, thus, hence, indeed, besides,* and *therefore.* Frequently used transitional expressions are: *for example, i.e., in addition, in fact, in the meantime, however,* and *on the other hand.*

He was proud of his achievement; however, it did not come without hard work.

She passed all of her finals; in addition, she earned the highest grade point average in her class.

D. Between contrasting statements:

It is true in peace; it is true in war.

The walls are light brown; the ceiling is cream-colored.

He eats ice cream; I eat spinach.

II. USE A SEMICOLON BETWEEN CLAUSES IN A COMPOUND SENTENCE, INCLUDING THOSE JOINED BY COORDINATING CONJUNCTIONS, WHEN ONE OR MORE OF THE CLAUSES CONTAINS COMMAS

A. When clauses in a compound sentence are not joined by a coordinating conjunction:

The committee was to consider wages, hours, and job descriptions; its decisions would be used by the administration as guidelines.

By agreement, the two groups would equally fund the project; it would be managed by a joint committee, with two delegates representing each group; a professional manager would be hired, and exercise an equal vote with the representatives.

B. When clauses in a compound sentence are joined by a coordinating conjunction. The eight most used coordinating conjunctions are *and*, *but*, *for*, *not*, *or*, *so*, *still*, and *yet*.

The girls, who were all good athletes, wanted to play on the football team; and they wanted an equal voice in the team discussions.

The swamp, two miles wide by four miles long, was just outside the town; yet no one, not even old Harry Townsend, had ever been to its center.

III. USE A SEMICOLON BETWEEN WORDS OR GROUPS OF WORDS IN A SERIES WHEN ONE OR MORE OF THE SERIES ELEMENTS CONTAINS COMMAS

The class included Jennifer, age 5; John, age 4; Marilyn, age 7; Doris, age 5; and Wendy, age 6.

They went to Denver, Colorado; San Francisco, California; and Tucson, Arizona.

IV. ALWAYS PLACE SEMICOLONS OUTSIDE OF QUOTATION MARKS OR PARENTHESES

Davy had read the chapter entitled "Soldier Boys"; he assumed the rest of the class had read it, too.

The new books are in (I didn't think they would ever come); will you pick one up for me if I give you the money?

V. DO NOT USE A SEMICOLON

A. Between an independent clause and a dependent clause:

They bought a new car which they used to drive to Michigan for her graduation.

[No semicolon after car.]

B. Before a modifying phrase beginning with a participle. Participles are adjectives derived from verbs. Present tense participle verbs end in "ing" (crying, running). Past tense participle verbs most often end in "ed," "t," "en," or "n" (ordered, went, held, taken, sewn).

The boat was long, <u>extending</u> a full 50 feet beyond the dock.

[A comma, not a semicolon after "long."]

The leaves are gone, <u>blown</u> from their branches by the high winds.

[A comma, not a semicolon after "gone."]

UNDERLINE

In typed or written manuscripts, a single line under the text is used to indicate titles, names, and foreign or individual words the writer wishes to emphasize, that would call for an italic typeface if set in type.

I. **UNDERLINE THE TITLES OF BOOKS, PERIODICALS, PAMPHLETS, PLAYS, MOVIES, LONG POEMS, MUSICAL COMPOSITIONS, WORKS OF ART, AND THE NAMES OF SHIPS, TRAINS, AIRCRAFT, AND SPACECRAFT WHEN USED IN TEXT**

He spent three days of his vacation reading Steinbeck's East of Eden.

They discontinued publication of Popular Computing last month.

As far as I know, he has the last remaining copy of The Public Speakers Society's 1925 pamphlet, One Hundred Short Introductory Remarks For Speakers.

Last week we went to see the play The Fantasticks at the community college.

Terms of Endearment won the Academy Award for best picture in 1983.

The second week's assignment in English 101 is to read Milton's Paradise Lost.

The second opera of the season was The Magic Flute by Mozart.

Gainsborough's painting Blue Boy is displayed at the Huntington Library in San Marino, California.

I served on the Navy Destroyer USS James E. Keyes.

The Southern Pacific's train El Capitan begins its journey in Los Angeles.

The B-29 Superfortress Enola Gay dropped the world's first atomic bomb on Hiroshima.

The spaceshuttle Columbia made its first landings on the dry lake bed at Edwards Air Force Base in California.

(1.) In typset text, these same examples would be set in italic type instead of underlined.

(2.) Descriptive or attributed titles of art work are not underlined.

Titian's portrait of the Duchess of Urbino, because of its lovely nude subject (the body of the Duke's favorite playmate with the head of the elderly Duchess) is popularly known as The Venus of Urbino.

II. UNDERLINE FOREIGN WORDS OR PHRASES NOT COMMONLY USED IN THE ENGLISH LANGUAGE

Foreign expressions in common use are usually found in the body of collegiate dictionaries. Additional familiar foreign expressions are listed in the "Foreign Words and Phrases" section at the back of the dictionary.

In reply, he said, "audi alteram partem."

[hear the other side]

"What you have here is an enfant gate," he said.

[spoiled child]

They dined en famille.

[at home]

(1.) Quotations entirely in a foreign language are not underlined.

(2.) Foreign language titles preceding proper names are not underlined.

(3.) The proper names of persons, places, institutions, etc., written in a foreign language are not underlined.

III. UNDERLINE LETTERS, WORDS, OR NUMBERS WHEN THEY ARE USED IN A SENTENCE FOR OTHER THAN THEIR MEANING

The ph in physics is pronounced as if it were an f.

The 33 on the sign looked like 88 from a distance.

(1.) These same letters, words, or numbers may be set off with quotation marks instead of underlining. In printed text, they are usually set with an italic typeface. The same style (underline, quotation marks, or italic type) should be used throughout the document.

IV. DO NOT UNDERLINE. INSTEAD, ENCLOSE IN QUOTATION MARKS

A. The titles of short stories, essays, articles in periodicals, and manuscripts in collections.

B. The titles of chapters or other divisions of a book.

C. The titles of unpublished papers, theses, and dissertations.

(1.) For the purpose of this rule, published material will carry a publisher's imprint on the cover or title page; unpublished material will not.

D. Television and radio programs.

E. The titles of short poems and songs.

V. DO NOT UNDERLINE (AND DO NOT ENCLOSE IN QUOTATION MARKS)

A. The titles of series, or the names of editions.

B. The titles of diaries, manuscript collections, or memoranda.

C. The Bible, or titles of its books or parts, or other sacred texts.

D. Musical compositions identified by the musical form and the key, with or without an identifying number.

VIRGULE   /

A virgule (known also as a diagonal, slash bar, slant line, shilling mark, or solidus) is a mark of separation, and may be used to divide two alternatives, or to separate lines of poetry that have been run into the text. The virgule is also used in other, related ways as a mark of punctuation.

I.   USE A VIRGULE

A. To separate choices or alternatives:

> He may have candy and/or fruit.

> Commonly used correlative conjunctions include either/or and neither/nor.

> Are you taking French for a grade, or on the pass/fail system?

(1) When indicating alternatives, no spaces are used before or after the virgule.

B. To separate lines of poetry that have been run together and inserted into the text:

> In "Gerontion," T.S. Eliot expressed familiar themes when he said, "Think now / She gives when our attention is distracted / And what she gives, gives with such supple confusions / That the giving famishes the craving. Gives too late / What's not believed in, or if still believed, / In memory only, reconsidered passion."

(1.) When marking the end of a line of poetry, use a space before and after the virgule.

C. To separate equations that are written in-line rather than set off from the text:

$$E(X) = \frac{a+b}{2}$$ *would be* $E(X) = a+b/2$

$$\frac{39+48+54+67}{4} = 52$$ *would be* $39+48+54+67/4 = 52$

(1.) The virgule may be used for writing all fractions, particularly those not found on the standard keyboard.

5/16   4/5   9/10   1 3/4

D. To indicate successive time periods:

winter 1985/86   1066/1067   fiscal year 1965/66

E. To designate month, day, and year (or day, month, and year) in informal writing:

10/1/81   for October 1, 1981   *[American style]*

1/10/81   for 1 October 1981   *[European style]*

F. As a symbol meaning "per" when used to indicate "for each":

35 gal/min   *[gallons per minute]*

50 bbl/day   *[barrels per day]*

12 boxes/carton   *[boxes per carton]*

A GUIDE
FOR THE USE OF
CAPITALIZATION

Capital letters are used to mark the beginning of sentences in written text. Important words in the text that serve as proper names for people, places, or things are also capitalized. Both of these uses serve to make written language more understandable to readers. The most common uses of capitalization are illustrated in the following guidelines.

I. The pronoun "I" and the interjection "O" are always capitalized

Do you think I did it?
Next week, I am going to Memphis.
Hear our plea, O mighty king.
We thank thee, O merciful God, for our blessings.

> *Note: The exclamation "oh" is capitalized only when used as the first word in a sentence.*

II. Capitalize the first word and all principal words in addresses, opening salutations, and complimentary closes in correspondence

Mr. Guy Taylor
Taylor & Taylor Company
123 Main Street
Hunter Beach, CA 92648

Dear Mr. Taylor
Dear Madam,
Sincerely yours,
Yours truly,

III. Capitalize the first word of complete sentences, sentence fragments, direct quotes, and lines of poetry

Complete sentences

Now that you're inside, take a seat.

Yesterday was Jane's birthday.

Sentence fragments, when they represent complete thoughts

"When did he go?"
"Yesterday."
"Take the shovel?"
"Yup."

"But he just . . ."

Sentences enclosed by parentheses when the sentence stands alone

He closed the shop before I got there. (We will catch him tomorrow, you can be sure of that.)

John left the store after making his purchase. (He bought a rain coat.)

Do not capitalize sentences enclosed by parentheses when they are contained within a sentence.

John left the store (he bought a rain coat) after making his purchase.

Direct questions within sentences

The question is: Should I go, or send John?

He wants to know, Now, or next week?

Direct quotes, when they are complete sentences or sentence fragments expressing complete thoughts

"I don't think I'll go."
"Why not?"
"Have to mind the store."

When I saw him he was yelling, "This way!"
The other man yelled, "Hurry, bring the hoe!"
"Bring the lamp so we can see," said Roy.

When a quotation is interrupted, the first word of the second half is not capitalized unless it is a complete sentence

"What the heck," said George, "is going on?"
"I'm not sure," said Jack. "We're going over now to find out."

Do not capitalize the first word of a quotation fragment when it is grammatically dependent on a sentence in which it occurs

He asked the brand, "so next time I'll know what to buy."

She ended the sentence, "and please write to me about your vacation plans."

Do not capitalize the first word of an indirect quotation

He asked me the brand, so that next time he would know next time what to buy.

She ended the sentence with the request that we write to her about our vacation plans.

Poetry — Capitalize the first word of each line of poetry unless it is purposely written in lower case by the author

There is a lady sweet and kind,
Was never face so pleased my mind:
I did but see her passing by,
And yet I love her till I die.
— Anon. 17th Cent.

but

> With them, in spirit,
>> we also go forth
> from the sweet peace
> of our beloved firesides
>> to smite the foe.

— Mark Twain
The War Prayer

IV. Capitalize proper nouns and adjectives, and their abbreviations when they have one.

Proper nouns name a particular person, place, or thing.

Common nouns name any one of a class or group of persons, places or things without specifying a particular one.

Proper Adjectives are derived from proper nouns, and from proper nouns that are used as adjectives.

When in doubt consult the listing in the main body of a dictionary for capitalization of proper nouns and adjectives.

Examples:

COMMON NOUN	PROPER NOUN	PROPER ADJECTIVE	ABBREVIATION
country	Germany	German	Ger.
city	Los Angeles	Angelino	LA
month	February		Feb.
day	Monday		Mon.
man	John Keefauver		J.K.
company	Portland General Electric Co.		PGE

A. PEOPLE

The names of persons are capitalized

Evan Thomas   Murial Hart
Bob Miller   Karen Fawbush
Janice Briggs-Hartford

Capitalization of the particles *de, della, der, du, l' la, van* and *von* used in family names varies. When possible, determine the form used by the person named.

In American and English usage, particles preceding family names are usually capitalized

James De Priest
Patti LaBelle
Di Maggio (Joe)

Alfred Du Pont
Dick Van Patten
L'Amour (Louis)

In European usage the German particle *von* and the Dutch *van* are never capitalized

Franz von Papen   -and-   von Papen
Jan van Riebeeck   van Riebeeck

In European usage the French particles *de* and *du* and the Italian *di* and *da* are lower case when preceded by a first name or title. They are either capitalized or dropped, depending on local custom and usage, when the family name stands alone

Duke de Richelieu
Pietro da Cortona
Georges de La Tour
Giuseppe di Lampedusa

(De) Richelieu
(Da) Cortona
La Tour
(Di) Lampedusa

The first letters of the *Mac, Mc,* and *O'* prefixes used with Irish and Scottish family names are always capitalized

Don McAllister
Jeanette MacDonald
McGovern

Sean O'Neil
Bessie McCoy
O'Connor

Personified nouns (when the name of a thing or abstraction is represented as having human qualities or power) are capitalized

Old Man Winter   Mother Nature
It was Fate that brought us together.
We are all the victims of Time.
The Chairman opened the meeting.

B. TITLES

Formal titles and ranks are capitalized when they precede a person's name

Senator Bradley
Sergeant Roy Ashton
the Earl of Kent
Doc Lindstrom
Chairman of the Board Iacocca

Treasurer James Jackson
Queen Elizabeth
Sheriff Bridges
Nurse Cali

Abbreviations of titles and other designations that follow a name are capitalized if they are also capitalized when spelled out

John Henry, Jr.   David Goldberg, M.D.
George Henderson, D.M.C   Martin Whent, Ph.D.
Michael Rogers, Attorney at Law

Formal titles are capitalized when used in place of a person's name, or when referring to a specific person

I spoke to the Senator yesterday.
Take this speech to the Governor.
The General would like his car brought.

Formal titles and organizational names are capitalized when addressing correspondence

Mike Burton, Professor of Management
John Kramer, Sales Representative
Vicki Price, Design Coordinator
Cary Gardner, Records Department
Brian Garrison, Emerald Microware Co.

Formal titles are not capitalized when used in a general or plural sense, or when they do not refer to a specific person

A company vice president called me.
We polled the senators.
I took the baby to the doctor yesterday.
When you see a lieutenant, salute.

Formal titles used as appositives (to restate, amplify, explain, or further identify the noun or pronoun that precedes or follows it) are not capitalized

James R. Miller, a company vice president
Rose Page, club treasurer
Mike Burton, professor of management
Elizabeth, queen of England

Titles of family relationship are capitalized when they precede or take the place of a person's name

Cousin Tim   Aunt Hilda
Grandma Jackson   Uncle Roger Hunt
I bought it for Mother.   I know Grandpa wants one.

Titles of family relationship are not capitalized when used with possessive nouns

Cathy's son   Roger's brother
my mother   his uncle
their grandmother   your father

C. ADJECTIVES

Adjectives derived from proper nouns are capitalized

Edwardian era	Italian opera
Euclidian geometry	Russian vodka

Adjectives designating race, nationality, or tribe are capitalized

Canadian	Australian
Apache	Hispanic
Eskimo	Negro
Caucasian	Asian

Adjectives indicating color of skin, and proper adjectives of general usage are not capitalized

black	white
bushmen	islander
nomad	highlander

Adjectives derived from proper nouns that have acquired a meaning of their own through common usage are not capitalized

macadam (road pavement)	italicize
watt (electric unit)	brussels sprouts
swiss cheese	chinese blue
french fries	pasteurization

D. PLACES

Compass directions are capitalized when part of a specific place or regional name

South America	Midwestern Nebraska
The Far East	South Carolina
Northern Hemisphere	the South

Compass directions used as common adjectives or when referring to direction only are not capitalized

south of France	northern Europe
western U.S.	eastern approach
He drove west	they flew southeast
down south	

Geographical place names are capitalized

Tropic of Capricorn	Africa
Gulf of Guinea	Singapore
British Isles	Equator
Arctic Circle	Port Morresby
Grand Canyon	Newport Peninsula
Kansas City	King County
San Gabriel Mountains	Colorado River

Nouns used as common adjectives to describe geographical places are not capitalized

the tropics	canyons of the west
the county court house	the southern oceans
the state of Oregon	the local port
the lakes region	the Pacific coast of Oregon
the Yosemite valley	the Cascade mountains
the Columbia and Willamette rivers	

Note: Geographical nouns used as common adjectives in legal documents are usually capitalized:

the City of New York	the State of Kansas
the Commonwealth of Massachusetts	

The names of streets, parks, buildings, and other prominent landmarks are capitalized

Chrysler Building	Empire State Building
Kent County Court House	Senate Office Building
Golden Gate Bridge	Rogers Park
Hansen Museum of History	Johnson Creek
Smothers Winery	Spenser Farm
City Hall	Police Station
Main Street	Seventh Avenue

Proper nouns used as adjectives to indicate local landmarks are not capitalized unless part of a formal name

post office	museum
opera house	library
the bridge	the park

Political division names are capitalized when used in a formal sense

the Roman Empire	Clackamas County
the Third Ward	Fifth Precinct
United Kingdom	European Common Market

Political division names are not capitalized when used informally

the empire's growth	the county's responsibility
the ward voters	the precinct office
a common market	his kingdom

Descriptive place names are capitalized when they specify a particular place or region

the New World	the Dust Bowl
The Big Apple	the Gulf Coast
the Wheat Belt	the Bay State
the Bowery	Old Town
Chinatown	Down Under

E.THINGS

The names of vehicles are capitalized

Queen Mary (passenger ship)
Columbia (space shuttle)
Voyager (space capsule)
Miller American (racing power boat)
Spirit of St. Louis (airplane)

Taurus (car model)
El Capitan (train)
USS James E. Keyes (naval ship)

Political party, business, organization, institutional, popular movement, and religious group names and their popular nicknames are capitalized

General Motors
Labor Party
Lutheran Church
United States Army
Transportation Department
American Legion
the Far Left

Kemper Life Insurance Co.
University of Oregon
Assembly of God
the Coast Guard
Communist Yugoslavia
Women's Movement
Veteran's Rights

Governmental and judicial bodies, both national and international, their administrative arms, and their acronyms are capitalized

the Supreme Court
Commerce Department
City Finance Office
Department of the Interior
United Nations (UN)
Internal Revenue Department (IRS)
Environmental Protection Agency (EPA)
Los Angeles County Municipal Court
National Aeronautics and Space Agency (NASA)

the Executive Branch
Department of Public Works
Office of the Mayor
Maryland State Police
World Health Organization (WHO)

Historical period and event names, and the names of holidays are capitalized

World War I
Renaissance
Bronze Age
Chicago Fire
Good Friday
Roaring Twenties

Spanish-American War
Battle of Britain
Election Day
Fourth of July
20th Century
Third Reich

Historical or important law, document, prize, and award names are capitalized.

Medal of Honor
Atlantic Charter
National Book Awards
Social Security Law

Nobel Prize
Treaty of Kent
Emmy Awards
Canada Trade Bill

The titles of published works and their divisions are capitalized

The Thesis Writer's Handbook (reference book)
Life on the Mississippi (novel)
Personal Computing (magazine)
Swinging Down the River (chapter)
Ode to Beauty (poem)

Note: The articles a, an, the, etc., are capitalized only if they are the first word in the title of a published work.

F. RELIGIOUS TERMS

Words and terms directly denoting the Diety and Jesus except *who*, *whose*, and *whom* are capitalized

He	the Almighty
Jehovah	Him (but himself)/ Lord
Thee	Divine Savior
Messiah	Son of Man

Names for the Bible and other sacred writings and their parts; and names of confessions of faith and of religious bodies and their adherents and words specifically denoting Satan are all capitalized.

Mass	Communion
Holy Scriptures	The Word
Koran	New Testament
Ten Commandments	Gospel
The Lord's Prayer	Apostle's Creed
Episcopalian	Christian
Jewish	Book of Mormon
Job's Daughters	Knights of Columbus
Devil	Father of Lies
Satanic Majesty	Leviticus
Book of Mark	Prince of Evil

G. OTHER

Days of the week and months of the year are capitalized

Monday	Wednesday
January	August

Seasons of the year are not usually capitalized

winter	spring
summer	fall

The expressions B.C. and A.D. are capitalized

465 B.C.   A.D. 1989

The expressions A.M. and P.M. may be capitalized or in lower-case letters (a.m., p.m.); either form is acceptable as long as the writer is consistent with the form used

10:45 A.M.	-or-	10:45 a.m.
2:00 P.M.		2:00 p.m.

Trade names, variety names, and names of market grades and brands are capitalized

Plexiglas (trade name)	Choice beef (market grade)
Green Giant (brand name)	Sugar pea (variety)

PROOFREADER'S MARKS

The symbols below are used to mark desired changes on manuscript or typeset copy.

⌄ ⌃		Put in letter, word, or punctuation mark
ℓ		Take out letter, word, or punctuation mark
stet		Leave in copy previously marked to take out
⌒		Close space
#		Put in space
∽		Transpose (words or letters)
¶	¶	Begin new paragraph
no ¶	no ¶	No paragraph
⟨		Run together (or no paragraph)
⊙		Insert period
⊏	⊏	Move to left
⊐		Move to right
⊐ ⊏		Center
≡		Make capital letter(s)
lc. ⫽	lc.	Make LOWER case letter(s)
ital.	ital.	Underline, or set type in *Italic*
s.c. ≡	s.c.	Set type in SMALL CAPITALS
B.F. ∼∼	B.F.	Set type in **Boldface**

A SELECTED GLOSSARY
OF TERMS USED IN
THE PUNCTUATION HANDBOOK

absolute phrase

a phrase within a sentence that adds meaning, but has no clear grammatical relationship; as when adding narrative or descriptive details:

He saluted the passing flag, his heart beating rapidly.

His task completed, George put away his tools.

acronym

a word formed from the initial letters or syllables of a compound title or word:

ZIP code (from Zone Improvement Plan code)

NASA (from National Aeronautics and Space Administration)

radar (from radio detecting and ranging)

adage

a short, pointed, frequently humorous statement used to illustrate a point.

adjective

a word that changes, limits, or otherwise defines or describes a noun or a pronoun.

adverb

a word that changes, limits, or otherwise defines a verb, an adjective, or another adverb.

adverbial clause

a group of words containing a subject and verb that does the work of an adverb, usually answering such questions as How? When? Where? Why? Under what circumstances?

Mary drove away because the people made her nervous.

If he doesn't watch out, he could get hurt.

appositive

a word or group of words that restates, amplifies, explains, or further identifies the noun or pronoun that precedes or follows it.

classification of words
in English, and in other languages, many words are classified into groups according to their use. Nouns, for example, serve primarily as the names of persons, places or things. Verbs express action, and adjectives are used to define or describe nouns and pronouns.

clause
a group of words with a subject and a verb, and used as part of a sentence. There are two kinds of clauses; independent and dependent.

An independent, or main clause, though a part of a sentence, is grammatically independent of it:

George didn't know it yet, but his raise had
been approved.

He turned slowly around; he knew he couldn't
draw his gun fast enough.

A dependent, or subordinate clause, depends on the rest of the sentence to complete its meaning:

George, the man who fixed the furnace, didn't
know it yet, but his raise had been approved.

He turned slowly around, carefully raising his
hands; he knew he couldn't draw his gun fast
enough.

complement
a word or words that completes the meaning of the verb in a sentence, usually answering the question "who" or "what."

compound noun
words linked to form the name of a person, place, or thing, and used as a noun (see also compound phrase below).

father-in-law	ex-husband	government-in-exile
first-born	stay-at-home	John-boy

compound phrase
a descriptive phrase containing three or more words:

following John's example	with his knife
light as a feather	to be first in line

compound sentence
a sentence made up of two or more independent clauses, each of which expresses a complete thought, and can stand alone as a sentence. The clauses in a compound sentence are joined by a comma, a coordinating conjunction, or a semicolon.

compound word

two or more words written as one (baseball, bookstore); two separate words joined by a hyphen and expressing a thought more than, or different from, the words used individually (penny-wise, break-in); or a root word joined to a stressed prefix (ex-husband, pro-administration).

conjunctive adverb

an adverb used to join thoughts in a sentence. *Then*, *however*, *thus*, *hence*, *indeed*, *besides*, and *therefore* are some commonly used conjunctive adverbs.

conjunction

a linking word that ties together clauses, phrases, or words. *And*, *but*, *for*, *yet*, *or*, *nor*, *so*, and *yet* are examples of frequently used coordinating conjunctions.

consonant

any letter of the English alphabet except the vowels *a*, *e*, *i*, *o*, and *u*.

contraction

a word formed by shortening another word or combining two words and replacing missing sounds or letters with an apostrophe. *Can't* (from can not), *we're* (from we are), and *don't* (from do not) are examples of contractions.

coordinate clause

clauses of equal type and importance linked together in a sentence:

She felt reluctant to go on the plane;
she was excited by the trip.

coordinating conjunction

words used to connect words, phrases, clauses, and sentences. *And*, *but*, *for*, *or*, *nor*, *so*, and *yet* are the most frequently used coordinating conjunctions.

correlative conjunction

two conjunctive structures used to form a parallel construction:

George not only washed the dog, but also cleaned out the garage.

They neither appreciated nor acknowledged the gesture of recognition.

declarative sentence

a sentence that makes a statement (as opposed to a question).

dialogue

a conversation between two or more persons.

digressive statement
    a statement not specifically associated with the subject of the sentence or text in which it appears.

gerund
    a verb ending in "ing," and used as a noun:

        Susan was driving last night.

homonym
    words with the same pronunciation but different meanings.

imperative sentence
    a sentence that gives a command or makes a request

        Open the door.

        Please give me the gun.

indefinite pronoun
    a pronoun referring to one or more things or persons:

one	no one	some
all	few	something
everybody	other	any

independent clause
    a group of words with a subject and a verb, and used as part of a sentence, but grammatically independent of it:

        George didn't know it yet, but his raise had been approved.

        He turned slowly around; he knew he couldn't draw his gun fast enough.

inflection
    a change in the form of a word to indicate case (we—us), gender (hero—heroine), quantity (cat—cats), tense (is—was), person (I—we), and other distinctions used in the English language.

interpolation
    an explanation or comment added by the author.

maxim
    a general truth, fundamental principle, or rule of conduct.

modifier
    a word or group of words that, when used with other words, makes their meaning more exact by restricting or limiting their definition.

nonrestrictive

a group of words with a subject and a verb, used as a part of a sentence, and dependent on the rest of the sentence to complete its meaning:

George, the man who fixed the furnace, didn't know it yet, but his raise had been approved.

He turned slowly around, carefully raising his hands; he knew he couldn't draw his gun fast enough.

noun

a word used as the name of a person, place, or thing.

object

that toward which the action in a sentence is directed:

John drove the car.

[Car is the object of drove, the verb.]

parallel word construction

elements in a sentence that are of equal importance and expressed in the same grammatical form:

Their good health was the result of frequent exercise, a high fibre diet, and adequate sleep.
[Parallel; each item is written in the same grammatical form.]

Their good health was the result of frequent exercise, a high fibre diet, and their habit of getting adequate sleep.
[Not parallel; the first two items are the same, but the third changes form and makes the sentence awkward.]

parenthetical

an amplifying or explanatory word, phrase, or clause inserted into a sentence, and usually set off by commas, dashes, or parentheses. An amplifying or explanatory sentence inserted into a text.

participle

an adjective derived from a verb. Present tense participle verbs end in *"ing"* (crying, running). Past tense participle verbs most often end in *"ed," "t," "en,"* or *"n"* (ordered, went, held, taken, sewn).

past tense

action in the past.

personal pronoun
a pronoun denoting a person or persons:

I	he	she	you
it	we	they	

phrase
a group of words without subject or verb, used in a sentence to modify or explain its meaning.

predicate
the verb and associated words used in a sentence to complete a statement about the subject of the sentence:

John drove the car.

preposition
a word that connects a noun or pronoun with the main body of the sentence:

He stepped aboard the boat.
*[Aboard is the preposition, boat, the
noun, is the object of the preposition.]*

prepositional phrase
a group of words that connect a noun or pronoun with the main body of the sentence:

They used the ladder in place of the
ruined stairway.
*["In place of" is the prepositional phrase,
"stairway," the noun, is the object of the
prepositional phrase.]*

present tense
action in the present.

pronoun
a word used in place of a noun (he, she, it, they, etc.)

proper noun
a word or words naming a specific person, place or thing

George Stevens	Crystal Lake
Oregon	The Citadel

restrictive
a word or phrase that restricts the meaning of a sentence:

The man who spoke to them represented the
Navy Department.

sentence
> a group of words, usually including a subject and predicate, which makes a statement, or asks a question. A sentence may sometimes consist of one word, with subject or predicate implied in the context of its use or expression.

sentence fragment
> an incomplete sentence, or a part of a sentence which has been separated and punctuated as a separate sentence.

sic
> Latin for thus—used in text to indicate that a mistake was copied the same as it appeared in the original.

tense
> the indication of time, past, present, or future.

transitional expression
> an expression used to connect thoughts in a compound sentence. *In addition*, *in fact*, *i.e.*, *e.g.*, *in the mean time*, and *on the other hand*, are transitional expressions.

verb
> a word or group of words used to express or assert something about a person, place or thing.

vocative
> a word or expression indicating the person addressed:
>
> > Mother, I need you over here!
> >
> > "Help me, Bobby, I'm slipping."
> >
> > "You, on the ladder! Come down.

vowel
> any of the letters *a*, *e*, *i*, *o*, or *u*.

MAIL ORDER FORM

Please send me the following books.

_____ copies of *The Punctuation Handbook* at $4.95 ea.

_____ copies of *The Thesis Writer's Handbook* at $10.95 ea.

Shipping: $1.00 for the first book and .50¢ for each additional book.

I am enclosing my:

☐ Personal Check for $_____

☐ Money Order for $_____

☐ I can't wait 3-4 weeks for 4th class mail. I am enclosing $2.50 postage for the first book, and $1.25 for each additional book for First Class Mail or United Parcel Service delivery.

Deliver to:

Name _____

Address _____

_____

City _____

State   Zip

Mail the completed form to:

Alcove Publishing Company
P.O.Box 362
West Linn, OR 97068

Photocopy this page and use the copy to order books by mail.